Life in the Highlands and Islands of Scotland

Life in the Highlands and Islands of Scotland

COLIN MACDONALD

Part One

ECHOES OF THE GLEN

Part Two

HIGHLAND JOURNEY

THE MERCAT PRESS
EDINBURGH

Echoes of the Glen first published 1936
Highland Journey first published 1943

This edition first published 1991 by
Aberdeen University Press

Reprinted 1993 by Mercat Press
James Thin, 53 South Bridge,
Edinburgh EH1 1YS

© William MacDonald and Margaret Newton 1991
ISBN 008 0412246

Printed by BPCC-AUP Aberdeen Ltd

PREFACE

When Eric Richards and I were researching material for our book *Cromartie; Highland Life: 1650–1914* (Aberdeen University Press 1989) we were hard-pressed to find any authentic voices from the generations of tenants on the Cromartie estates. Our sources remained obstinately limited to the factors and the landlords. The silence was almost complete until the Crofters' Commission of 1886 took evidence from Cromartie tenants. Then Eric discovered one of Colin MacDonald's books, long out of print but still to be found in the north. Colin's father had given evidence to the Napier Commission (1883) as a representative of the crofters from the Cromartie estates of Strathpeffer. Colin was born at just about that time. His books and other writings were all we could have wished—a Cromartie estate crofter, a knowledgable and erudite man who became a senior Land Officer with the Department of Agriculture for Scotland and, later, Gaelic-speaking member of the Land Court. We sought out copies of his four books, the first two of which are reprinted here, and we made good use of them. Just before going to print we were introduced to Colin's daughter, Dr Margaret Newton, living with her husband on the ancestral croft on the Heights of Inchvannie, near Strathpeffer. She generously shared her family photographs with us, so we were able to illustrate our book with the MacDonald croft house and family and other estate tenants who had merely been names to us before.

We were able to trace back MacDonalds as tenants of the Cromartie Barony of Strathpeffer to the early eighteenth century when several of that name were in the various townships. The township of Inchvannie, held jointly by many tenants was on the flat fertile strath, and about 1780 it was cleared and made into a large farm. The tenants of the township were given the option, which most of them took, of becoming crofters on the Heights, then renamed the Heights of Inchvannie. There is no actual documentary proof that the MacDonalds of that resettlement were the ancestors of Colin, but his family tradition has it that they were. He claimed that his family along with a family called Rose, who also figure in early rentals, had been original settlers on the Heights. The land was held free for a few years on condition that a house was built and the ground cleared of stones and cultivation begun. Then a small rent was claimed, small but hard to gather from seventeen acres of unbroken moorland. Their first house was a long-house, shared by their cattle, and its site can still be seen, built of the boulders cleared from the land.

A thin prosperity and very hard work enabled the early nineteenth century MacDonalds to build a better one, and then in about 1900 the small solid and comfortable house which still stands was built by Donald and his son Colin, and local men. This massive continuity is impressive, as is the value placed on education and on simplicity: impressive but not exceptional in the Highlands and Islands. But Colin had the story-teller's gift and the ability to record his tales. They came straight from experience and from the border between the oral traditions of gaeldom and the modern media-dominated world, from the crofters and the Gaelic speakers whose way of life was hard and honest. You will never read anything more authentic.

Monica Clough
Glen Urquhart

INTRODUCTION

The suggestion that the books written by my father between 1936 and 1949 should be reprinted brought great pleasure to my only surviving brother Bill, William MacDonald of Dornoch, and to me. I am delighted to have been asked to write an introduction to this re-issue of the first pair of his four books.

So here I am, sitting and writing by the fire in the house built by my grandfather nearly a hundred years ago, on the croft on the Cromartie estates where our ancestors have been tenants since the eighteenth century, and possibly for longer. The house is on the high south-facing slope, the Heights, between Dingwall and Strathpeffer. It commands a spectacular view. To the south lies the valley of the Peffrey river backed by the long range of Knock Farrel, the Cat's Back and Cnoc n'Eglais, with glimpses of the Monadhliath mountains and the Grampians beyond. East lies Dingwall with the Black Isle behind it. Westward is sheer beauty: Castle Leod nestling in trees, where the present Earl of Cromartie still lives, the charming Victorian spa village of Strathpeffer, and the peaks of the western hills.

My brothers and I had always admired father's books with their fund of information, humour and tales of the past, so many of which we had heard told and retold in our childhood. We knew, however, that there was more to his writing than mere entertainment. As the *Inverness Courier* put it in 1943 after publication of *Highland Journey*:

> When Colin MacDonald published his first book *Echoes of the Glen* we considered it to be such an important contribution to the story of social life in the Highlands with its vivid and faithful portrayal of the characteristics and daily living of the Highland people that, in a leading article on Highland matters, we recommended everybody interested in Highland problems to read it and take it to heart. The same may be said of *Highland Journey* for nobody who wants to understand the Highlands and the Highland people can afford to neglect it.

Offspring of generations of Ross-shire crofters, Colin MacDonald left school at a little over thirteen, and worked his father's croft until at the age of twenty-six he matriculated at Marischal College, Aberdeen. He was then on the staff of the Aberdeen and North of Scotland College of Agriculture: he worked for the Board, later the Department, of Agriculture for Scotland and finally became Gaelic-speaking member of the Scottish Land Court. He was a man large in stature and mind, generous by nature and with a delightful sense of fun. His upbringing and the many jobs he had undertaken as a boy and young man—herd boy, shepherd, drainer, fencer, roadmaker, lumberman and many more besides—had made him a very practical and down-to-earth man, but deep in his soul there was something of the poet. He savoured words and was deeply moved by the beauties and miracles of nature. He had perhaps a slight eccentricity in the matter of dress because, except at funerals, weddings and such serious occasions, he invariably wore a plus-four suit, usually of a crotal colour beloved of the Hebrides and tailored by the Fifty Shilling Tailors of happy memory. The plus-fours were worn at Head Office in Edinburgh as well as on his many field trips to the Highlands and Islands. Accompanying this somewhat conspicuous outfit were stout hand-made shoes with welt and soles which projected like a gutter round the uppers. A 'fore-and-aft bonnet' of the same tweed as his suit completed the outfit. In the days of tram-cars he had a method of crossing roads—even Princes Street in Edinburgh—which brought heart flutters to relatives, and to drivers, but nevertheless worked for him. Glancing briefly to ensure that no vehicle was within striking distance he would set out with long deliberate strides and cross unflinchingly to the other side, confident in his assumption that any on-coming traffic would slow down for him.

In 1913 his eldest sister, a schoolteacher, brought to the croft for the summer holidays a friend who taught in the same school. She was Margaret Stewart Young from Crieff in Perthshire. The following year she and my father were married and spent over six years in Thurso, where my two elder brothers, Colin and Bill, and I (christened Margaret but known as Paddy) were born. It was after my father's transfer to the Head Office of the Board of Agriculture for Scotland in Edinburgh that my youngest brother was born. At that time my father was trying to wean an alcoholic friend from his weakness and by way of encouragement he said that if his friend would keep sober the expected baby, if a boy, would be called after him. The bribe must have worked because this squirming new life was given the names Lewis Gordon Grant MacDonald—but at home he was always Sandy.

My mother was gentle and self-effacing, very supportive and with great inner reserves of strength. My father was the first to admit that it was her influence and encouragement that allowed him to develop in the way he did. He was a wonderful story-teller and could hold an audience enthralled. To his credit he could take a story against himself with the greatest good humour. Colin MacDonald was a tolerant man but pomposity, hypocrisy and 'Man's inhumanity to man' could rouse his impatience or rare anger. Education in its widest sense ranked high with him and he and my mother made considerable sacrifices—for in those days there were no university grants—to fit the four of us for careers in medicine, dentistry and veterinary sciences. But it was the informal education which remains in my memory. Long weekend walks over Edinburgh's Braid Hills, and the Blackfords and the Pentlands where birds, flowers, trees and animals were studied and such things as the rules of golf, the rotation of crops and the chances of fishing, and the like were touched on. There was that Sunday when he and I, in the interest of an article he was writing, walked miles round central Edinburgh, both old and new towns, to discover which streets were paved with Caithness flagstones. Research for another article involved a hunt through the telephone directory for surnames which were also the names of colours. A fascinating tapestry emerged of Greens, Blacks, Silvers and Scarlets, Whites, Golds, Browns, Blues and Pinks. Museums were visited and my mother was encouraged to take us at half-terms to the Border Abbeys, or to Stirling Castle and Cambuskenneth Abbey.

My father's thirst for knowledge was insatiable and the house was full of books of all kinds—dictionaries, quotation books, atlases, bird books, wild flower books, collections of poetry, history, mythology; the works of Burns, Scott, Dickens, Shakespeare and John Buchan and—my father's inseparable companion—*Para Handy* by Neil Munro. I well remember the excitement when we took delivery of the new 1929 edition of the *Encyclopaedia Britannica*, all 24 volumes of it in its exceedingly shiny 'mahogany' bookcase. This was something he could ill afford but which he longed to acquire. There were few days when he did not look up something in one or other of its volumes. I still have this set of books, battered, dog-eared and patched: much loved and still in frequent use.

Life in Edinburgh in no way lessened my father's love of, or interest in, the family croft on the Heights of Inchvannie. He continued as tenant and arranged with neighbouring crofters to have the use of the seventeen acres of land. The house was lent rent-free to anyone in need of a temporary home on condition that they kept it wind and weather-tight and that they moved out for the six weeks of our school summer holidays. He wanted to ensure that we were familiar with country as well as town ways. To my brothers and to me the Heights has always been a very special place. When school closed for the summer holidays, uniforms were tossed aside: large trunks were filled with blankets, sheets, pots and pans: a compartment was reserved on the morning train from Waverley station and into this, northward bound, piled two adults, four children and 'Sporran' the family Cairn terrier. Excitement rose as familiar landmarks brought us nearer and nearer to Achterneed station. There a neighbour, Jock, would meet us with horse and cart to take the luggage up the hill, but not for us youngsters the sedate pace of such transport. After a day of sitting in the train the steep open road called and we scampered this way and that, renewing acquaintance with familiar places and covering two or three times the distance plodded by the shaggy-footed shire horse. As the boys grew older they cycled north, taking with them a small tent and camping a night *en route*. These holidays were spent in primitive but blissful conditions and, barefoot, we roamed the hills, helped with hay-making and learned how to hoe turnips and to make ourselves useful at harvest time. From quite an early age an annual pilgrimage to the summit of The Ben was one of the highlights of the holiday. (Ben Wyvis is always The Ben to those in its shadow. It is over 3,400 feet high.) We chose a good day—there seemed to be so much sunshine in the 1920s and 1930s—each took a knapsack with food, drink and reference books and possibly a fishing rod. We would set out about 9 a.m. and return about 6 p.m., weary but happy, rejoicing in the weather, the wonderful views and the many interesting things we had seen. Sometimes we were rewarded by a sprig of white heather, more rarely white bell-heather. On one particularly hot day about half way up the Ben my father, clad in ancient plus-fours, produced a pair of tiny folding scissors and begged a family friend who was with us to hack off the lower parts of the plus-fours to produce instant shorts. Thus attired and with a knotted handkerchief to cover his bald head he was able to enjoy the expedition to the full.

We got to know our crofting neighbours and great characters many of them were. Two of my favourites were Mairi à claidheamh (Mary of the Sword) and Dannie Phadraic, both were MacDonalds but unrelated to each other or to our family. Mairi was a tiny bent person, in her eighties when I was a girl, with bright eyes, no teeth and plentiful conversation. She took snuff and Sandy and I used to love asking what her favourite brand was, in order to hear her invariable reply: 'Ach, m'eudail [my darling] the black snuff with the white dottacks.' Once every week she would cover her long dark skirts with a large snow-white starched apron and walk the two miles to Strathpeffer for bread and other 'messages' and trudge back up the long steep road weighed down by her purchases. She showed us the kist in which she kept her 'Clae's against the daith'—the garments in which she was to be buried. She never referred to toes, they were 'the fingers on my feet'. Dannie was a stone mason, and a wit. He was a great gardener and no lady ever left his house without a "bookay' of flowers: roses, maidenhair fern, and other blooms (including myself at the age of 8 or 9). One of his many sayings was 'Never turn your back on a lady or a ladder'. Dannie was looked after by his sister Mary, a gentle creature, one of the most beautiful women I have known.

Bob Aird, tall lean and eagle-eyed, and his diminutive wife Mary (a cousin of my father) were great friends of ours. It was on their croft that we learned to turn our hands to any task, and to feel at ease among the cattle and with the huge shire horse. Many were the feasts of home-made scones and pancakes with raspberry jam, washed down by scalding tea from a milk-pitcher, after helping at hay-making or harvest. My poor mother! During the holidays she had to feed a hungrier than ever brood with the inconvenience of an old black range and a few iron pots. Never a word of complaint did we hear from her. The boys kept the family pot boiling by snaring or shooting rabbits, with which the countryside was grossly over-populated. Sandy and I collected the milk daily from the only farm on the Heights.

These Highland holidays were magical and must have had a profound influence on us because when war service was over and circumstances permitted, Colin became a general practitioner in Skye, Bill took over the dental practice in Dornoch and I joined the Strathpeffer medical practice. Sandy's heart was in the Highlands but he did not come home from the war—the Anzio beach-head claimed his young life.

When working days were over it was back to the croft for my mother and father. My mother viewed the move away from Edinburgh and a large circle of friends with some trepidation, but for my father's sake she went north. It was not long before the glorious views, the tranquil pace of life, the charm and fascination of the changing seasons cast their spell upon her. She became devoted to the place and the people. Alterations were made to the house to ensure comfort and convenience as they grew older. Electricity was installed, water from the well was pumped to the house, larger windows made and a bathroom and a new kitchen were fitted up. The old range disappeared from the living room to be replaced by a fine open fireplace with back-boiler. (Oh, the luxury of running water, and hot at that!)

There followed a period of great contentment filled with writing, gardening, walking and enjoying the endless streams of visitors who came from far and near. Neighbours always found an open door and a welcome. The floor of the living-room was deliberately covered with a washable rubberoid material, so that his crofter friends would not be frightened off by fear of dirtying a fine carpet with their muddy boots.

Ill health, pain and several operations marred the last few years of Colin MacDonald's life, but his articles continued to appear in various national and local newspapers. The pleasure he took in family and friends was undiminished. In spite of the pain I think his verdict would have been 'It's been a grand life and never a dull moment.'

Now read on and, if you will, take pleasure in his writings.

Margaret MacDonald Newton
Heights of Inchvannie
Strathpeffer, Ross

Part One

ECHOES OF THE GLEN

OR

MAC-TALLA NAN GLEANN

CONTENTS

FOREWORD

Much of what is contained in this book appeared serially a few years ago in the *Ross-shire Journal* and the *Highland News*, and I am indebted to the editors of these papers for permission to reprint.

I am also much indebted to Mr Alastair MacKillop, Edinburgh, for putting the finishing touches to the Gaelic bits.

The tales and sketches are from actual life as it was lived amongst crofters in a Highland glen some forty to fifty years ago. Personal recollections of that period are particularly interesting because of the striking contrast in type, character, and outlook to be found amongst the people who then formed a crofting community.

The railway had just recently extended one of its spreading tentacles to the far north; compulsory education had but recently begun its revolutionizing career: and there was a general widening of the physical and intellectual horizon. So that, at that time there were to be found in the average Highland glen three main classes of people.

First there were the old, who were the last generation in Scotland of the quite illiterate. Generally, they were the descendants of those who had settled in the district following the upheaval caused by the Rebellion of 1745. Prior to that event, the clan system with its more or less defined territorial occupation prevailed throughout the Highlands. With the clan system, too, went a minimum in the way of arable cultivation. The easier pastoral system was much more congenial, and beef, mutton, venison, and fish formed the staple food. When girnals

or larders needed replenishing there was always the
favourite sport of helping themselves by foray on their
more industrious neighbours of the machairs.

But the Rebellion and the severe enactments which
followed it put an end to the old order. No more was it
possible for the Highlanders to supply the family needs
by recourse to the sword. In the absence of roads and
railways food imports could come only by boat, but in any
case there was no money to pay for them. Necessity is
indeed a hard taskmaster. It forced the ex-clansman to
manual labour. He had to turn to the tilling of the soil.
But even here there were limitations; for the extent of
arable land was meagre. Thus it was that the Highlander
was compelled not only to cultivate but to reclaim. For
a people so unaccustomed to work they did prodigies in
that direction. They trenched the virgin earth, they
drained it, they removed stones from it, as huge ramparts
of stone dykes still testify; they limed it, they manured it
and made it "rich to grow." From 1750 onwards, for
over a hundred years, this work of reclamation went on
and it is no exaggeration to state that in 1870 seventy-five
per cent. of the whole of the arable land in the Highlands
had been laboriously achieved in that way. It should be
noted, too, that the arable area in 1870 was considerably
in excess of what it is to-day—for much of what the people
so industriously reclaimed has been allowed to revert to
broom and heather.

These old men and women were purely Gaelic-speaking
and many of them did not understand a word of English.
In some respects they were undoubtedly ignorant and
parochially-minded. Their chief concern was with crops
and stock and weather and their neighbours' affairs. On
the other hand, although unable to read or write they
were conversant with interesting old tales and keenly
appreciative of such Gaelic poetry and songs as they might

hear recited or sung at weddings and other convivial gatherings. Moreover, the very exclusion of those old people from the knowledge that is in books made them entirely dependent for the formation of character and the adjustment of their lives and actions to the world around them on the intelligence, common sense, and charity with which nature had endowed them. Nor was there lack of "the spark of Nature's fire" in many of those old men and women. I can recollect many of them now, who possessed a mien, a dignity, and a solidity of character that no mere book-learning can ever bestow.

Then there were the middle-aged, the majority of whom had attended school in their youth for longer or shorter periods; but as attendance was not compulsory, and as the summer and autumn offered opportunities of earning much-needed money at herding and harvest, their school-days were usually confined to the winter months. A rudimentary knowledge of the three R's was the extent of their learning at school, and many of them allowed this knowledge, so painfully acquired, to lapse through lack of use. A few, on the other hand, had grasped with greedy clutch this new-found joy. It was a key that could open doors of new worlds to them, and they never ceased to use it. Such were the outstanding men of the district and the acknowledged leaders in all movements calculated to be for the good of the community.

As for the young generation, they, willy-nilly, went to school from the age of five to fourteen. Encouraged by poor but ambitious parents, and inspired by dreams of their own, the great majority of them sought diligently to acquire such education as would give them a higher market-value in the wider world around them. Equipped with that, and with a good physique, in addition to the virtues of decency, frugality, and honesty ingrained in their natures by the circumstances of their upbringing, they sought and got employment in many walks of life that drew them away from the Highlands. Year by year the cities claimed them; the colonies; foreign countries; in fact the human drift from the north had set in. And, whether for the ultimate good or ill of those who went, or of the nation as a whole, there can be no doubt whatever that, of the various factors which combined to produce the now attenuated Highland population, compulsory education was by far the greatest.

Just as a matter of interest I have measured accurately the extent of drift in the Strath of my youth and it is shown briefly thus:

	No. of Crofts	Total Population	Population under 20 years
In 1888	57	228	102
In 1936	41	130	33
Decrease	16	98	69

All my life I have been in close contact with crofters. For the first twenty-six years of it it was my privilege to have been one of a crofting community. My oldest and some of my most respected friends are there. Moreover, ours was the *ceilidh* house of the Glen. I can therefore fairly claim to have knowledge of my subject.

It has to be emphasized, though, that the *ceilidh* stories and the conversations as I heard them were in the Gaelic. Even the best English translation or rendering lacks much of the original *blas* (flavour or relish), but that just can't be helped.

There isn't much in the way of dialogue, but where dialogue does occur Highlanders are not made to speak Lowland Scots. That must be disappointing to many, but the truth is, Highlanders do not speak that way. They mostly speak good, if slow and strongly accented, King's English.

Moreover, unlike much that I have read concerning the Highlands, what is written here is not culled at second-hand or fanciful, but from personal experience and fact. Of course that may have rendered it less readable, but—

> *'S fhearr an fhirinn na'n t- òr,*
> *'S cha toil leam a' bhrèug.*

Or as it may be rather lamely rendered in the less expressive tongue—

> Truth transcends treasure;
> The false I despise.

C. MacD.

CHAPTER I

The Daily Round—Plain Fare—Peats in the Making—Look
before you leap!—Exit the old Fuel

THE daily round on a croft included—and still includes—
a good deal of hard work.

Money was always scarce; so were luxuries; but there
was generally a sufficiency of good plain food. This
combination of hard work and plain fare—with occasional
relaxations—went far towards producing a community
that was a poor field for a doctor. One neighbour that I
particularly remember, whose almost invariable breakfast
for over fifty years consisted of brose and milk and oatcake
and butter, and whose supper was a repeat of breakfast
with porridge substituted for brose, carried on his face
the rosy bloom of robust health right through to within a
few weeks of his death at eighty-seven, and his only
physical troubles were the result of such gastric indiscre-
tions as accompanied the celebration of New Year's Day
and such occasions.

Every season as it came round brought its own particular
activities. In spring there was the usual bustle associated
with ploughing and otherwise preparing the land for the
sowing and planting of crops; that was mostly men's
work. Summer brought with it turnip-thinning and hay-
making, at which both sexes gave a hand. It also brought
peat-cutting, which was one of the events of the year.
Often there was a neighbourly co-operation in this work;
two, three, or more families would form a squad that
worked together until they had cut peats sufficient for the
requirements of all concerned; and anyone who has never
had "a day at the peats" has missed a joyous experience.
There would, indeed, be exquisitely aching limbs and

14

backs after the first day of that hard work, but these were only subjects for joke and laughter.

The peat-moss in our case lay some four miles distant from the nearest house; the road to it was up a rough cart-track that led, first through the township, then through a shady fir-wood, and finally through two miles of heather. The whole squad would be afoot by five o'clock of a sunny summer's morning and ready to start off by six. There would be two or three older folk and maybe a dozen young people in all. There would be baskets packed with oatcakes and scones, fresh butter, home-made jam, hard-boiled eggs and—choicest of all—"speldacks" (a variety of the finnan haddock of particularly delicious flavour) for dinner and tea. And the banter and the laughter and the light hearts with which they walked the miles to the moss!

By noon, peats sufficient for some six months' fuel for one house would be cut and spread on the banks to dry; and appetites would be so keen that they would not have quarrelled with much less toothsome fare than was then provided. And oh! the ecstasy of that meal, spread on an emerald bank by the side of a purling burn, with the larks pouring out their souls in song in the blue vault overhead!

After dinner the older folk would rest for half an hour while their irrepressible juniors indulged in "soft-peat battles," that are infinitely more ludicrous in their facial "results" than snow-balling. Or, if there was an "innocent" from the south amongst the company, the catch of *leum nan tri fòidean* (the three-peat jump) would be tried out. For this practical joke—highly diverting to the onlookers and even laughed at by the victim—a spot was chosen at the edge of a deep peat-hag which contained a pool of black, peaty water. Those in the know would start a competition in "standing" long-jump; they jumped from the edge of the hag, and landed on the lower level across the pool. When the competition got very keen an expert would suggest that much longer jumps could be achieved if the start was made from a slightly higher level. To demonstrate his theory he would lay three hard peats one above the other on the heather close to the edge of the hag and parallel to it. He then stood on top of the peats and jumped. But he had to be very careful to spring almost vertically so as not to disturb the peats by the backward pressure of the toes; he just managed to clear the pool as a rule —sometimes he did not, and I have seen the biter bit! But, assuming no such initial catastrophe, the "innocent" was allowed a try. He—or she—never suspecting a trap, stood on the peats and jumped in the ordinary way—with disastrous results! The backward pressure of the toes at the moment of taking the spring caused the piled peats to tumble backwards and the athlete to take an involuntary header into the black mess below!

Sleep came without rocking that night; but the muscular pains and aches of next morning were in a class by themselves! However, another hard day at the peats was an effective, if heroic, remedy.

Scarcely any coal was used, and the annual fuel requirement of the township ran to 2500 loads of peat. As the years went by the difficulty of getting squads increased. Coal had to be resorted to, and by 1925 had so completely ousted the old fuel that in that year not one load of peats was burned in the whole of the Strath.

CHAPTER II

HARVEST was the busiest and most anxious season of the
year, yet it had a cheery atmosphere too. There was a
full family muster at the work which was of such vital
importance to all; everyone from eight to eighty gave a
hand. On the larger farms in the valley reaping machines
were in use. "Self-delivery" reapers were at that time
just coming in, and their revolving wings, besides perform-
ing the work of the second man, lent an added appearance
of activity to the field. But—with the exception of one
proud possessor of an antiquated "tilter"—all the crofters
cut their crop with the scythe. The day of the heuk had
just passed.

The scythe gang consisted of three people: the
"scyther," who cut the crop with such rhythmic sweeps
of his awkward-looking implement and laid it in an
orderly row by his left side; the "lifter" (usually a
woman), who gathered the crop into sheaf-size and laid
it on bands deftly made by herself from a small handful
of straightened straws; and lastly, the "binder-and-
stooker" (either sex), who tied the sheaves and stooked
them.

Given favourable conditions—a standing crop, a dry
day, and a gentle breeze—the gang would finish an acre
in a day of ten hours. Sometimes, when neighbours
joined forces at harvest as they did at peat-cutting and
there might be as many as six gangs working together, the
harvest-field presented an animated scene as the six

17

scythes, side by side, but each one on the right, back a yard from the one on the left, bit their way into the standing crop with a rhythm and timing that resembled the measures of a good-going song.

The state of the weather at harvest was, of course, the great factor which determined the time necessary for the attainment of that coveted last-cut handful of the year's crop, the *Maighdeann Bhuana*, which was duly decorated with gaily-coloured ribbons and hung on the kitchen wall till New Year's morning, when it was presented to the old mare in a spirit of mixed fun and solemnity.

In all but exceptional years the middle of October saw the crop all under broom thatch and *sioman* (straw rope). And then what romping fun we youngsters used to have running round the stacks playing *Cluich-nan-cruach* (the fun of the stacks)! It was keenly exciting, this stalking and chasing each other round the new-made stacks by the light of *Gealach bhuidhe Feill-Mhicheil* (the yellow moon of Michaelmas). The fun was liable to be spoilt, though, by the older lads and lassies retiring to dark corners for some quiet "coortin" (*suiridhe*)—much to the disgust of the wee ones—until they grew older themselves!

A few loads of sheaves were destined never to go into a stack. They were put straight into the barn for early threshing. This was for the double purpose of providing a straw supper (*Muillean Fodair*) for the beasts, whose pastures were now rather bare, and the household with the first oatmeal of the season. I suppose the beasts will still require to get their supper, but I'm thinking there is not the same demand for the *Min-Chorca* that used to taste so good!

After harvest there was a rush to get the potatoes lifted before Hallowe'en, for it was rather a discreditable mark to have potatoes still unlifted on the first of November. By this time, too, the first oatmeal of that year's crop would be in the girnal and there was a general feeling of security against the coming winter.

Winter was ushered in by the celebration of Hallowe'en; a festival of joyous adventure for the youths who formed raiding bands that "stole" neighbours' carts and ploughs and swingle-trees, and, by a process of interchanging wheels and axles, etc., contrived to give a few puzzling days to the owners. Anything in the nature of malicious mischief was debarred by the etiquette of the fun, but those few crofters who were foolish enough to resent this somewhat inconveniencing but harmless youthful frolic might rest assured of added and special attention when next Hallowe'en came round. And we were specially fortunate when two of our principal oppressors happened to be at variance with each other and not on speaking terms. That was a heaven-sent opportunity of achieving an amazing mix-up of carts and wheels and axles and ploughs and socks and swingle-trees which it took the hostile owners weeks to unravel; indeed sometimes the riddle could be solved only by the helpful intervention of one of the original but unsuspected perpetrators!

On the other hand, neighbours who didn't resent our frolics, and who left their ploughs and carts in the open, were seldom molested. There was no fun, for instance, in running off with anything belonging to *Uilleam Ruairidh*, for *Uilleam* left his gear unchained and unprotected and would never say an angry word if we went off with the lot.

So, instead of "stealing" *Uilleam's* gear, fantastically dressed and with blackened faces, we would pay a friendly call, announcing our arrival with a fusillade of turnips on the door.

Uilleam's attitude was not the result of calculating diplomacy; he was a kindly old man, living all by himself —and his dog Sharpy—genuinely fond of young folks and with a delightfully sympathetic understanding of their ways. He could read fortunes, too, in the white of an egg —a much more reliable medium than mere cards or tea-cups—and many a merry winter evening did the lads and lassies spend in *Uilleam's* cheery kitchen as he "saw" their various fortunes in the bubbles of the *Gealagan*.

One morning after Hallowe'en *Eilidh Dhonn's* chimney would not draw for the reason that *Maoilean's* washing-pot had been placed upside-down on the lum. Two of us climbed on to the roof and removed the obstruction. We had the grace to feel a little guilty on receiving much praise and a handful of "lozengers" from dear old *Eilidh*—for well we knew how the pot had got there!

Then there was the day the *Taillear Fada* and his wife slept in "*An latha rinn sinn moch-eirigh*" ("The day we did the early rising")—as himself used facetiously to refer to the incident.

It took a lot of doing, but we did manage without being discovered to plug up the windows and round the *Taillear's* door with a plaster of soft peat so that not a *dideag* (peep) of light could enter the house. As the *Taillear* never possessed a clock, but regulated his rising and retiring by the light of the sun, the ruse succeeded beyond our brightest expectation. It was the persistent *ranail* of the beasts in the byre that at last impelled the *Taillear* to open the door—and there, to his astonishment, was the sun at twelve o'clock!

CHAPTER III

As winter progressed towards the shortest days of the year, field work lessened, and there was opportunity for attending to the hundred and one things that needed repair or renewal. Leather harness needed sewing; belts required to be mended; hoes and rakes needed new teeth or handles; corn riddles required new bottoms or frames; turnip and potato baskets made of wild willow were repaired or made anew; the family boots had to be patched and soled—in fact there was scarcely a limit to the number of such indoor and necessary occupations on a well-managed croft.

Yet winter was not all devoted to work, and there was a surprising number of ways in which the long winter evenings could be made to pass pleasantly.

Despite the frowns with which the majority of clergymen of that day regarded dancing, youth would out, and so would dancing. One winter, when there had grown up in the Glen a young generation who knew no dancing because of the ecclesiastical opposition which had for several years suppressed tentative efforts at organizing a dancing class, a few lads set the ministerial wrath at defiance. They engaged a dancing-master, and, as there was no suitable hall available for their purpose, they arranged with an elderly crofter of youthful daring for the use of an old thatched barn. The barn had only an earthen floor and its roof showed generous patches of sky; but our heroes clubbed together and between them raised funds and labour sufficient to repair the roof and put in a wooden floor. That was a memorable winter;

practically every young person in the place joined the class—and in those days we *danced*.

To me those modern dances introduced from the U.S.A. are an anæmic exhibition. There is nothing to them at all. You just go slithering your feet along the floor in any old way you choose. There does not appear to be any definite relationship of step to music. The main effort is in the direction of avoiding effort; and, if you please, after but a few minutes of this wildly unexciting stuff the musicians very considerately stop to give the poor things a rest. But the latter clap their hands in dull unison to signify their wish to carry on a little longer. So the music and the inanity start off again!

But where are the dances of forty years ago? Quadrilles and Lancers with their stately grace and timing? The Highland Schottische that in its first part was the epitome of accurate step-control, and in its second stage demanded such chivalrous skill in steering clear of calamity in the joyous swinging swirl? Petronella? How your top couple used to race "down the middle," warm hand in hand, and then "back again and waltz round." You could be danced properly to one tune only; but that tune was an inspiration, and it was unworthy of us to dub it as we did, "The Cat took the Measles and she died, poor thing"!

And the romp of Rory O'More!—and the quaint deferential gallantries in Sir Roger de Coverley—better known as the Haymakers' Jig!

Polka! Pas-de-quatre! Circassian Circle! Flowers of Edinburgh! These are some of the names that we then responded to so heartily, and that now recall our fondest memories.

But high above them all, in actuality and retrospect, stood and stands the Scotch Reel and Reel o' Tulloch. For that was more than a mere dance: it was a medium for expression of national and individual character. When the master of ceremonies announced the magic name the floor filled in a flash, and from the initial sweeping curtsy to the glorious final flourish it was an inspired poem of physical activity and spiritual satiety. Oh, Jimac o' Davie! that used to stamp out "time" with your tackety toes (for a real reel, pumps are a futility) so that you inspired Geordie's elbow to magic with his fiddle—which in turn inspired you to higher and still higher abandon of heel and hand, and hoochs that rose in grand crescendo to the culminating crash. . . . What would you say to the so-called dances of to-day? To the Foxtrot, the One-step, and the Two-step, with their slithering feet and timeless, tuneless pusillanimity? I can hear your scornful "*Air falbh leo! Cha'n fhiach iad!*" ("Away with them! They are worthless!")

There was a never-to-be-forgotten grand finale in the shape of a ball in the village hall—in close proximity to the Manse! Whatever credit fell to be ascribed to the clergy of those days would certainly not include an item for *intentionally* adding brightness and happiness to the lives of their parishioners.

CHAPTER IV

VERY little notice was taken of Christmas Day and it was
not until the eighties that the first of January began to be
celebrated in our circle as New Year's Day, and even in
those houses where the new fashion was adopted there
was a celebration on Old New Year's Day too. Many
families did not take to the new fashion—in their own
homes—for twenty or thirty years after that. Indeed,
there is a remnant of respect for Old New Year's Day in
the shape of a neighbourly dram still to be met with on
the east end of the Strath. For many years both fashions
were observed in one house or another, with the result
that there was a more or less continuous celebration from
the night of 31st December till the 13th January. However, whisky cost only 2/3 per bottle—"Special" 2/6—and
it was whisky! There would be first-footing and feasting
and singing and dancing to surfeit.

But the event of New Year's Day itself was the game
of shinty.

There was no limit to the number which might form a
team. Everyone was enlisted on one side or another, and
it was not uncommon to see in the game men of seventy
and boys of seven. There might not be much method or
combination in the play of a team, but there were great
individual players who could do miracles to the *cnag* (ball)
with the aid of a home-made *caman* which was treasured
for years for this annual outing.

One game I remember was captained on the one side
by a man of sixty years of age and the other by a sixty-two-
year-old. They had been opposing captains for years and

the closest of friends all their lives. Both were over six feet and as lean as a lath. They met on the field of play about eleven o'clock, each carrying his trusty home-made *caman*. Of course, several drams had already been downed and many *slainte mhaths* and *Bliadhna-mhath ùrs* (Good-healths and Good-New-Years) exchanged.

The method of selecting sides is interesting. The two captains stood facing each other. *Dònull* held his *caman* by the middle and threw it vertically towards *Uilleam*, who caught it where he could with one hand. Then each in turn took a hand-over-hand grip of the *caman* towards the top. The last to get a grip at the top and be able, with that grip, to swing the *caman* three times round his head had first call on the crowd for his side. They then called in turn till everybody was enrolled. Then off went jackets—which were piled to form "hail-posts" at either end of the field, and then . . . !

Modern hockey players consider modern shinty a wild and dangerous game. I wonder what they would think of the shinty served up by the grandfathers! Even on a New Year's Day "friendly" play would be wild enough, but should it be a real match between rival parishes, then indeed it was no field for falterers.

Foul?—There was none. No quarter given or asked.

"*Cluich suas! Sid thu Iain! Buail am Bug . . . !*"—(I'm not translating that one).

Skin and hair went flying in real style. A bloody face or limb was a mark of honour, and by the end of two hours' fierce encounter few indeed were scathless. At the New Year friendly generous "revivers" were resorted to frequently during the match, but so hard was the game that every man was as sober as a judge by one o'clock, and partook of an amazing meal of broth and beef and potatoes which the goodwife of the house had prepared in three large washing-pots.

CHAPTER V

A School for Orators—Terror in the Dark—The Haunted Rock

OUR Strath was rather singular in that, since the early seventies, it had a properly constituted and well-conducted Debating Society, which met two or three evenings each week from October to April. For the first twenty years the Society had rather a precarious existence. It had plenty spiritual heat but no material home. One winter it met in the smiddy. For some years an old thatched barn was its temple. Again a granary housed it for a while; and one winter, when the local stationmaster was its president, the Highland Railway waiting-room sheltered its enthusiastic members. Moreover, at the end of that session the proceeds of a collection were applied to purchasing paraffin in substitution of the Company's paraffin consumed throughout the winter. There seemed to be a kindlier contact between railway officials and the public in those days than is possible with the present soulless combine—and no whit less honesty.

Later—as recent as thirty-nine years ago—the Society became sufficiently strong and enthusiastic to erect a small hall as its permanent headquarters. There followed a period of much activity and progress; then decay; and now, for over twenty years, not a vestige of the old Debating Society—only the little hall—sadly forsaken—but for its ghosts. . . .

In addition to the debates there were magazine-nights, hat-nights, draughts, etc. A youth was eligible for membership on attaining the age of fifteen, and no Member of Parliament ever took his first seat with keener pride and apprehension than did our initiates on their first night.

A young member was not compelled by rule to speak

other than very briefly during his first session, but in subsequent years it was obligatory on everyone to take a responsible part in debate. There were some, of course, who never became fluent or interesting speakers, but there were several who did, and who could express their well-considered opinions in concise, consecutive form and cool collected manner that stood them in good stead in future years in various walks of life.

Talking of ghosts . . . A hardy annual of our debates was: "Are ghosts real or imaginary?" On that night —despite previous experience of the creepy spines and terrifying dreams that were sure to follow—there would be a full muster. I forget most of the hair-raising examples cited in support of the affirmative, but I well remember the unadmitted but obvious chumming on the way home after a "ghost night." One such night, after a succession of real bonnet-lifters, my heart was in my throat during the quarter of a mile I had to go after parting with my pals. It was one of those nights of Egyptian darkness that we get in late autumn, with not a breath stirring, and so utterly dark you couldn't see your hand a foot from your nose. All of a sudden I was tripped off my feet and fell flat on my face on something soft and warm! There was a grunt, and then to my horror the soft thing wriggled below me and there came the most agonized "*Baaow*" of a cry I had ever heard. In frantic terror I let out a howl that must have out-yowled the immediate cause of it, and caused my friends to making yelling inquiry as to what on earth was the matter. With an effort I gathered my wits and lit a match. There was—a neighbour's indignant black stirk! It had selected the middle of the road as its bed for the night, and in the darkness I had tripped over and fell plunk on its grass-distended stomach!

Here is one of the ghost stories I do remember. It was

told by a brother of Maggie's, and with much better effect than it can be written.

Johnnie was the "lad" with the head shepherd up at the Glen. He came from farther west the country, where at that time there was a thoroughgoing belief in ghosts and the supernatural. At the Strath there was an awfully bonnie lassie who had aroused in Johnnie the high-pulsing surge of youthful love. Be he never so tired after a day on the hill, or in the fanks, Johnnie, every Saturday night, tramped the three miles that separated the Glen from the Strath, to worship at his shrine. But never once—unless in broad daylight—did he take the short cut along the railway that wound through "The Rock" with its awesome crevices and eerie buttresses that rose abruptly to over three hundred feet. Even in daylight, for Johnnie, "The Rock" was the veritable home of demons and witches and lost souls. One Saturday he was long delayed on the hill by a "jibbing" ewe—that most exasperating of brutes that will not join the general drove and run before the dog, but turns and stamps its foot in defiance; causing much embarrassment to the collie and inspiring most shepherds to astonishing heights of poetic execration. Well, that night Johnnie was very late in getting home, and, despite a hurried toilet and a gulped meal, it was almost dark before he started off for the Strath and Annie.

Instinct advised the long way round. Love urged the short cut through "The Rock"; and the strongest proof that can be adduced of Johnnie's far-gone condition is that love won. With fast-beating but stout heart he made for the opening at the west end of the frowning cliffs. Heavens! it was darker than he thought! And there were swirling gusts of wind that sometimes blew him forward, sometimes held him back, and anon would nearly snatch the bonnet off his head. A sudden hoot from an owl nearly made him scream. His spine went youkie at the clattering descent of some stones sent a-rolling by goats which frequented "The Rock." He dared not look up: with bent head and half-shut eyes he held steadily on. Now he was nearing the most dreadfully dark part of that horrible place. Another hundred yards and he would be past the worst and would run like a hare for the other end. Just then, out of the pitch-black night it came: a terrorized blood-curdling scream, that echoed and re-echoed through "The Rock"! It was too much for Johnnie's already taut nerves: with a moan of abject terror he turned and fled: fled from that infernal chasm of devils and foul fiends, back to the west entrance, and on by the long roundabout way over bog and burn and heather to rejoin the railway a good half-mile beyond "The Rock." Here, out in the open, the darkness was less profound; and to make up for lost time Johnnie set off down the line at a steady trot.

Nearing the station—some two miles from "The Rock" —Johnnie caught up with Maggie, the head shepherd's daughter, who was also Strathward-bound on shopping bent. Mightily relieved to have company he fell into step. Soon it dawned on Johnnie that Maggie (who had not a scrap of his belief in ghosts and witches) must have come through "The Rock" very shortly before he made his effort that had ended so disastrously. Had she heard anything? Curiosity set him speiring.

"Did you come through 'The Rock'?" he inquired.

"Yes," said Maggie. "Did *you*? But of course you wouldn't!"

"Well," said the embarrassed but truthful Johnnie, "I meant to, but I didn't. I—— But didn't you *hear* anything when you came through?"

"Hear anything? No; of course not. What would I hear?"

"I'm telling you," Johnnie heatedly asserted, "I wouldn't go through 'The Rock' in the dark again if you were to give me the Cromartie Estate!"

"Don't be a fool, Johnnie," said the practical Maggie.

"Fool!" said the outraged Johnnie. "I'm not a fool, and I'm telling you that if there wasn't murder done in that rock to-night there will be before long. I was half-way through when I heard the awfullest yelling and screaming!"

It was then a queer expression came on Maggie's face: a light as of understanding; and then she began to laugh and laugh, till she was nearly hysterical with laughter.

"What the devil are you laughing at?" inquired an angry Johnnie.

"Oh, Johnnie! I'm laughing at you—and at myself—and at the whole thing! Wait till I tell you. When I got to near the end of 'The Rock' to-night, all of a sudden out of the darkness in front there swooped up something like a big white sheet. It rose over my head and swished down at my back—I could feel the cold 'wind' of it on my neck. It all came on me so suddenly that I'm afraid I did scream like a scared schoolgirl."

"Yes, yes," said the excited Johnnie; "but what is the meaning of a white sheet on a dark night in 'The Rock'? And"—derisively—"how did a white sheet get there?"

"Well," said Maggie, "I was annoyed to think that I had screamed like a frightened lassie, so I turned round to see what it was; and it was this—no doubt thrown out from a train, and certainly caught up by a gust of wind" and the frugal Maggie produced from her basket—a page of *The Scotsman*!

The evidence was indisputable, and not a little humiliating to poor Johnnie; but on a dark night not even his love for Annie could ever entice him through "The Rock" again.

CHAPTER VI

The *Ceilidh*—Patronymics—The Land League

BUT the pastime par excellence of the winter months was
the *ceilidh*. It seems incredible that nearly fifty years can
have elapsed since those well-remembered *ceilidh* evenings
with their kindly gossip and stories of events and characters
of long ago.

Of all words and institutions, this of *ceilidh* is surely now
the most misrepresented and abused! It never gives me
real pleasure to say anything nasty of anybody, but I
cannot help thinking that those Highland Associations of
the South which in recent years have been foisting on
their members and the general public those so-called
ceilidhs of theirs have much to answer for.

A *ceilidh* where you have to pay to get in!—in a hall!
—with a platform!—and a chairman!—in a boiled
shirt!—and the folks all dressed up!—and a programme!
—and set speeches!—and everyone so mincingly polite
with the mimmery of a formal concert! *Mo Naire! Mo
Naire!* Call it a gathering. Call it a concert. Call it
a Highland Concert if you will: but do not call it a
ceilidh.

A *ceilidh* was not a fore-ordered thing: it was a natural
growth. Only round a kitchen peat-fire could it flourish.
Nobody was bidden. Anybody came. There was
absolute social equality. The sartorial peak never rose
beyond a clean collar and brushed whiskers. The talk
just came—easily—naturally. One topic led to another.
Each was free to talk or listen. Although, naturally,
some excelled, never was the *ceilidh* a "show-off" place
for the individual. There was utter camaraderie, utter
"off-guard." There was an easy friendly understanding

atmosphere about the *ceilidh* that I have never quite met in any other kind of gathering—and when they rose to go, "*cabhag air do thilleadh*" (hasten your return) from *Bean an tighe* (the housewife) adequately expressed everybody's sentiments.

Perhaps nothing can so emphasize the equality that pervaded the *ceilidh* — and throughout the crofting community for that matter—as their mode of addressing each other. There was no "mister" at all. One man to another was just *Dònull* or *Ruairidh* or *Alasdair* or whatever his Christian name was. Two of the same name were distinguished from each other by some special qualification, as *Mòr* (big) or *Beag* (little), or it might be by the addition of his father's or grandfather's Christian name or craft. An art or craft, even if not practised in the family for generations, might still be the distinguishing patronymic. Often, indeed, the legal name of a person was practically forgotten. There were more than a dozen old people in the Strath whose proper names I never knew until curiosity set me inquiring—and then, some of those I asked weren't too sure!

A married woman, whether widow or wife, was addressed as the wife of her husband. If her husband's name was—or had been—*Dònull*, she was addressed as "*Bean Dhònuill*"—with a tendency to add the distinguishing patronymic of her man.

Even neighbouring children adopted this mode of address towards their elders—and never with disrespect. Unmarried women were invariably known by their Christian names. To be addressed as "Miss" was a great joke.

It was when the big snowstorms came that real good *ceilidhs* were possible, because then no outside work could be done and responsibilities were limited to the feeding of the beasts and barn-work. Then when night came—

often, it seems now, with a bright moon shining over a world of white, but at intervals darkened by wild showers of drifting snow—one after another of the neighbours would drop in. Inside there was a blazing peat-fire that sent its welcome warmth to every corner of the kitchen. The bairns were gathered round a table busy at lessons. The goodman had pulled in the old armchair to the fire-side and adjusted his spectacles—bought from a pedlar for one-and-sixpence and a fill of tobacco, and by the simple test of efficiency equal to any .modern lenses costing two guineas—preparatory to having a pre-liminary glance at the contents of one of the local news-papers. It might be the *Ross-shire Journal* (still flourishing) at that time execrated by all crofters for its Tory views on the land question, but bought weekly because of the necessity of finding out the moves of the enemy. Or it might be that staunch supporter (now defunct) of the land agitation the *Invergordon Times*. The goodwife, whose amazing variety and volume of work went on from early morning till late at night, and whose robust health and intense interests made her life a real joy compared to the drab existence of the working man's wife in the city, would probably be knitting or sewing or darning.

There was no formal knocking at doors in those days, and the first indication of an arrival for the *ceilidh* was the sound of thumping and stamping of feet outside, and finally of slapping with a broom or heather besom to remove the snow from boots and leggings. Then a loud hail: "*Cò tha stigh?*" (Who is within). "That will be Dònull; let him in," the goodman would say to one of the bairns. Someone ran to open the door and to smile a welcome.

In the course of the next hour half a dozen others—and sometimes more than twice that number—would arrive.

A more homogeneous lot it would be difficult to imagine;
yet they were a study in contrasts.   Nearly every man was
a rank individualist and only subscribed to another's
opinion if, after critical discussion and mature consideration, he felt he was justified in doing so.

At that period there was a strong move on the part of
crofters throughout the Highlands to obtain statutory
fair rents, security of tenure, and the right to compensation for permanent improvements effected on their
holdings.   Branches of the Land League had been formed
in nearly every parish, and feeling between crofters and
estate factors ran pretty high.   I shall not discuss here the
merits or otherwise of the case on either side, but no one
who witnessed the *ceilidh* on an evening when the activities
of the Land League were under discussion can ever forget
the scene.   Seated in his armchair by the side of the fire,
with the eyes and ears of the whole *ceilidh* circle giving him
rapt attention, the goodman would read what one of the
papers had to say about the matter in its leading article, or
what others' views were as expressed in "Letters from
Correspondents."   A short paragraph would be read,
then the spectacles would be removed, and, changing to
the Gaelic, the reader would make the point crystal-clear
to his audience in their mother-tongue.   When the point
was thoroughly taken by all, the process would be repeated, again and again, until the end of the article was
reached, and then everyone joined in general discussion.
It was indeed an impressive scene.

CHAPTER VII

Ceilidh Stories—The *Caileag Bheag Bhàn* (Little fair-haired lassie)—
Uisdean Mòr and *Mairi Bhoidheach* (Big Hugh and Bonnie Mary)

DÒNULL was one of the outstanding men of the *ceilidh*.
He would come in stroking and blowing the snow from
his red beard. He was a low-set, sturdily built man,
the embodiment of health and vigour and the kindliest
of neighbours—although very critical of those who slept
long of mornings! He himself was up at five A.M. summer
and winter. His chimney put up the first smoke in the
parish. He could tell to a minute when the others smokes
went up, and after many years of close observation of the
point he had by this gauge arrived at a rough estimate
of the relative worthiness of every family in the place. He
had practically no book-learning, but he had a wonderful
knowledge of Gaelic songs and sayings; and for native
intelligence, wit, and humour I have seldom met his
superior. Dònull had a rare knack of gathering news,
and as he was a born *raconteur* his way of retailing it was a
lesson in elocution. Moreover he had a retentive memory,
and could quote from such Gaelic bards as Duncan Bàn,
Rob Donn, and Ross of Gairloch with unerring aptitude
to the tale in hand. He was the only farmer in a district
of crofters but he entertained no snobbish views of social
superiority on that account and was always "one of
ourselves." Old and young welcomed Dònull to the
ceilidh, for his presence assured them of an interesting and
merry evening.

We bairns just loved to lure Dònull on to telling the
story of—

THE CAILEAG BHEAG BHÀN

or

THE LITTLE FAIR-HAIRED LASSIE

The *Caileag Bheag* was really an ancestor of Dònull's own, and the story came down to him from his mother, who had got it from her grandfather:

Away back in the distant past the people of Dònull's clan were at strong enmity with a clan who lived three days' journey away. Fights and forays between them were of frequent occurrence. One day didn't the *Caileag Bheag Bhàn*—then only two years of age and the darling of the district—go amissing. High and low they searched for her; by the burn-side, in the heather, in the woods. But never a trace of their darling could they find, and sore, sore were their hearts for many a long day.

Eighteen years later a young man of Dònull's clan was returning from the wars in Holland. For short cut he chanced going through the old enemy territory. But he had to go warily for, if discovered, he might never reach home.

He was stealthily winding his way up a burn-side where the hazel bushes, open spaces, and sparkling fern-fringed pools were transformed by the afternoon sun into a veritable fairy-land. Suddenly Tormaid Og stood spell-bound! Across the clearing by the side of a pool, clad in dress of green bracken and with a garland of wild flowers in her hair, stood the most beautiful *Caileag* he had ever seen! But she was no immortal.

Utterly unconscious of his near presence the *Caileag* began to sing in a voice—oh! so sweet and tuneful! And, to Tormaid's amazement, the song was a croon of his own clan!

Fearful lest he should frighten away so lovely a creature

Tormaid decided on a ruse. When she came to the end of a verse in which the mother asked the little one—now on the point of sleep—what had she to be afraid of—for would not the big brothers of the clan keep her safe, Tormaid remembered the response that came from the big brothers and this he sang in low melodious voice. The response came so naturally that at first the *Caileag Bheag* did not seem to realize that it was an actual human being who made it. But before she could take alarm Tormaid Og said:

"Fear not, *mo chaileag Bheag Bhàn*. A friend is near you. Nay, not merely a friend but a kinsman. For surely those features and tresses of yours belong not here but to my clan. And the croon?" said he. "Where learned you the croon that is ours?"

Assured by the friendliness in his voice the *Caileag* explained that she had thought she belonged to the local clan and that they were all so good and kind to her; but that of late she had been dissatisfied, and a yearning for she knew not what had come over her. As for the croon, she did not know where it came from. It and the music of it just "swam into her heart" one day.

But Tormaid pointed out that it must be the unconscious recollection that came to her of what her mother used to sing her to sleep with as a child.

Events followed joyfully after that. The *Caileag Bheag Bhàn* knew Tormaid Og was speaking truth and straightway went home with him to her own people. Great was the rejoicing amongst young and old.

For a time there was fear of a raid by the ancient enemy; but it soon transpired that the latter were as fond of the *Caileag Bheag Bhàn* as were her own people; and as the great desire of both sides was for her happiness they agreed to enter a friendly compact—and so ended the old enmity for ever.

Of another type entirely was Dònull's story of—

UISDEAN MÒR AND MAIRI BHOIDHEACH

or

BIG HUGH AND BONNIE MARY

Uisdean was a strapping lad of twenty-five and foreman on one of the big farms in the valley.

Mairi was twenty-two and dairymaid at the same place. She lived with her widowed mother in a cottage half a mile from the farm and was just as nice and bonnie a lassie as you could meet on a day's journey.

For five years Uisdean had been courting Mairi but for some reason or another had never come to the scratch. It began to look as if he might prolong the courting stage indefinitely. Needless to say, this prospect did not please Mairi. The *Maighstir* (Master), too, an observant, kindly old man with whom Mairi was a great favourite, had taken stock of what was going on and was getting impatient at Uisdean's dilly-dallying.

Every term day the maighstir would say to Mairi, " I suppose I will be losing you, *'Mhairi 'ghalad*, by the end of the next term?" But ever it was the same doubtful reply.

Then one evening the maighstir and Mairi put their *comhairle cuideachd* (consulted together) and things began to happen next morning.

It was the day of the Muir-of-Ord Market. By five in the morning the maighstir was ready for off, grey pony and *breacan* (plaid) all complete. Then of a sudden he remembered! He shouted for Uisdean.

"Uisdean," said he, "run as fast as your legs will take you to Mairi's house and ask her if she will do me the favour of lending me a hundred pounds till to-morrow. I need the money for the Muir to-day and I forgot that this was a bank holiday!"

Uisdean opened wide his eyes and stared. Then he scratched his head and concluded that the maighstir had gone insane! But anyway, the maighstir was insistent.

"Off you go!" said he in well-simulated wrath, "and don't stand there like a choking hen!"

And to humour the madman Uisdean ran off on his fool's errand.

Mairi was just leaving home for the day's work when Uisdean arrived.

"It's a fine morning, Uisdean," Mairi greeted him with a becoming flush. "But what is all the hurry? Is anything wrong at the farm?"

"Wrong," exclaimed Uisdean. "If the maighstir hasn't gone off his head!"

"Indeed! Indeed!" said Mairi. "It's myself that is sorry! And how has it taken him?"

"Taken him!" said Uisdean. "Hasn't he sent me here like a fool to ask if you will lend him a hundred pounds for the Muir-of-Ord to-day!"

"Ach! and is that all?" retorted Mairi, apparently greatly relieved. "And why should he be off his head to ask that? Indeed it is myself that will lend him the money and welcome. Come you in for a minute till I get it."

Uisdean was dumbfounded but followed Mairi in amazement into the cottage. Mairi went to her *ciste* (trunk), took out a fat roll of one-pound notes, and deliberately counted out a hundred of them. Then said she to the now nearly petrified Uisdean:

"Are you sure it was only a hundred he wanted because he is welcome to more?"

Uisdean was just able to assure her that it was a hundred pounds the maighstir had mentioned.

"Off with you, then," urged Mairi, "and don't let the decent man be late for the market!"

Uisdean and Mairi were married at the next Martinmas term, and they lived happily to a very old age. I happen to know and esteem their descendants this very day.

Mairi always kept ten one-pound notes rolled over a wad of newspaper locked away in her *ciste*. But she wisely never told Uisdean that that was the maighstir's wedding present, or that these and the hundred pounds she "loaned" on that memorable morning had been given her by the maighstir the night before for that very purpose—and to bring a laggard lover to the point!

CHAPTER VIII

Seumas the Philosopher—Calum: a Close Shave—Sian: the
Protective Charm

ANOTHER outstanding character was *Seumas*. He was
comparatively well educated and had a small but select
library. He got two or three weekly papers and one
monthly magazine—Stead's *Review of Reviews*—and sometimes he had American and other foreign papers and
periodicals sent to him from friends abroad. Seumas did
not come often to the *ceilidh*, but when he did come mere
gossip was taboo for that evening. Stories of pioneer life
in Canada or Australia and political or ethical disserta-
tions were his sort of contribution, and I can yet see the
eager interest of the less well-informed as they listened to
his graphic discourse. Seumas was at once the best and
the worst crofter in the district. He always had good
crops and stock and was held in great respect by his
neighbours, but accomplishments in which other men
took supreme pride—for instance, a straight furrow or a
well-built stack—were matters of utter indifference to him.
I have seen him nearing a "finish" in his lea ploughing
with the unploughed rig yards wide at one end and run
to nothing at the other, and "a straight like a corkscrew."
When I mildly twitted him on the point he laughed
unconcernedly, and told me that it was only when I
mentioned the matter he realized he *was* ploughing; he
had spent the whole forenoon just following the horses
and absently turning over the ground, but his thoughts
had been occupied with some poem of Burns, the run of
which he had been trying to get right!

"But," said he, "although the furrows are crooked the
oats will grow just as well as if they were straight"; and

so they did, for he always used the best of seed and kept his land in a high state of fertility.

On another occasion I was giving him a hand with the leading-in of the harvest; he was building the stack and I was forking on. He kept up an interesting conversation all the time and I had to warn him repeatedly that the stack was going agee. He did try to rectify matters, but usually overdid it until, when nearly finished, the stack had assumed rather a weird shape; but the builder's concern was with something in Russia. Just as the last of the standing sheaves were being fitted in at the top the whole structure came toppling to earth—with the architect half-buried in the ruins! To most stackers such a happening would have seemed a calamity, but my philosophic friend merely grasped an armful of sheaves, started to build again on a new foundation, and proceeded with the tale of Siberia!

CALUM: A CLOSE SHAVE

Calum came from the west end of the Strath. He was an old soldier and had been with the Seaforths in Egypt at the battle of Tel-el-Kebir. His stories of personal encounters and blood and battles were of a kind that made Buffalo Bill's exploits seem comparatively anæmic. How we revelled in Calum's stories!—in the telling of which I am convinced he never sacrificed colour and effect for veracity. But one could not doubt the truth of that time when the great big Dervish with a ferocious face ran at Calum with the very obvious intention of plunging a long-hefted spear through his entrails; or of how Calum, partly in terror and partly because his Highland blood was up, side-stepped smartly—he always emphasized the celerity of that particular side-step—and turned the tables by plunging his bayonet—a grand "third point with the lunge"—right into his assailant's diaphragm until the point came out at the back! I can still hear the squelch with which that son of Pharaoh fell in his tracks. But not before his spear (deviated somewhat from its true aim by the accident to its owner) had pierced the side of Calum's body just outside the ribs. The wound soon healed up, but the *ceilidh* puzzle was: how did Calum come to be wounded at all? For had not his old neighbour, *Mairi Mhor*, put the *sian* on him before he went away to the war? —the *sian* which was a sure shield against all injury by enemy missiles? However, it was comforting to reflect that that one small wound was the only evidence of its inefficacy; and, indeed, taking into consideration the size and ferocity of this particular Dervish, was not the slight wound rather a proof of its *efficacy*?

CHAPTER IX

An Taillear Fada and his "Alteration"

AND who that ever saw—and heard—the *Taillear Fada* (The Long Tailor) could ever forget him? The *Taillear* was actually six feet six inches in height but he was so thin —we used to say we would thread him through a darning-needle—that he gave the impression of being over seven feet at least. His voice was something unique: it had only one tone and volume and these were of such stentorian character that they would make the best efforts of a sergeant-major on parade seem feeble. When, therefore, as frequently happened, the *Taillear* and his wife had a difference of opinion over some domestic detail, and when the argument was conducted—as it usually was—out-of-doors, all the neighbours within a mile radius could listen-in with the greatest of ease and be thoroughly informed as to the *Taillear's* opinion of his consort. Her retorts might be inaudible to the listeners but judging from the ire they seemed to arouse in her husband they must have been very much to the point. As I grew older and got to know this strange couple intimately I was surprised to find that they got on very well together and were really quite fond of each other. I could only conclude, there-fore, that those wordy wars were merely a sort of training for "keeping their hand in" at the art of crushing retort— an accomplishment in which both were ever expert.

When the *Taillear Fada* came to the *ceilidh*, the others generally manœuvred him into telling the story of that time he went all the way to Edinburgh Hospital for the "alteration" (operation) to his leg. He rode part of the way on "Rory," a very small horse for such a long-legged man. One of Rory's successors that I remember was also small, and when his master bestrode him the long legs just reached the ground; and when the rider wanted to dismount he did so by the simple process of standing on his toes and commanding Rory to "go on"—which Rory did—leaving his master standing on mother-earth behind him.

I will not tell here of the adventures on the journey south, but the experience in hospital must be touched on. The first problem was an adequate bed; the one that had been prepared for him was too short. When that was ultimately overcome there was trouble about the sheets: the patient complained that they were cold and "slippery." But the matron was firm, and sleep in sheets he had to—for the first and last time in his life. Then when the doctor came to see the patient, and turned down the bed-clothes for the purpose of examining the leg, he gazed in astonishment and exclaimed, "Good Lord! What a length!" Shortly afterwards that doctor went out and brought in another, who immediately on viewing the *Taillear* exclaimed, "My God! What a length!" And yet a third doctor was brought in and his first remark was "Good Lord! What a length of a man!" These outspoken comments on his person annoyed our friend, but he restrained his anger and said not a word ("*Cha dubhairt mi guth!*"). But when, on the morning of the "Alteration," he was put into a wagon and wheeled through to the operating theatre where there were several "stoodants," and when the latter on seeing our hero whispered practically in chorus, "Good Lord! what a length of a man!" it was too much for the *Taillear*, who raised his head and addressed them firmly—and do not forget the voice—"Com, com, you there! What you are going to do, do it, and never mind your 'what a man!'— and non of your cloryforum for me neither!" It was in the early days of chloroform and it had been suggested to the patient that some of the new drug should be administered to ease the pain. But the patient would have none of it, and the bone was exposed and scraped, and the only indication of pain on the part of the *Taillear* was that he chewed a bit off the sheet—and he didn't like sheets anyway!

CHAPTER X

Alastair: inspired—Ranald and the Rooshian—Prison Life
made easy—The Spirit of the Glens

ALASTAIR was a general favourite throughout the neighbourhood. He seldom missed a *ceilidh*, but his usual
rôle there was that of appreciative listener. His philosophy seemed to have led him to the conclusion that it
wasn't worth while holding on to any point of view so
strongly as to involve one in a quarrel or heated argument.
It is true that occasionally—perhaps twice in the course
of a year: once when the stirks were sold and again on
the rent day—when a certain degree of victory over the
ills of life had been attained, anyone who put any proposition to this usually complaisant man would find that
he had caught a Tartar. For under the inspiring influence of a few hours in the village inn Alastair would
argue any point with anybody! Not in a nasty spirit,
but in a jovial, loquacious, and delightfully witty manner
so utterly unlike his usual quiescence that he would hold
the stage for that evening.

Telling of Alastair brings his neighbour, Ranald, to
the memory. Ranald's prestige in the *ceilidh* circle lay
in the fact that he had been in the Crimean War. This
old campaigner had lain with the British Army for months
outside Sebastopol. The siege was a long, drawn-out
affair, and a certain degree of friendship grew up between
the soldiers on either side, but more particularly between
the opposing sentries, a number of whom had got to
recognize each other and "conversed" by signs and
actions in quite a friendly way.

But there one was highly unpopular black-bearded
"Rooshian" who was given to express his contempt for

the British by gestures which have a common meaning in all languages. This man, as he did sentry-go on top of the city wall, had often roused the ire of the British sentry opposite by his insulting "language," and there had been many threats of reprisal; but there was a strict order that no shot was to be fired except for the purpose of giving the alarm of some serious movement on the part of the enemy. The insults, therefore, went unavenged until one day, when Ranald was doing sentry-go, the "linguist" surpassed his previous efforts by raucously clearing his throat and expectorating in Ranald's direction; then he put his thumb to his nose with fingers outspread, and finally—a new "phrase"—he turned his back and smote with his hand that part of the anatomy which is normally sat on. This enraged the Highlander, who shook his fist and pointed to his rifle to indicate that if the insult was repeated he would shoot. The Russian must have reckoned that this was just an idle threat because he proceeded to repeat the insult down to the last detail; at which moment Ranald snatched up his rifle, took hurried aim, and fired. He was a noted shot, and on this occasion proved up to his best standard, for he registered a bull's eye on the offending hand and its tender underlying support—to the extreme discomfiture of the guardian of the city, who gave a loud yell, disappeared round a corner of the ramparts, and was never again seen on that section of the wall.

But the report of the shot roused the whole British Army; buglers sounded the "stand-to" and there was general commotion. Ranald realized that he was "for it" and promptly reported the facts. He was put under immediate arrest and was called to account the following morning. Fortunately the officer was a fellow-Highlander; questions and answers were in Gaelic, and when Ranald described the final insult and how he could not stand it any longer, and just let the Rooshian have it, the officer exploded with laughter, clapped Ranald on the shoulder and exclaimed, "By Gad! you were quite right, and I would do the same myself too!—but I'll have to put you in guard-room for a week all the same." The punishment was lightened, however, by the fact that Colonel M—— called round to see the prisoner every morning, surreptitiously bringing along with him a toothsome bite of food—and a gill of the spirit of the glens. When we read in school the rather prosaic history of the Crimean War and the Siege of Sebastopol we felt a sort of contempt for the official historian. But of course, that poor man did not have the advantage of that knowledge of colourful detail which we of the *ceilidh* had.

CHAPTER XI

The Genii of the Sandpit—A Foolish Old Man—A Wise Old
Miller—Trouble in the Timber-yard

WE had some simple old characters that you could only
find in country places and in those days: simple-minded
survivals of an illiterate age. They were not by any
means of the parish-fool type. Some of them indeed, in
some respects, were wittier than people who considered
themselves vastly superior. Most of them, too, were
prodigious workers at so-called "unskilled jobs." It has
to be admitted, though, that their "culture" was of a
rudimentary standard. Nearly all of them were ready
to go on the spree at every opportunity. They were also
primeval in the matter of self-discipline in other respects,
and given to furious bursts of rage and anger. Of this
latter class was Moigean, a much-bewhiskered chubby
little mannie, who for half a century was the genii of our
sandpit. It was from this sandpit that all the sand
required at the building of the grand new houses in the
Strath was taken, and it was Moigean's job to prepare
it and count the loads removed. He would carefully
remove the layer of soil from the top, undermine the
"face" for a "fall," and then separate the gravel from the
sand by laboriously shaking the mixture through hand-
riddles.

Never was labourer more honest or loyal to his employer
than Moigean. He guarded the sand as zealously as the
manager of a gold-mining company would its precious
metal. Knowing this, and purely for the purpose of
getting Moigean into a rage, some of the carters would
arrange their timing so as to arrive at the pit when its
protector was at his dinner in his not far away house. Of

course they never "got away with it," as even while he munched his dinner Moigean would have an eye and an ear to the pit. Out he would come in deepest wrath and there would be a tremendous row, and a subsequent report to the forester of a successful foiling of wicked thieves!

This passionate disposition of poor Moigean was of course a gift from heaven so far as the boys at the school were concerned. The sandpit had a wide "face," usually semicircular at the top and anything from twenty to thirty feet high. On a day that Moigean would be busy at the bottom we would apply our favourite form of torment. Approaching the top of the pit by a wide detour we would creep stealthily towards it, and, well spaced round the edge, we would lie flat on our stomachs to peep down on the unsuspecting and industrious Moigean. Out would go a head and neck (shrouded in bracken camouflage) at the north side of the pit and its owner would start a chant designed to imitate the noises made by a pig:

"Moick—oick—oickan!
Moick—oick—oickan!"

Down would go riddle or shovel and up would go Moigean's dander at first sound of the hated chant. He would grasp stones from the gravel heap to hurl at the offender. But just as the first stone was thrown that head was withdrawn and another jutted out at the south side to start the "Moick—oickan" chant. And so it would go on, the offending face never near the place that the enraged Moigean threw the stone at. This baiting game usually ended by Moigean following us up to the school to lodge a complaint. As it was impossible for him to identify any boy—and of course we all denied the charge— the master took the safe way of giving us a good loundering all round.

Young fiends? Yes: I rather agree. That is what most schoolboys can be. But they can be quite the opposite, too. If only that old ass of a man had had the sense to remember—

> "Sticks and stones may break my bones,
> But names can never hurt me,"

—and acted accordingly—in other words, if he had taken no notice we would at once have lost all interest in the sport. His neighbour the miller knew how to handle boys. We were quite prepared to torment him, or anybody else that would fly into a rage; but the miller gave us handfuls of *sgileadh* (oat kernels) and showed us through the kiln and the mill, so we were mostly good friends.

When he grew too old for the heavier work in the sand-pit Moigean was transferred to the saw-mill as a sort of yardsman. Here his heaviest job was counting the stobs or slabs or rails that were loaded on to customers' carts. His instinct for protecting estate property was as strong here as in the sandpit, but in taking count he was rather handicapped by his inability to count beyond the dozen. This he did audibly in Gaelic: "*Aon, a dhà, trì, ceithir, coig, sia, seachd, ochd, naoi, deich, a h-aon-deug, DUSAN!*" Moigean would triumphantly announce, putting a pebble in his pocket to mark each dozen. When the load was completed the trouble would start.

"*Sin agad ceithir dusan gu leth*" (There's four and a half dozen to you), Moigean would assert.

"*Ceithir dusan gu leth!*" the wicked ones would exclaim. "*Cha dian mise dhe ach da fhichead's ceithir-deug*" (I can only make fifty-four of it).

Solemnly the pair would count the stobs again. Moigean was confirmed in his four and a half dozen—and the tormentor in his fifty-four. Soon the dispute grew hot; there would be several counts but no agreement. Nothing would do but that Anderson the forester must come and settle it—and it was a matter of supreme pride with Moigean that the forester never found *him* wrong in his count "*Na meirlich!*"

CHAPTER XII

Angus of the Second Sight

THERE was another of the *ceilidh* coterie—Angus—who deserves special mention, for I believe if ever a man had the gift of second sight this man had it. He had eyes that just looked into and clean through you. He had a fine contempt for the ordinary conventions; he might call in to the *ceilidh* and sit smoking and gazing into the fire for hours without contributing one word to the conversation; then he might get up and leave abruptly with or without a brief *oidhche mhath* (good night). On such occasions it was impossible to say whether or not he was in any degree conscious of what the others were talking about. I am nearly sure he was not, for I have often seen him after maybe an hour of absolute silence and intense fire-gazing suddenly look up towards the company and, irrespective of whether someone was still talking or not, begin to address them on some subject connected with the supernatural.

Angus openly claimed to have the power of foreseeing events and to have frequently been assisted in the performance of Herculean tasks by supernatural agencies. When this man began to talk we youngsters just "froze" in our seats. The lesson-books might still lie open before us but our every absorptive mental faculty was concentrated on the words of the speaker, and shivers ran up and down our spines as the tale unfolded. It was usually a story of some supernatural experience of the speaker himself—of knocks which foretold deaths; of wandering lights which preceded national or international calamities; or of phantom funerals met at certain points of the road. I confess that, even last autumn, as I passed one of these spots at the quiet dark hour of midnight an involuntary "creep" wriggled up my spine and seemed to up-end the few remaining hairs on the top of my head.

It is true that most of the tales were of the past, so that we were not in a position to check their veracity or the teller's powers of divination, but there were two incidents for the truth of which I can vouch.

The first came right closely under my own observation. I shall merely give the facts and attempt no explanation —for the simple reason that I sought diligently for one for years, quite unsuccessfully.

Angus was a very industrious man. He would occupy any spare time in reclaiming parts of the croft which were still in the rough. One November he put in several days reclaiming a rough belt near the high road. In the process he encountered a huge boulder buried its own depth in the earth. Angus dug down and round about it until it was quite exposed. I inspected it closely and made a rough calculation of its measurements and weight. As it was roundish in shape only an approximate weight could be arrived at, but I am sure it weighed not less than two tons and it may have been nearly three. It lay in a pit just its own depth below the ground, *i.e.*, its top was on a level with the surface of the ground and its bottom lay in a hole some five feet deep. One evening at dusk, coming along the road, I stopped to talk to Angus who was sitting smoking on the boulder and pleased that he had now fully exposed it. I remarked that of course his next step would be to blast it.

"I will not blast it," he said curtly.

"Anyhow," I said, "you will have to break it to pieces somehow before you can get it out of that hole."

"I will take it out whole," he said, "and that before to-morrow morning." As he had now assumed that mysterious manner I knew so well, I said nothing further and went home, smiling to myself and certain that the stone would still be there when I passed in the morning. I had had a hard experience of levering boulders out of the ground, and I knew very well that no combination of lever and fulcrum and "purchase" that could be applied to that stone by as many men as could get effectively round it would lift it out of that hole; and Angus was alone.

Next morning at daybreak I passed along by that road again, and words are quite inadequate to express my astonishment at seeing the stone lying on the surface of the ground beside the hole and the hole empty! And Angus was standing beside the boulder, that now looked even bigger than before. There was an expression of quiet triumph on his face and before I could utter a word he said in Gaelic, "I told you I would do it, and there it is."

"But," I asked, "how on earth did you do it?" He looked me straight through the eyes and said in the way so characteristic of him, "*Thog mi mach i—ach fhuair mi cobhair!*" (I lifted it out—but I got help!—meaning from a supernatural source). This incident kept the men of the Glen guessing for the rest of their lives. Close investigation of several possible explanations gave not a ray of light and I leave it at that.

The other incident was told to me by my uncle who was an eyewitness of it, and who hitherto had been sceptical of Angus's claims as a seer—but who, if the subject ever cropped up afterwards, declared that there was "something in it," as he could never forget the Achnasheen incident. Here is the story.

It happened when the Dingwall and Stromferry railway was being built in 1871. A number of people from the Strath were employed in various capacities at the making of the railway. Hundreds of navvies from all over Britain and Ireland were employed there. One day Angus and my uncle were engaged along with a gang of navvies of mixed nationality at a rock-cutting west of Achnasheen station. The navvy gang's conversation was of the choice order usual to that fraternity; but Angus worked in silence and never took any part in the ribald profanity around him. Just before dinner-time one day, when the language had attained to a deeper degree of profanity and blasphemy than usual, Angus suddenly threw down his pick and started back with an exclamation. All stopped to look at him. He was now gazing intently at the rock-face and perspiring freely. After a few moments he walked to the bank and put on his jacket. He then turned to the gang and said in that quietly dramatic way he had, "You men! instead of using such dreadful language should be saying your prayers, for by this time to-morrow death will be amongst you. I saw blood on the rock!"—and without another word he walked away.

The incident awed even that crowd of toughs for a few minutes, but when they knocked off for dinner they made it the subject of rude jest, and by night had forgotten practically all about it.

But next day at eleven o'clock, while the same gang were working in the same cutting, a "dead" blast exploded in their midst. One man was killed on the spot and another seriously injured, *and the blood of both was on the rock*.

CHAPTER XIII

Dark Doings—*Snàth Sgochadh Fèithe* (The Spraining String)—
Stopping Blood—A Sick Cow and *Bùrn Airgid*—Sacrifice of the
Black Cockerel—Horror in the Glen—The *Corp-Creadha!*—The
Death of Superstition

In the days of which I write recourse to the occult was
frequent. Should a person sprain a wrist or ankle, or a
beast a tendon, a friend went as a matter of course to *Bean
Choinnich an Fhidhleir* (Kenny-the-Fiddler's wife), for a
snàth sgochadh fèithe. Elsewhere in this book a full description is given of the making of this wonderful "spraining-
string." The string was tied loosely round the damaged
limb and he was a brave man who questioned its efficacy!
I have personally gone to the old lady for at least a dozen
of her famous strings. The first time was for my brother
when he fell off a horse and sprained his ankle. The last
time was for Kenny Grant's mare's hind leg—a sprained
tendon.

Old Ann had the power of "stopping blood"—a most
valuable accomplishment. When a school chum of mine
got his foot cut badly with a broken bottle and the thing
continued to bleed and bleed—well, the lad who was with
him at the time—Johnnie C.—just ran as hard as his legs
would carry him to Ann's cottage. Ann immediately
"did and said 'something'" and assured the messenger
that the bleeding had now stopped—which, as a matter
of fact, it had! Ann died only about thirty years ago.

Then there was a very old *Cailleach* whom I can just
remember—*Mairi Mhor*—who had the rather rare gift of
putting the *sian* on a man. She "treated" Ranald before
he went to the Crimean war, and never a scratch did he
receive throughout the whole campaign. Mairi's gift

was also resorted to by Calum before he went to the Egyptian war. Calum had hairbreadth escapes by the dozen and the only hurt he got was a scratch on the ribs from a Dervish spear—but that was not to be wondered at, as I have told in another chapter.

In 1892 my father bought a cow at the Muir-of-Ord Market. Within a day or two she developed a bad cough. Soon it was evident that the cow had been "doctored up" for sale and that she was really in a bad state of health. As usual in such cases—professional veterinary advice being rather expensive—the local "vet." was called in. Now this man, a crofter in the Strath, though an amateur, had undoubtedly a wonderful skill in veterinary science. Moreover, his skill was ever at the service of his neighbours without fee or reward. In this case Davy tried every likely remedy he could think of. But the cow grew worse. He then suggested to my father that, all ordinary cures having failed, he would like to try *bùrn airgid* (silver water). My father consented, qualifying the consent with "If it doesn't do any good it can't do any harm."

I was only very young at the time, but, sensing there was something special afoot, I determined to see what I could. So, keeping well out of the circle of light shed by the stable lantern which my father carried, this is what I saw and heard. The conversation was all in Gaelic, but for convenience I will render it in English.

Said Davy to my father, "Get me a wooden vessel, a piece of silver money and something of gold."

My father went away and in a few minutes returned with a wooden trough, a half-crown, and my mother's wedding-ring, and handed the lot to Davy.

"Now," said Davy, "half fill the trough with spring water."

My father did so, at the well, and brought it to the byre.

At this stage, on tiptoe with curiosity, I nearly blundered

by approaching too close to the scene of operation; but I just managed in time to withdraw from the circle of light. Yet I could clearly see what took place.

Davy dropped first the half-crown and then the gold ring into the water. With a stick he stirred the water about. He then passed his hands repeatedly over the vessel in true Hey! Presto! fashion, and muttered a *duan*, of which, I regret, not a word could I make out. Then dipping his hand in the water, he carried it, dripping, over above the cow's head and sprinkled her neck with the *bùrn airgid*. He repeated the process until the whole of the spine from head to tail was liberally sprinkled. The while he sprinkled he muttered his *duan* or whatever *Beannachadh* (blessing) it was. Finally, he turned to my father and said those words which will always stick in my memory:

"*Well, a Dhomhnuill, mar dian sin feum dhi, cha'n urrainn mise an corr a dheanamh*" (Well, Donald, if that does not do her good, I can do no more for her).

The artistic finish to the foregoing would be to record that by morning the cow had quite recovered. A regard for truth, though, compels me to state that when I went to the byre early next morning the cow was dead.

One summer's day, when I was very young, yet able to drive the horses in the harrows, I was employed in that occupation. I was surprised to see a number of people— men and women—dressed in their Sunday best wending their several ways towards a neighbour's house. First I thought it must be for a mid-week prayer-meeting; but then I wondered how it was I hadn't heard of such. While still wondering I was further puzzled to see both my own parents leave home, also all dressed up. Now, a country boy resents on-goings like these without knowing the reasons for them. But I was too far away from anybody to shout and ask what was afoot.

About an hour after the last visitor had disappeared into the neighbour's house the whole lot came out again and skailed solemnly homewards. My parents came towards home and I made sure of being at a point with the harrows where I could intercept and interrogate them regarding such mysterious on-goings. My father merely waved me aside and said, "Ask your mother." But Mother was disinclined to divulge anything and the most that I could get out of her was that she "might tell me again." Later that day I wormed it out of her.

"Ach!" she said, "if you must know, we were just trying to do something to help J.'s lassie M."

This girl, by the way, who was about eight years of age, had for two or three years been subject to very distressing fits, and the story my mother told me was as follows:

An old woman of the Glen, wise in certain mystic rites, had, after consultation with the child's parents and an elder of the church—a most worthy man—decided that one of these rites should be performed in the hope of effecting the cure of little M., all efforts by the medical profession in that direction having utterly failed.

The first requisite was an all-black cockerel—which must be an "offering." Fortunately an aunt of mine possessed such a cockerel and at once offered it for the occasion.

The next point of material importance was a knowledge of the exact spot on which the wee lassie had had the first fit. This was known to her parents. It happened to be in the lobby of their house. This lobby was at that time floored with Caithness flags. With the requisite material and knowledge assured, invitations were sent to selected neighbours—all known to be very friendly disposed towards the afflicted family—to attend to take part in a semi-sacred semi-sacrificial rite. They met in the parlour. A short religious service of prayer and praise was conducted by the elder. Then one of the Caithness flags was removed with pick and crowbar from its place in the lobby. A hole was dug. The black cockerel, with legs tied together, was placed in the hole. The earth was returned so that the cockerel was buried alive. The flag was replaced. A prayer was addressed to the Deity pleading for the removal of His afflicting hand from the house of His servants. The crowd skailed homewards. . . .

How I laughed when I got the story! "Really," I protested, "you don't believe in such nonsense!"

"I don't know whether I believe or not," was my mother's reply, "but we were asked to go and we couldn't refuse. Besides, one never knows."

I remained utterly sceptical and waited confidently to hear of the next fit so that I could rub the ridicule into my parents. The opportunity never came. That little girl is now a robust matron with a grown-up family; and never one further seizure did she have since the day of the sacrifice of the black cockerel.

That's a much more artistic finish than the last one, and it, too, has the merit of being true.

Practices involving contact with the occult were usually resorted to only with a benevolent motive—to mend a limb, to cure a disease, to arrest loss of blood; to release a person or animal from evil influences; to confer immunity from bodily injury, etc. It is true that the very necessity for some of these—for the release from evil influences, for instance—implied the existence in the neighbourhood of some people with evil gifts and intentions. One or two I knew were discredited with having and using the evil eye—which caused not a little trouble to man and beast; but such cases were infrequent. That, perhaps, is why the one case of undoubted malevolence in my experience stands out so clearly in my memory.

There was in the Glen at that time a certain functionary of much power and influence. To put it mildly, this person was not beloved by the community at large. While still middle-aged he contracted a severe illness, and though no hearts would have broken had he been permanently called hence, it came as a shock to the Glen when it was learned that someone had actually gone the length of positive and active enmity. One evening while two natives were going through a wood and along a burn which ran through it, didn't one of them catch sight of something peculiar lying at the edge of a pool and partially covered by over-hanging ferns? On closer investigation the men realized that the object was nothing other than a *corp-creadha* (a monstrous effigy in clay, stuck all over with nails and pins). It bore an unmistakable likeness, too, to the man who was ill. The running water had already caused a considerable wasting of the clay. The news went round the district like wildfire and there was little doubt in the mind of every native that, had the *corp-creadha* not been discovered—and destroyed—the life of their unbeloved would have ended at the moment when the running water of the burn had disintegrated the last remnant of the gruesome effigy.

In these days of "enlightened" learning it is a convention to smile in a superior sort of way at the "superstitious" beliefs of our "ignorant" grandparents. The floodlight of scientific research has left no dark eerie corners in which belief in such things as Evil Eye, Witches, or Second Sight can survive; and the many occult charms and rites commonly resorted to in the Highlands less than half a century ago are now merely a matter for cultural interest—perhaps! Yet as one knowing the Highlands intimately, and its people and their language, I assert that often only lip-service is paid to the modern convention; and that beneath the surface—not much beneath at that—a substantial measure of belief in the old superstitions still survives.

Quite recently, I talked with an old lady in Ross-shire who showed me a small piece of elm twig she had carried for ten years in the pocket of her skirt as a protection for her cow against the evil eye of an unfriendly neighbour. When I smiled, and urged it was ridiculous to believe either in the evil eye or in the efficacy of a bit of elm as a precaution, she retorted that before she had resorted to the elm twig two cows in succession had "gone wrong" on her—one in the udder, and the other took fits—and I might laugh as I liked but she would carry her elm twig!

CHAPTER XIV

The Long Trail—Keeping a Lykehouse—Brightening the Burial
—Hens and Hymen—A Word on Dram-drinking—Births—The
Howdie and some Statistics

A GLANCE at some of the vital aspects and outstanding
events of what I call the Long Trail—meaning the
journey from the cradle to the coffin—may be of interest.
A coffin suggests something doleful—but that's as it may
be; and to end on the lighter note I take the coffin end
first.

Generally, it may be taken that the Reaper with the
Scythe did not manage to get in his blow at the inhabitants of the Glen till they had reached a ripe old age.
Rarely indeed was it otherwise. In these circumstances,
although due and genuine sorrow was evinced at the
passing of an old neighbour and friend, there was a
certain sensible and philosophic attitude in regard to the
matter which tended to lighten the grief.

Up till about twenty-five years ago an occasional
"lykehouse" was still "kept." Ten years earlier the
custom was general. That is to say, when a death
occurred a number of neighbours and relations sat up
each night with the afflicted family while the body lay
unburied. Nor was the company by any means a doleful
one. Each person on arrival viewed the corpse and
touched its forehead—a precaution against unpleasant
dreams—and made some remark that was half of regret
yet tinged with happy memories of the departed. Then
he or she sat round the fire with the others and joined in
general conversation. Never was much *bròn* (wailing)
allowed into tone or talk. If the departed formed the
topic of conversation at all it was only to touch on events

brave or jolly or comical, in which he or she had been the ringleader. An occasional dram was sent round and did its share in achieving the underlying object of the lyke-house—a mutual "cheer-up" in a mutual sorrow—but never have I seen anything approaching drunkenness or conduct in the slightest degree unseemly.

The same can be said of funerals. It would have been a disgrace to bury any old person without at least one dram for all the mourners at the lifting and another at the churchyard—and one or two later at the house, for special friends and relations—but I have never seen an instance in our glen that would give any basis for the well-known joke about the man waking from a drunken sleep in a ditch and being in doubt as to whether his condition had been occasioned by a wedding or a funeral.

Weddings were big affairs in those days. There were no weddings in the church; that for us would have been sheer *mòr-chuis* (swank). Every bride was married from her mother's "room"—the parlour of the house—or in the little local "Hallie." The neighbours were invited practically *en masse* and all came who could. Presents were numerous and a good mixture of the ornamental and useful. Hens were a special feature—very sensibly designed towards helping with the wedding feast. On occasion a present took the form of a carcass of a sheep or a roast of beef—very useful too—but hens were the chief victims of our Hymeneal celebrations. Days before the great event they were handed in at the door in pairs and pairs and pairs till a truly amazing total was some-times attained.

Before the "Hallie" was built the biggest barn or granary in the vicinity of the house was requisitioned for the dance. Of the old-time dancing I have treated elsewhere in this book. Here I need only say that dancing reached its high-water mark at the weddings!

There was a lot of musical talent too, which lay dormant in a number of people until kindled to life by the wedding dance and the heart-warming and courage-inspiring "refreshments" which accompanied it.

I cannot give the same certificate for sobriety at the weddings that the funerals earned—but, truth to tell, a dead-sober wedding was (and is) a dull affair!

While on the subject of dram-drinking there is a point I want to make—and emphasize. From our earliest years we were accustomed to handling and tasting whisky. Boys of ten years and younger—aye, and girls too—were offered a dram by their parents on New Year's morning and on other occasions. They were by custom expected to take the glass in hand, say "*slainte mhath*" ("good-health") and just taste the fiery spirit. When they grew up they were allowed to exercise their discretion as to the amount taken. I have often heard it urged that it is highly dangerous to allow young folks to taste intoxicating liquors on the ground that it tends to create a liking which is apt to develop into a crave for drink, and so make undesirable citizens of them in later years. There may be physiological or pathological facts which go to support that view. I do not know. But I do know that of 257 people born in the Glen over a period of some thirty years —and to 90 per cent. of whom whisky was freely offered from their very early days—less than half a dozen reached anything approaching the reprobate stage with drink.

On the other hand I know of several cases where the custom of early familiarity with whisky undoubtedly had the effect of influencing a man towards a strictly temperate life—cases where youths in their late teens or early twenties for once failed to gauge their "safety mark" and went ingloriously over the score—to their such intense mortification that they were on guard against drunkenness for the rest of their lives.

Nowadays a birth in the Glen is a rarity. Not so in the last thirty years of the nineteenth century! In that time, to 43 mothers were born, as near as may be, 257 children—an average, by the way, of six per family. There was one family with only one child. The largest family mustered eleven juniors. Families of from five to eight were the most common. There was only one childless married woman.

In the majority of confinement cases a doctor was not sent for at all. In the great majority of cases where a doctor was called in he appeared at the house hours after the "arrival" and when the "howdie" had made all safe for mother and child. Quite recently I read in the papers of a proposal to introduce new legislation which is intended to ensure that no other than a doctor or trained midwife shall officiate at a birth. I do not quarrel with the wisdom or otherwise of such a law, but I do wish to state the rather striking fact that of the 257 children and 43 mothers mentioned above only three children died at birth and not one mother died in childbed.

Very probably the natural, healthy life led by the mothers in the Glen—fresh air, plain feeding, and an amplitude of interesting duties—contributed in no small degree to their own and their offspring's almost complete immunity from serious trouble at so critical a time. But, on reflection, it seems to me there was more than that in the explanation. Amongst country mothers, in those days at any rate, child-bearing was regarded as a perfectly natural and normal function, and as such—assuming ordinary common-sense care and precautions—did not involve them in any really serious danger. They were clear of the paralysing mist of morbid dread and neurotic fears with which the function of child-bearing has come to be surrounded. . . . But I had better get off dangerous ground and let the matter rest on my facts!

CHAPTER XV

Old *Feills*—*Feill na Manachainn* (Muir-of-Ord Market)—A Tale of a Suit—*Feill Chailean* (Colin's Market)—A Day of Cloudless Pleasure

IN "The Trysting Place," towards the end of this book, a description is given of the Muir-of-Ord Market—*Feill na Manachainn* as it was sometimes called. The *Manachainn* had reference to the Monastery at Beauly near which was the stance of an older market. Later the market was shifted to the Muir-of-Ord some two miles farther north, and although the Gaelic name of the new stance was the *Blàr Dubh,* with many people the old name of *Feill na Manachainn* persisted.

The advent of the auction mart sounded the knell of the "Muir-of-Ord." In the years before the war it had degenerated to little more than the selling and swapping of a few superannuated horses and a fight or two amongst the tinkers. But in the eighties it was still the Falkirk Tryst of the north.

I retain one vivid recollection of this market. It was on a day in June forty-four years ago. The preceding evening I was thrilled to the marrow when my mother told me that it had been decided I should accompany father on the morrow with the stirks to the Muir-of-Ord Market; and that, if the stirks made anything over six pounds apiece I would get a new suit! That night gave me my first experience of insomnia.

At five next morning I was up feeding and grooming the stirks. We were off at six on our eleven-mile drove. By ten o'clock we were duly stanced on the Muir.

Then came the weary waiting for offers. For nearly two hours not one of the scores of drovers gave us more than a passing look.   About noon a big man with a blob nose came along.

"Aye, man," said he to my father; "what are ye seekin' for the stirks?"

"Six pounds five shillings apiece," was the reply.

"Ye mean six pounds five shillings for the *two*," came the withering retort as Blob-nose walked away.

An hour later a man with a smug, sickly, sanctimonious smile came along.

"How much for the stirks, good man?"

"Six pounds five shillings apiece."

"You mean five pounds six shillings apiece?"

No reply from my father other than a look of scorn.

Several dealers then came along in quick succession, but the best offer was five pounds ten shillings.   Then another dreadful hiatus.   We were on the point of starting for home at six o'clock when he of the blob nose reappeared.   The nose had by this time acquired somewhat of a carnation colour.

"I'll gie ye six pounds apiece, maister," said he, "and that's a pound too much."

"Off home with them," was my parent's reply.

Had I been wearing boots my heart would no doubt have dropped into them.   As it was, it just seemed to ooze out of me altogether as I headed the stirks for home. I had gone maybe a hundred yards in that direction when Blob-nose bawled, "Here, maister! I'll gie ye yir price but there'll be a lucks-penny."

I stopped.   My father turned round.   The two met. "Haud oot yir haun'," said the drover.   Out went the left palm.   Twelve golden sovereigns were deliberately counted into it; then two crowns.   One of the crowns was handed back as lucks-penny.   The two principals shook hands.   Like shot I about-turned the stirks in the direction of their new owner.

We walked the eleven weary miles home. I slept a round and a half of the clock and next week I got my first real new suit.

One by one the other old *Feills* of Ross-shire died out. They were interesting landmarks and we have nothing quite like them. Many of them were associated with some saint or other and no doubt originally were of a semi-sacred character although in later years they came to be regarded merely as stock markets, and finally degenerated into holidays where cheap-johns, merry-go-rounds, and sweetie stalls held sway.

Feill-Mhàrtainn had a wide vogue, marking as it did the Feast of All Saints on the first day of November— *Oidhche a' Shamhuinn*. The *feill* itself is no more, but there is still a relic of old-time ploys amongst country boys on that night—the night of Hallowe'en.

Feill Mhìcheil was another of the big markets but there was a good deal of variation in the actual day of observing it in different localities. Practically not a vestige of *Feill Mhìcheil* remains in Scotland; but Michaelmas is still one of the English quarter-days.

In the spring of the year—2nd February to be exact— *Feill Bhrìde* was celebrated. It was still quite a feature of the year too. There is still occasional reference in Scottish farm leases to *Feill Bhrìde* as Candlemas and it has prominence as Candlemas in the English and the Roman Catholic Churches.

Then there were the more local markets—*Feill a' Pheabair* (The Pepper Market) was one; it died out in Ross-shire in the seventies.

Feill Èideachan was originally the special market at which the women bought ribbons and laces and such finer articles of apparel as they could not weave at home, and at which the men got themselves properly equipped with the "harness of war"—body armour, shirts of mail, etc.—for the purveying of which the smiths and armourers were in attendance and did a roaring trade. But *Feill Èideachan* had lost all its original significance long before my time.

Feill Seònaid (Janet's or Jessie's Market) was another that is just outwith my recollection but which was a favourite with the previous generation. Who exactly Seònaid was I could never discover, but her market held long sway in the north and did not quite die out till the early eighties of the last century.

But so far as the youngsters of forty to fifty years ago were concerned there was only one survival that counted, and that was *Feill Chailean* (Colin's Market), the very mention of whose name revives a flood of youthful memories. It was held on the second Tuesday of August —by which time, by the way, the blaeberries should be at their best—and how our excitement grew as *Latha Feill Chailean* approached! For weeks in advance every penny was a prisoner, to be liberated on that great day. I have often wondered if any bairns ever got greater pleasure out of less coin of the realm than we did at *Feill Chailean*!

We could scarcely sleep the night before. By six o'clock in the morning as many as two or three dozen of us—boys and girls—dressed in the best togs we could muster, including boots as a concession to town gentility, would start off for Dingwall, whose High Street would be lined with stalls on which would be heaped such an assortment of toys and "goodies" as we would only see at *Feill Chailean* and in our dreams.

Some of the keepers of the stalls might be strangers but many came there year after year. In this category Harry-the-Jew's Wife reigned supreme. She was old when I first saw her but she never seemed to grow older. As to form, she was ample and ugly, but she had a kindly streak in her, too, and her goodies were the best on the *feill.* Her *pièce de resistance* was a yellow candy-rock that we knew by a euphonious if somewhat inelegant name of our own. At the start of the day there would be a veritable mountain of this candy-rock on the end of her stall. But customers came in queues. As each came along the old lady chipped a piece off with a little iron hammer and handed it over, *sans* paper, *sans* palaver, in return for the tendered copper. By evening the mountain would have vanished.

Our funds were never great in those days. If the older ones had command of a shilling on the morning of the great day they were passing rich. The younger ones ran down to mere pennies. But with judicious selection it was wonderful what a few pence would purchase. With eightpence at *Feill Chailean* I have bought:

A pistol	1d.
A box of caps	½d.
A watch	2d.
3 sugary biscuits	1d.
1 lump of the famous candy-rock . . .	½d.
2 minutes on a swing	2d.
A fourth-share in a bottle of lemonade . .	1d.

—and a day of cloudless pleasure that only a boy can buy.

CHAPTER XVI

Days of Independence—*Lath a' Mhàil* (Rent-Day)—Gugan and his Donkey

In these days of distressing unemployment it may seem odd to urge the need for holidays. But there is a world of difference between a real holiday and enforced idleness; and even now there must be many urgently in need of relaxation from the daily round, the common task that eternally keeps their noses to the grindstone.

For most of the women in the Glen, from the day they were married till the day they were laid to rest in the old churchyard, anything in the nature of a real respite was practically unknown. It must not be inferred from this that on the whole they lived unhappy lives; far from it; for theirs was that life of service to others in which the greatest happiness is to be found. But oh! how they must have longed for an occasional week off the chain, those brave self-sacrificing women.

For the men, apart from New Year's Day, the two great holidays of the year were the day of the games and rent-day—*Lath a' Mhàil.*

The games afforded to the men an opportunity of putting on their Sunday suits, a real enjoyable day witnessing, or taking part in, the various sports, and a trouble-banishing spree at the finish. They were held in the district cow-park, and for the twenty-odd cows that were put to summer grazing there the games-day was a holiday too; for on that day they were sent to another field where for the first hour they were happy in the exercise of true bovine curiosity sniffing out the mysteries of a stale ditch and later gloried gastronomically in the fresher pasture which the new field afforded.

Another tenant of the games park was Jeannie—a donkey belonging to an old character who went by the name of Gugan. For weeks Jeannie would be as docile and well-behaved as the best lady-visitor at the Strath. But that was only part of her guile, just to allay suspicion and blot out public recollection of her past misdeeds. Then when Jeannie reckoned that the cow-owners' recollections were sufficiently dim, she played her joke.

In the dead of night she would nibble and chew the rope with which the gate had been tied as an extra "safety," and by dawn would have the knots untied. Then with uncanny skill she shot back the bolt and pushed the gate open. The visitors at the Strath that morning would be entertained by the appearance of a number of cows strolling in bands in front of the shops and wandering round the Pump Room. Altogether Jeannie's joke never failed to cause a degree of annoyance to the cow-owners and amusement to others that must, I am sure, have given herself an impish satisfaction; for, having liberated the cows, she herself remained innocently in the park.

The day of the Highland Gathering was one of the most popular of the year. There we could see the great Donald Dinnie's Herculean prowess with hammer and *cabar*, and our then local star—still very much in the flesh —Kenny Whitton, with his extraordinary athletic versatility. Then there was Dunkie MacDonald, another "local" who had broken the world's record vault at the Paris Exhibition, and could still, with the help of a drop of courage which he deliberately sipped from a "bottlie" kept in his pocket for the purpose, usually out-vault them all.

Another of the outstanding ones was Merchant, yon little high-jumper from Aberdeen, who used to give us a laugh by walking back under his own jump wearing a tile hat on his head!—and there still would be inches to spare.

But not a few of us went to the games to satiate our

music-starved souls (the clergy frowned on all but psalm tunes) with the flood of melody which poured from the pipes of young Johnnie MacDonald and Willie Ross, who were winning prizes even then—and who now, as Scotland's veteran Pipe-Majors, are universally acclaimed two of the greatest descendants of MacCrimmon.

For the boys of the glen only *Feill Chailean* rivalled the day of the games in the whole year's round.

A boy might pay his entrance money like the rest, but that was only when he was in funds—or was unfortunate. There was a nice shading of honesty—or the reverse— about this matter of paying to get in. When a boy hadn't the price he just didn't go. He went to the woodie for a feed of geans instead, and pretended he preferred geans to games. When he had the price of admission and no more he would walk in as bold as brass, not by the regular entrance but from the far side of the park. He selected the moment for advance, though, with a nice regard to the position of the patrolling Bobby. If Robert had an eye to promotion, or was afflicted with conscience scruples in the way of abstract honesty, the ruse seldom worked; in which case our hero would advance straight towards the arm of the law and proffer the price of admission— pleading ignorance of the rule that admission was by the gate only! But if Dame Fortune smiled and he was left with the shilling to regale himself at the stalls his conscience salve was the same as that of the respectable citizen who goes off the street cars without paying his fare —nobody asked him to pay!

On *Lath a' Mhàil* every man donned his Sunday suit, paid his due, took off his dram from the factor and looked the world in the face. And if he took several more drams and indulged with his fellows in a hilarious and belated home-coming—what of it? *Lath a' Mhàil* was his day of independence.

It was in this spirit that a band of worthy neighbours I remember so well, having "cleared their feet with the factor," would repair to the *tigh-osda* (inn) and, in the course of a day of unshadowed bliss, consume as much *uisge-beatha* (whisky) as ultimately led their physical feet into obvious trouble. The metamorphosis which John Barleycorn effected, changing men of staid, reticent, rather serious cast into happy-go-lucky creatures bubbling over with mirth and wit and humour, was something to marvel at and highly interesting. It was a gradual process; each dram did its little bit to put the *bodach* out of them, until at last, one by one, they were indeed:

"O'er a' the ills o' life victorious."

The very atmosphere of that day seemed to affect *Donncha Beag*; the frown flitted from his face before the first dram. Not so with *Fearchar Fada*, who had a head "like cast iron" that stood the subtle influences amazingly. But when at last this stronghold did succumb it was no half-surrender!

Thus elevated and equipped—for each took a bottle in his pocket—it was only half a crown—late in the evening the gang would start their homeward way. It was no Marathon, that journey home; it must have been about the record in slow motion. Points in morals and philosophy had to be discussed. There were fine theological values to adjust. And that necessitated sitting down— which they did frequently—at the side of the road.

By midnight they would arrive at the road-end where the first break in the party must take place. That called for a special sederunt; just a wee *deoch an doruis*; much protestation of friendship and "*Mo Rùn Geal Dìleas*" ("My Faithful Fair One") from *Dònull a' Chiobair* if he had arrived at the singing stage. *Lath a' Mhàil* was the only day in the year that *Dònull* was ever heard to sing;

but on that day he put a wealth of love and longing into that beautiful Gaelic song that gave the key to the reason for his single state. Long years before there had been a "*Rùn*" in his life. She had not proved "*dìleas*"; she had gone away and married another. But never once did *Dònull* think or say a hard word of her; and every year on *Lath a' Mhàil* he paid loving tribute to her memory.

As the ceremony had to be repeated at each parting of the ways it told rather heavily on Iain Dearg and "Maoilean," who had farthest to go. Indeed that pair usually spent what remained of that night in a fashion from which worldly care was gloriously excluded — the end of a perfect day!

"Shocking!" exclaims your rigid moralist. Is it, indeed? Well, maybe it is; and maybe that is what our heroes themselves thought of it in the grim realities of next morning—a sore head and a sorrowful wife. But is that all? Is there no other side to it? Does not some psychological and physiological lesson lie somewhere in the conduct of these otherwise most worthy of men? Is not excessive hilarity the inevitable result of excessive monotony? Can you blame your dog if he makes a riotous frolic of his own day off the chain?

CHAPTER XVII

Contrasts in Comforts—Weirs and Dam(n)s—Bogaran the Post—
A Sort of Sermon

DOUGIE used to warn us boys seriously against the degenerating influences of the physical comforts and conveniences which were creeping into the world even in his time.

" *Gaireas an latha-diugh! Ubh, ubh! Co ris tha 'n saoghal a tighinn?*" (The luxuries of to-day! Och, och! What is the world coming to?) he would exclaim if he saw a boy wearing boots in June, or gloves at any time. He had some biting words for cushions and spring mattresses, warming the hands at the fire, and such-like *gaireas.*

I wonder what Dougie would say now! The bare wooden seats of the trains of not so many years ago have evolved into the luxuriously upholstered divan of to-day. The pan of "hot" water on which our feet used to freeze has given way to the steam pipe or electric heater.

Our grannies used to coax the *cruisgein* to shed its faint flickering light that threw mysterious shadows in the room. Now we tip the electric switch to get instant and dazzling illumination. And so it is in every direction. Truly, if bodily comfort were the measure of contentment we have made rapid strides in that way in the past half-century.

And look, for instance, at the postal facilities we now enjoy. Perhaps the wonderful perfection of the postal system throughout the Highlands to-day may be fairly regarded as a fitting memorial to the amusing persistence of the late James Galloway Weir, M.P. for Ross-shire. For years that gentleman was the bane of the Postmaster-General and the Scottish Office. When J. G. developed a mania which took the form of an urge for a daily delivery of letters, or a new footpath or pier or boat-slip, or whatever it might be, and once he started the campaign, nothing would divert him from his purpose. He might get snubbed and ridiculed, but back to the attack he would come, again and again, until at last, out of sheer exhaustion, they would give him what he wanted. So notorious was he in this way that there appeared in some of the newspapers of that time the rhyming effort of an M.P. wag which ran something like this:

> The weary Weir with queries queer
> The question-paper crams;
> Oh! was there e'er another weir
> That caused so many dam(n)s!

Now there is not a *bodach* or a *cailleach* in the Highlands but takes it as a matter of course that a postman delivers the letters daily at the door. In the old days Bogaran was our postie. From the present standpoint it cannot be said that he "delivered" the letters at all: he merely took them from the town post office and left them at the smiddy or the shoemaker's shop or the railway station, where you could go for them or leave them––or chance it that a neighbour might bring them along. Sometimes letters would lie at the smiddy for months, and would get so black with the soot and the handling that you could hardly make out the address; but very likely the most neglected ones were "just accoonts."

Bogaran's official duties were the least of his activities. Starting at seven in the morning, with his little pony and trap, he collected letters for posting from the station and two or three letter-boxes *en route*. He had to wait three hours in town for the incoming mail but was much too frugal to waste the shining hours. Before leaving home in the morning he had filled the trap with a variety of produce from the croft. Potatoes, eggs, chickens, honey, vegetables, and goats' milk (he always kept goats) were his usual items of trade in the forenoon. Then, before leaving for home, he would haggle with the fishwives at the Cross over a deal in herrings or haddies or speldacks which he sold at a not too modest profit on his journey up the Glen.

But Bogaran was an obliging old fellow. The number and variety of commissions he undertook daily for people by the way was astonishing. At every road-end someone would charge him with one errand or another:

"A bottle of cough mixture from Hay's—the black stuff, not the pink."

"Tell Rory to come with his scythe to the cutting of the hay to-night."

"Get a white pirn from Heckie Crawford's—a strong one for gallows buttons."

"Throw this coulter in at the smiddy for sharpening—and don't forget to bring it back."

"There's a bit of crowdie here for my sister in the toon." (The crowdy was sweetly fresh but rather insecurely held in a cabbage-leaf.)

"Ask MacMillan when Ali Mòr's watch will be ready."

These would make a fair daily sample. Never once did he make a book-note of such errands: he just carried them in his head, yet seldom did he make a mistake. But I'm afraid the picturesque obliging Bogaran would ill fit in with the cold efficiency of the postal service of the present day.

Each successive generation seems to need more support from its parents than the previous one. Well do I remember how our parents used to contrast the luxurious way in which we were brought up with their own Spartan rearing. They would condescend on details too. *We* had loaf bread nearly every day of the week while *they* had it as a treat on Sundays.

Butcher meat, that in *their* youth was an item for the
New Year menu and for wedding feasts and funerals, *we*
regaled ourselves with on every Sunday and occasionally
through the week as well!

And in the matter of education and of boots and clothes
and holidays it was the same: we didn't know how well
off we were!

Yet I sometimes smile to think what our bairns would
say if they had meted out to them the same standard of
"luxuries" that our parents considered so "soft" that it
was bound to spoil us! For nowadays young men and
women are still at school or college at an age when their
grandparents were rearing a family; and during the
whole protracted period of their education they receive
as their common due a standard of spoon-feeding that
would scandalize those old worthies. Whether or not
they will live happier lives or prove better citizens in
consequence is extremely debatable. I incline to the
view that, as a general rule, and having regard to the
average economic standard of his class and generation,
the more a boy is spoon-fed the more he is unfitted to
stand square to the world on his own legs. In any case,
that has proved in the main to be true of the youngsters
who filled the benches in our little school of fifty years ago.
In very few instances indeed did the comparatively
pampered ones manage to sprachle up the brae of life;
whereas I can think of dozens at the other end of the scale
who did; not necessarily, indeed, in true worth, or in
the cardinal virtues, but in what the world popularly calls
success.

What the result will be of the present-day pampering
of youth I do not pretend to be able to see. But possibly
it will be less disastrous than we sometimes fear. After
all, pampering is a relative term, and the problem which
the process involves is not confined to any one generation

—although successive generations of anxious, well-meaning parents seem to regard it as peculiarly their own, and are apt to shake their heads and utter gloomy forebodings for the future.

But even if pampering does prove disastrous, are we to blame those who are but the recipients of parental indulgence? Surely if blame there be, that is the portion of the parents, who are simply going with the stream in this matter. Now, a certain amount of going with the stream is inevitable; or at least, going against the common current is so difficult a course that the majority of parents do not seriously attempt it. To be more or less like your neighbours is always a comfortable and comforting position, and I do not blame parents who try to be that. But they are certainly unfair when they seek to ascribe to their offspring any bad results of their own system of training. Whenever an unsatisfactory situation arises it is a common human failing to plead "not guilty" and point the finger of reproach at the other fellow. Parents as a class are prime sinners in this respect. They are apt to think and say quite a lot about the child's duty to its parents; but often it would be more to the point to remember the parents' duty to the child. Dash it! The kid had no say in the circumstances that made him a member of the family: it was his father and mother who undertook that responsibility; and to me it seems comically illogical for them to seek to evade that responsibility by calmly transferring it to the bairn. No, no, Mummy!—and no, no, Dad, too! That won't do. You have a much greater responsibility towards little Jimmie than little Jimmie has towards you; and if you discharge it efficiently, but, above all, honestly and fairly, Jimmie is not likely to let you down . . . *Gabh mo leisgeul!* If this chapter hasn't turned into a sort of sermon!

CHAPTER XVIII

Smuggling—A Drop o' the *Creutair*—Guest of His Majesty—
Safety First

LARGELY a fruit of the "Forty-five," the rigorous efforts towards the suppression of illicit distilling were never too popular with the people of the Highlands. The natives of the north very naturally resented that drastic interference with their liberty; just as they resented having to encase their legs in ridiculous tubes of cloth instead of leaving them bare to the winds of heaven in the kilt. Consequently only in the eyes of the law was it ever held to be a crime to cheat the gauger. In fact, the man who succeeded in making his own drop of the *creutair* despite the vigilance of the gauger and his staff was regarded rather as a hero in public estimation.

Of course, that spirit is now quite dead . . . eh? Oh! yes, of course . . . maybe. . . . But maybe there are two or three places that I know of, far up by the burn-side in the higher corries, where the "worm" is not yet rusty and the *poitdhubh* has no holes in its bottom . . . maybe . . . but I better no' be saying! And maybe the story that follows is just a figment of the imagination?

Quite recently I was staying over the week-end "somewhere in the North." The gaugers had been busy for days searching the neighbourhood. One of them spoke to me in the village street. He told me all about their activities; they were hot on the track of the smugglers. While we were talking an old friend of mine came along. We exchanged courtesies in the Gaelic. Then I asked him what he and his neighbours were doing at —— to keep the men of the knickerbockers so busy.

"For the love of heaven," said he in the Gaelic, "watch

what you are saying! Do you know who is standing beside us?"

"Fine that," said I, "but the poor *creutair* hasn't a word of the language."

"Are you certain?" he inquired.

"Quite," I assured him. Then I added, "He tells me they have given all of you such a fright that not one will dare go near the bothy again this summer."

On hearing this, my friend looked at the sky as if he were searching for signs of the weather; then, "If himself is of that opinion let him continue it," said he; "but if yourself could be doing with a drop of the right stuff, maybe I could get it for you to-night!"—and maybe he did!

And maybe I know an old blacksmith who is an artist at shaping certain "utensils" and in giving them an aged appearance so that when they are judiciously distributed and "hidden" in the moss, and when they are subsequently "discovered" by an "honest native" who reports the find to the authorities, their reward value is considerable. Maybe . . . just maybe. One has to be very canny about these matters.

But my next story is an old one and no harm can come of telling it. I can vouch for its truth too.

Just over a hundred years ago there lived on the Heights of Strathpeffer one John Macdonald. He was then about forty years of age. For many years John had kept two smuggling bothies going alternately. One was in *Coire 'Bhothain* and the other at the *Leth-allt* near *Cnoc na Bainnse*. He always played a lone hand, thus avoiding the usual pitfall of the smuggler—a babbling confederate. So that not a breath of suspicion blew his way, and all might have continued well had not a gamekeeper by an unlucky chance one day actually walked through the roof of the *Coire 'Bhothain* bothy and discovered John red-handed at his hobby. He was an unfriendly game-keeper that; he lodged information with the authorities at Dingwall.

After trial John was duly sentenced to be detained for a period of six weeks as an unwilling guest of His Majesty King William IV. John's wife walked to Dingwall every other day bringing food for the prisoner. A fortnight went by without incident. Then John had a brain-wave. The old jailer was well known to favour the cup that cheers; in fact he was possessed of a chronic and insatiable thirst—and on that John gambled—and won.

During the remaining four weeks of the sentence there was observed a gentleman's agreement whereby every evening after dark John's cell door was unlocked. John then proceeded by a quiet route to the *Cnoc na Bainnse* bothy and there worked strenuously and in complete safety until returning dawn warned him it was time to make for his prison again; which he did—bringing with him in liquid form the price of the old jailer's complicity.

As John's son put it to me, "The safest smuggling my father ever did was that time he was in Dingwall Jile."

CHAPTER XIX

The *Sasunnaich*—A Delusion—Primordial Instincts—Effective Remedy for Poaching—Ali Dubh and his Wiles—Barley Bree—The Professional—Cousin to George Washington—Setting a Thief to catch One—*Mo Naire !*

IT is late September. Once again the bloom is off the heather; the grouse are "packing," and the *Sasunnach* sportsmen treking south.

What an interesting interlude this annual visit to the Highlands must be in the lives of not only the "gentry" themselves but also of their retinue of servants, male and female! All thoroughly enjoy themselves, although indeed they never quite manage to grasp the educational and intellectual calibre of the Highland gillies and game-keepers and other natives with whom they come in contact.

The truth is that before these *Sasunnaich* come north they cherish the usual *Sasunnach* delusion that Highlanders are an ignorant, semi-barbarous people, in kilts and red whiskers. *Na Creutairean bochd!*—and they never get thoroughly to realize how much the boot is on the other foot. Further evidence of the inability of the *Sasunnach* to understand the Highlander is found in the ineradicable belief of the average shooting tenant that the average crofter is an inveterate poacher. That, of course, is absurd. The great majority of crofters have a feeling of sympathy for the usually impecunious laird and are very pleased that the poor man should make the most of his shootings.

Hares and rabbits on the croft are the crofter's to kill as he likes, of course. Moreover, all sensible lairds, knowing the damage hares and rabbits can cause to corn and turnip crops, are glad to see such pests rigorously kept under. But for feathered game like grouse, pheasants, and partridges the majority of crofters have no use at all. Apart from any other consideration, such fluffy things are bothersome to prepare and cook!

I'm not saying, though, but that once in a while, in an amateurish sort of way, some of us might indulge the primordial instinctive love of the chase. For the pursuit of game is older than man-made laws. In every male, to a greater or less degree, it is an inherited instinct, the occasional indulgence of which, even if running counter to the law, gives a peculiar joy to the individual. In saying this, I am no mere theorist; fine do I remember the thrill of the illicit hunt. The advent of a new game-keeper was but added piquancy—a gravy to my grouse.

It was our laird—confound him!—who put an effective end to my poaching (on his estate) over thirty years ago. For what did he do but invite every tenant with a gun to a day's shooting! It was the first time that had been done in our experience and you would scarcely believe how greatly some twoscore of us appreciated that invitation. Hitherto, our opinion as loyal Land-Leaguers of the laird, had he known it, would not have involved him in any expense in the way of larger-sized hats. And this invitation was in a way quite embarrassing! It was all very well to cherish a somewhat hostile attitude towards a laird whose relationships with the smaller tenants were of that aloof and condescending order so characteristic of lairds in general, but what was to be our attitude towards this man who not only gave us some good days' sport, but extended generous hospitality to boot? For those few days at anyrate we were as man to man, or, rather, we were a band of brother hunters with equal chances in the chase, eating food out of the same panniers and drinking drams out of the same flask.

Many a time since then have I wondered if the laird ever fully realized how much more effective than a dozen gamekeepers were those delightful days of camaraderie.

Ali Dubh was the one in our Glen who came nearest to the amateur artist in poaching. He had an uncanny knowledge of the ways of the wild. For him it was a positive pleasure to pit his craft and guile against the wariness of beast or bird or fish.

As a wee fellow I was one of Ali's worshippers and favourites. Occasionally he would condescend to initiate me into the wiles of the game.

As his name implied, Ali's colouring was black—beard as black as a crow. He was tall and lean, and lithe as a monkey. Even with age his wiry frame refused to carry an ounce of adipose. Ali was the only man I ever knew who could catch a hare by "circling" her. Should he, when walking over a lea field, spot a hare lying snug in her tuft of grass some twenty yards ahead, he never made the mistake of stopping to look or otherwise indicating that he had seen her. Oh no! That would have set her off on the instant. So Ali just glided into a trot, circling the hare.

Round and round he went, gradually lessening the circle and accelerating the pace. Puss would stare this way and that, not sure which way to break and clearly more than half hypnotized by the now swift gyrations of her hereditary enemy. Nearly always she hesitated too long. With terrific force and unerring aim, Ali— now circling on a five-yard radius or so—let fly the shortish stick he usually carried; and ten to one there would be hare soup in the house to-morrow.

That sounds quite easy, but try it! Many a time I did, and the hare would be off before I completed the first lap. There was some mesmeric quality about Ali Dubh which I did not possess.

Seldom did Ali use the gun. When he did use it he never wasted powder or shot. But there was an inconvenient advertisement in the noise of a gun; besides, it was a crude method compared with—say—the artistry of his grouse-catching plan.

It would be late in October. The harvest would be over—at least it would be all in except for a few stooks which Ali (most unfortunately!) hadn't managed to cart home. Soon the grouse would be sure to discover these stooks. Maybe only half a dozen of them came the first time, but with the true sociability of the aviary they informed the pack of the rare feast which could be had for the pecking. Next day at dawn the stooks would be literally covered with grouse.

And so they would be again the following morning. But then a queer thing happened. A grouse would quietly disappear between two sheaves into the middle of a stook; then another and another in quick succession, until maybe a score had mysteriously vanished. And then, to the wild alarm of the birds still feeding on the outside of the stook, Ali would crawl out from its inside—where he had ensconced himself an hour before dawn. With deft fingers he had drawn by the leg bird by bird to its doom!

I found that one much easier than catching the hare.

Then sometimes Ali would be solicitous for the partridges. That would be in the hard frost and snowy days of winter when the poor things had difficulty in picking up a decent meal. Ali, the Good Samaritan, would scatter three or four handfuls of barley near some hedge or bushes or stacks which the partridges were likely to visit during the night or early morning. How the poor hungry birds gobbled up that grain! So Ali continued his hospitality for two or three nights. By the fourth night there would be a veritable partridge jamboree, and if you went along early next morning you would get the laugh of your life, for there would be perhaps a score of paitricks as tight as lords, laughing and turning somersaults and with a devil-may-care look in their eye! But they could neither fly nor run away. So you took the poor things home to the fire. . . . Oh! I forgot to explain that an accident had happened to that last night's feed of barley; it had spilt into a bowl of whisky the day before and had lain there for eight hours before Ali remembered to take it out!

But Ali was just an amateur. Finlay was a professional; to what profound depths his cunning went I can only surmise. Finlay was not a crofter; he lived in the town. He was over middle age when first I remember him and continued to an old age actively engaged in the only profession he ever really loved. Over a period extending to nearly sixty years his total appearances before the Sheriff on poaching charges must have constituted a record. But what is the good of prosecuting a poacher anyway? Whatever corrective effect fines or imprisonment may have on the average transgressor of the law, to the real poacher they are only a temporary deterrent. This fact is tacitly acknowledged by those sensible judges who invariably allow the poaching delinquent so many days in which to pay the fine. In nine cases out of ten the wind is raised as a result of a more successful poaching expedition than the last one.

The most dramatic incident in Finlay's experience took place some twenty years before I can remember and while he was still a young man. Often did I hear my Uncle Sandy tell the story.

This uncle was grieve on a farm some two miles to the south of the town. One September morning at five o'clock Sandy as usual was first afoot, and seeing that everything was right about the steading. Suddenly into the barn came Finlay in a dreadful state of perspiration and fear. Quickly he told his tale. The previous night while poaching in the woods he was surprised by the gamekeeper. There was a bit of a scuffle. Finlay's gun was accidentally discharged. One of the keepers was killed. (This proved to be incorrect—he was badly wounded but recovered.) The alarm had been raised. The police and a band of volunteers had been hunting Finlay from cover to cover all night; but in the dark which precedes the dawn he had managed to shake them off for a bit. But they would be there soon. Sandy must hide him in the straw and tell the pursuers when they came that he had seen a man disappear into the wood beyond. Into the middle of a huge heap of straw crawled Finlay. Almost immediately along came the hunt. Poor Uncle Sandy!—who in the matter of lies was about on a par with George Washington. But he told a whopper that time—though indeed it was not without a lean to the side of virtue. Off went the pursuit into the next wood.

Finlay lay in hiding and was secretly fed by this worthy uncle of mine for three days. Then he headed for the south—not by the high road we may be sure. Inside a month a stalwart young man (now clean-shaven instead of wearing the beard which men in their early twenties then affected) offered himself for recruitment at the Edinburgh Police office. By what name he went I know not, but his physique was so outstanding that he was enrolled forthwith. Next day the smart recruit was on Princes Street in company with an old hand who was showing him round. At the Mound the older policeman took a photograph out of his pocket and handed it to Finlay.

"Here, young fellow," said he, "get your blinkers on to that, and if ever you see a man with a face to fit that photo arrest him. There's promotion there—for you and me."

Finlay took the photo. He looked at it long and hard, taking in its every line and expression—and particularly the beard. He then put it carefully in his pocket.

"Right," said he, never batting an eye. "I think I would know that fellow anywhere"—and well he might!!

For nearly two years Finlay patrolled the streets of Edinburgh as one of its most promising young policemen —diligently searching, we may presume, for the "wanted" Ross-shire poacher whose photograph he carried in his pocket. This is like the story of the sick cow: it has a poor ending. Finlay did *not* finish his career as Chief Constable of Edinburgh.

After nearly two years of meritorious service with the Edinburgh Police, and when the new Finlay might reasonably have hoped that all traces of the old one were safely obliterated, like a bolt from the blue came disaster. A youth from the north joined the police at Edinburgh. This creature happened to have seen the old Finlay on more than one occasion. He was an observant skunk, keen on promotion. Following a report by him, Finlay was arrested, tried, and convicted. The next nine months of his life he spent in durance vile; and the remaining sixty years of it as the most inveterate poacher I ever knew —a super-artist in his profession.

CHAPTER XX

In the eyes of the city artisan, whose judgment is based
on the *seaps* (guzzles) of butter, cream, fresh eggs, and
heather honey incidental to a summer's holiday, life on the
croft is apt to appear in roseate colours. To the crofter
and his family, conscious of the drudgery of mucking
byres, the heartbreak of a wet harvest and the pain of pulling turnips on a frosty morning, the colours are apt to be
drab. As usual the truth lies between the two extremes.
While the life is not all the cream and honey existence
imagined by summer visitors, the crofter is much better
off than he himself knows or cares to admit.

Often I have been asked the question, "But what *is* a
croft worth to the crofter? How much does it contribute
to the livelihood of the family?" Usually I answered the
question evasively because it did not permit of a brief or
definite reply. The answer depended—as it still depends
—of course, on the size and sort of croft, and the man in
charge; and even more particularly, perhaps, on the wife
in charge of the man in charge!

In our Strath the crofts varied in extent from one acre
to fifty acres, and the rents from less than £1 to £30.

Seventeen of them were too small to maintain a horse.
At the other extreme were a dozen crofters who kept "a
pair." The middle-sized ones kept one horse only, and
"paired up" for ploughing, etc.

As may be surmised, only the biggest type of croft was
sufficient to provide an adequate living for the family;
and seldom did the occupiers of the large-sized croft
resort to "outside" labour. While, as already indicated,

the return from the croft varied with many factors, the usual financial statement for a well-worked place of the largest type in the eighties would be very much like this:

INCOME

From sale of		6 six-quarter-old cattle at £10	.	.	£60	0	0
,,	,,	,,	20 lambs at 25/-	.	.	.	25	0	0
,,	,,	,,	50 hogs (wintered only) at 25/-	.	.	62	10	0
,,	,,	,,	4 fat pigs at 40/-	.	.	.	8	0	0
,,	,,	,,	½ foal (one each alternate year at £10)		5	0	0
,,	,,	,,	40 quarters oats at 18/-	.	.	36	0	0
,,	,,	,,	4 tons of potatoes at £3	.	.	12	0	0
,,	,,	,,	6 tons hay at £3	.	.	.	18	0	0
,,	,,	,,	120 doz. eggs at 8d.	.	.	.	4	0	0
,,	,,	,,	Butter, crowdie and sundries	.	.	5	0	0

Total Cash Income   .   .   .   £235 10 0

EXPENDITURE

Rent and rates	£30	0	0
Guano and bone meal	6	0	0
Artificial feeding stuffs	5	0	0
Grass and clover seeds	4	0	0
Smiddy	6	0	0
Ironmonger (for scythes, hoes, nails, oil, etc.) .	3	0	0
Saddler (for major harness repairs, reins, etc.) .	2	0	0
50 lambs bought for wintering at 12/6 . .	31	5	0
2 bought-in calves at £2	4	0	0
4 young pigs at 10/-	2	0	0
Stock service fees	3	0	0
Halflin's wages	14	0	0
Depreciation of implements (against renewals) .	10	0	0
Average annual loss by death in stock . .	10	0	0
Sundries	5	0	0

Total Cash Paid Out   .   .   .   £135 5 0

This, deducted from the total cash income of £235, 10/-, left for the family maintenance, say, £100. But in addition to that there was the value of home produce consumed or used by the family, including wool, made into tweed for clothing. Taking a family of six—*i.e.*, father, mother, and four resident children—I put five shillings per head per week as a fair figure. That works out at a total of seventy-eight pounds per annum, giving for the family maintenance in cash and kind a total of £178 in the year.

A further important consideration was that no house rent was payable; and yet another, that fuel could be had from the moss for the making.

On a middle-sized place the cash sales would be proportionally somewhat less. Those on a £12 croft would approximate a total of . . £100 0 0

But a halflin would not be required, so
    that the total pay-out per annum
    would be around £56 0 0

Leaving a credit Cash Balance of . . £44 0 0
The value of home produce consumed and
    used would be practically the same as
    in the other case £78 0 0

Which left for the man and his wife and
    family to live on £122 0 0

—in addition to the advantages of no house rent and free fuel. In these circumstances, with a view to improving the family financial position—advanced education for at least one of the family was an ambition in most homes— it was usual for the crofter himself, or members of the family while still very young, to engage in "outside" work that offered. Carting for building contractors, thinning and pulling turnips, haying and harvesting for neighbouring farmers, "gillie" work with the local shooting tenant, ploughing for horse-less neighbours, etc. etc.

In the case of the very small crofts the man-of-the-house was usually a tradesman—masons and joiners predominated—there was an occasional tailor and shoemaker. In our Strath the last weaver died before I was old enough to remember him. Even on a croft so small that only a cow, a pig, and hens could be kept, and where the "shift" was as little as one acre, the home contribution, consisting as it did of milk, butter, crowdie, eggs, potatoes, chickens, as much as five or six bolls of oatmeal and some very good ham, was very considerable; was, indeed, so considerable as to leave any fear of real poverty entirely out of the question. I never see the professional trained economist trying to reduce the value of a croft to figures, or hear lectures on microbes, but I think of *Ann a' Ghobhainn*.

Anna lived her long life in blissful ignorance of all the rules of the hygienist. Not since her mother washed her as a baby did Anna have a bath—except that involuntary one on that memorable occasion when, crossing the river on her way home from the peats in the fading light, she stepped on a lump of river-froth which she mistook for a stone and we had some difficulty in hauling her out. The extent of her daily ablutions was limited to her hands and face. Yet kindly neighbours who "prepared" the body when, at the age of ninety-two, Annie's cheery soul at last took flight, for years recalled the "blue-white skin, as beautiful as a child's."

Her bedroom window—which contained one of those "knotty" panes that produced the queerest distortions—was never once opened since it had been put in by Iain Donn nearly a hundred years before Anna was born; and that for the simple reason that Iain, unaffected by modern microbic theories, intended it only for the dual purpose of letting in the light and keeping out the cold. Yet Anna had a vigour of lung and peach-bloom complexion at eighty that few flappers, sleeping under the most modern hygienic conditions, can boast.

Her old brown teapot sat eternally stewing in the hot ashes of a peat-fire that rarely died out, and the tannin content of the black brew must have far exceeded the danger-point of the toxicologist; but neither Anna's teeth nor intestines seemed a whit the worse.

Anna died before the days of the Old Age Pension but she never accepted charity. From her visible means of support—the produce of a score of hens and an acre of land—a dietetic economist would no doubt prove to his own satisfaction, by an elaborate process of calculation and reasoning, that Anna could not possibly survive for more than a few months—but he would be wrong.

Yes, so far as supporting a family is concerned there is a *plus* factor in the economics of even a very small croft which it is impossible to reduce to figures.

While on the subject of economics it may be as well to add a word on the matter of food in conjunction with the daily round. Here is a typical case:

In winter the family reveille was around 7 A.M. The wife lit the kitchen fire—often that was merely a matter of reviving the peat embers that had smouldered all night —and set the porridge on the fire to cook, the while she milked the cows, fed the pigs and hens, and did some general choring.

Before breakfast, the man and one or two of the boys fed the cows, stirks, and horses, mucked out byre and stable, and tidied the place generally.

Breakfast, at 8 o'clock:

Porridge—with creamy milk.
Tea.
Oatcakes, girdle scones, butter (eggs too scarce and dear in winter).

After breakfast, and "The Books," those of school age were got ready—with as much joy then as now—for that tyrannical institution. There was no road to the school; we just went through fields, over dykes and fences and down by the side of a wood.

Into school at 10. Play hour 1–2. Out at 4; home at 5.

As we set off in the morning each carried in the "bag" the "piece" and bottle of milk that was to sustain us during the day. There were occasional big days when loaf-bread or a cookie figured in the piece, but normally it consisted of generous slabs of oatmeal bannock cemented together with butter or crowdie, or both. A healthy appetite is a wonderful sauce. It was a hard job holding up the piece till the play hour and what survived till then got the shortest of short shrifts.

Meantime, at home, weather permitting, ploughing was proceeded with, or pulling and driving of turnips. In stormy weather threshing and the feeding of beasts were the main activities. In the present day of oil-engine-driven mills, when the straw required for a week can be threshed in an hour, it is scarcely possible to imagine the demand on time made by threshing with the flail.

Thump, thump, whack! Thump, thump, whack!

Even yet I can recall the dull song of the flail going on and on and on. . . . What a relentless tyrant that implement was!

By noon the wife would have the dinner ready for those at home. Do not imagine that that is all she had done since breakfast-time! I have often tried to recall in detail just what the croft wife did in her long and active day but have always given it up as hopeless. But of this I am sure: that between baking, washing, milking, cooking, churning, sewing, darning, mending, tending hens and pigs and calves, and not infrequently giving a hand with field work, she was unquestionably the busiest person I have ever encountered. And with it all, she was usually the embodiment of health and good spirits.

Dinner:

    Potatoes—boiled in their skins.
    Salt herrings—from a barrel laid in at the beginning of winter.
    Tea.
    Oatcake, butter.

The meal after the bairns came home was usually a repeat of dinner, but it should be emphasized perhaps that a lot of milk was consumed by everybody.

Almost invariably on Sunday there was a broth and beef dinner, plus milk pudding *de luxe* (because of eggs and cream), plus tea.

Throughout the week, too, there was a surprising variety of relief from the salt-herring diet. Scarcely a week passed without a hare or rabbit being caught. There was always a hen or chicken available. Seasonally, magnificent fresh herrings were procurable, as well as "kessocks" and "garvies." Then in spring, when eggs were plentiful and cheap, we ate eggs by the half-dozen.

In addition to any garden fruit there was abundance of wild rasps, brambles, and blaeberries; and in our case the rather rare and delectable *Oidhreag*. This fruit rather resembles in form the loganberry. It grows on a strawberry-like plant amongst the heather and rarely fructifies below the 2000-feet altitude. One of the special days in the Strath was that day towards the end of July when we went to gather the *Oidhreagan*. Natives home on holiday looked forward to that day. I have seen as many as thirty of us set off in the morning, with ample provisions and pails and baskets, climb for three hours towards our favourite corrie, and in four hours more fill our pails and baskets to the brim with rich red *Oidhreagan* that made jelly with a sort of honey flavour. . . . Oh yes. Looking back over our menu of those days it seems to me we fared not so badly.

CHAPTER XXI

OUR crofters differed from most crofting communities in
the north in that they had little or no common pasture on
which to graze their stock. Our land was in the main
arable, and worked on a rotational cropping system very
similar to that practised on the large arable farms in the
valley. The plan of rotating crops instead of continuously growing the same sort of crop in the same field
year after year was practically unknown, or but rudi-
mentarily understood, in this country a hundred years
ago. Prior to then, little other than cereal or fodder
crops were grown, and after two or three years of the same
crop the land got so chokeful of weeds that the only hope
of cleaning it was by bare-fallowing—*i.e.* ploughing,
harrowing, and gathering off the weeds repeatedly
throughout the summer. By this method you did clean
your land, but you got no crop (except weeds!) off that
field that season. In this connection there must be a
surprising number even of present-day farmers who do
not realize how much they owe to the humble turnip;
for it was through the introduction of the "neep" that
their great-grandfathers gradually evolved a system of
rotating crops which is the basis of our now generally
admitted high standard of "clean" farming in Scotland.
Those observant ancestors of ours soon spotted that,
instead of bare-fallowing each field every two or three
years, they could, after clearing off the bulk of the weeds
in early summer, still sow a crop of turnips—which made
such palatable winter feed for cattle and sheep. By
careful hoeing and scuffling between the rows of turnips

throughout the summer they killed off the last of those hated weeds. Thus the growing of the new crop known as turnips gave them a whole series of advantages, *e.g.*—

Cleaner land.

An extra and most palatable winter food for stock.

Better-conditioned sheep and cattle in spring.

Capacity for wintering a greater number of live-stock.

Improved fertility resulting from folding sheep on turnips.

Cleaner and better hay and pastures from seeds sown out on the cleaner land.

More and better-quality dung (the farmer's best "bank" of all)—and several others with which I need not burden this book.

But, in short, the modest turnip revolutionized our whole system and practice of agriculture, with incalculable benefit to the country.

In the earlier years of the system of rotating crops the custom was to leave the "shift" in grass for one year only, so that there was the simple four-years rotation: turnips; oats (or barley); hay (or grass for pasturing); oats— and you went round and round that "clock." Later, the advantage of leaving the grass field unploughed for two years came to be appreciated (making a five-years rotation); and still later it was left in grass for three years, leaving you with a six-years rotation, thus: turnips; oats (or barley); hay (first-year grass); second-year grass (pastured by stock); third-year grass (pastured by stock); oats—so that you could depend on having the same sort of crop in any given field every sixth year; thus providing simple but infallible chronological data for settling various disputes or differences of opinion in regard to questions of local moment.

For instance: What was the age of the bride? The

howdie of the Glen would settle that conclusively by recalling that, on the night her professional offices were urgently required at the *birth* of the bride, she (the howdie) was unable to take the short cut through a certain field *because the night was wet and there was a crop of hay growing in that particular field.* Therefore, if in the year of her marriage there was a hay crop in that field again it was quite simple: the bride's age must be some multiple of 6—say 24. Of course, unkind suggestions might be made that she was only 18; or, worse, that she was 30 or even 36! But usually, with the hay as a basis, there was no doubt about the real age. On the other hand, if it wasn't hay but turnips that grew in that field in the year of the marriage, the original wet grass still settled the question, because, if the field were now in turnips, the bride was clearly two years *younger* than a multiple of 6— say $24 - 2 = 22$, or 28 (*i.e.* $6 \times 5 = 30 - 2 = 28$), and the general weight of opinion left no room for doubt as to whether twenty-two or twenty-eight must be regarded as the bride's true age.

Old Anna was our super-expert in the use of this rustic rule. Such controversial subjects as the age of Beelie Mòrs wife, of Murdo's cow, of Jock Stewart's mare, of Rory's cat or Bogaran's billy goat; or the years that had elapsed since the winter of the big snowstorm (when the sheep were smothered up at the Glen, and when a south-bound train conveying a wedding party from Strome to Dingwall and a north-going train with a funeral party bound for Skye were both held up in a twenty-foot drift below the nut-wood, and both parties danced all night in the waiting-rooms at the station to keep themselves from starving to death of the cold), and innumerable matters of like moment, all yielded to Anna's infallible memory and her inexorable application of the rule of the rotation.

"What's the good of spaikin?" Anna would demand of anyone brave enough to challenge her dictum. "You needn't tell me that she's only twenty-four. Wasn't I coming doon from Kenny Og's the very day that Donal's wife was going west to the birth? And wasn't Donal himself and the bairns lifting the taaties in the field at the Big Thorn? And didn't I meet Doctor Tricky [a disrespectful reference to the then parish medico who had the misfortune to bear the Christian name of Tregellus] coming over with his baggie at the station? And where is Donal's taaties now? Aren't you seeing them with your own eyes in the field next Simon's? And isn't it the year before last that they were in the field at the Big Thorn? And wasn't that four times roond since the year she was born? And isn't it two years more now? And isn't that twenty-six?—in October?—because isn't it lifting the taaties they was? What's the good of spaikin?" Anna would conclude, as with a snort she turned from an annihilated adversary.

And in face of such irrefutable evidence indeed, what *was* the good of "spaikin"?

CHAPTER XXII

Hell Fire

THERE is usually a conventional decorum observed in any reference to the religious life of our grandparents in the Highlands; their piety is always referred to as profound. Yet as one who has spent all his youth and the early years of his manhood right in the thick of it, I fear there is something of the enchantment of distance in that view.

Of religion, so called, we had a surfeit; but to an unbiased mind the form and dogma of it seemed of greater importance in the eyes of devotees than the tolerance and charity of thought and action which a religion should stand for.

That most of my old neighbours were sincere in their views I do not for a moment deny; but their religion, in both its theoretical and practical aspects, was but the reflection of their spiritual teachers' views, and in all conscience these, as a rule, were sombre enough to satisfy the most rigid Calvinist.

It was a cold, uncharitable creed they preached, which grudged any joy in life except what could be extracted from gloom. Their doctrine of "predestination" weighted us with a sense of the futility of effort. Present-day ministers who are puzzled at their empty pews can console themselves with the reflection that they are suffering from an inevitable reaction to the morbid ministrations of their professional grandfathers whose dominant note was Hell fire.

No description of life in a crofting community of the eighties of last century would be complete without some reference to the ever-burning furnace—provided by the Deity whose chief attribute was Love—for the eternal chastisement of sinners.

And I am an authority on Hell. It and all its lurid details were branded on my soul from my tenderest years. I can never forget, or remember without a shudder, the first word-picture of this dread place that a "minister of God," with all the solemnity which that profession then bestowed, so graphically disclosed to my horrified mind at the tender age of some five years.

It wasn't a mere reference to some dire place of punishment. Oh no! With unction he condescended on detail. It was a bottomless yawning hole with a red-and-blue lowe licking into every crannie of it, with the Devil in control of lesser devils whose sole function was to grab sinners and throw them into the hottest corner and roast them and roast them for ever and ever more!

It was this never-ending aspect of the torture that appalled me. It came to my mind that if I got only one short plunge into the fire and was then allowed to jump out and into a pool of cold water it would be bad enough, but bearable. But no fear! Down you were prodded by the Devil with a three-pronged fork and kept there for all eternity! Good God! I nearly fainted with fear. I remember I did cry out in sheer terror; but then I realized that to cry out in church might be one of the very sins that would certainly send me to Hell! So I pulled myself together.

Then a great hope came to me in the thought that, after all, one was only burnt in Hell if one were *bad*. So, thought I, "By gosh, I'll be good!" But then the most terrible fact of all came out when our spiritual adviser assured us that from the time before we were born it was written in the Book of God and foreordained whether we would burn in Hell or escape it! Even as a bairn I thought this rather discouraging. There didn't seem much point in trying to be good.

That night at bedtime I was the most scared wee fellow that the world ever contained. With tears I appealed to my mother for some ray of hope and comfort. But she, poor woman, had had the reality of Hell dinned into her all her life and could only hug me and hope that we were both on the list of the "chosen of God." It was a small crumb but I grasped it. What else was there for a wee fellow to do?

Looking back on my earliest years I can truthfully say that Hell and the fear of it was never far from our minds, and even on those few occasions when we dipped into some innocent frolic, Hell hung in the near background like a skeleton at a feast.

From churchgoing friends I am given to understand that Hell nowadays is rather disowned by the clergy—that, in fact, they are rather ashamed of the old institution and are inclined to the use of plausible sophistries calculated to reconcile the veritable thing Hell was in the view of the clergy of forty years ago with the allegorical thing into which it has now degenerated in the ecclesiastical mind.

Well, well! Other days other ways. But indeed I have difficulty in thinking kindly of the old Hell and those who preached it.

Notwithstanding the inescapability of Hell for those predestined to it, our moral mentors—most illogically, I thought—were ever urging all of us to "good" actions for the propitiation of the Deity, and surely none was more puzzling than in regard to our conduct on the Sabbath!

To seek to edify your mind on that day by reading Shakespeare or Scott was one of the unforgivable sins; but you were free to debase it in uncharitable gossip with your neighbour to your heart's content!

It was permissible to cut tobacco with a knife on Sunday, but not on any account might you cut a string or a stick, or even the vegetables for the broth!

You might wash your face on the Lord's Day; indeed you were expected to; but you were heading straight for perdition if you shaved it; or cut your nails!

If your boots were left unbrushed on the Saturday night, then unbrushed they must remain over Sunday if you wanted to escape eternal punishment! But you might brush your beard without risk.

There was no sin in taking the horses to the water to drink; but your neighbours shuddered for your soul if you reversed the process by taking the water from the pond to the horses! That was a very subtle one!

You daren't peel the potatoes on Sunday before cooking them; but, once boiled, they could be peeled with impunity!

Altogether, there was a fine, hair-splitting discrimination between the things you might and might not do on the first day of the week, that was always puzzling to myself; and no amount of Wee MacGreegor inquisitiveness in the way of "Whit wey, Ma?" ever shed much light on "The reason o' the cause an' the wherefore o' the why."

IF there is one class of fellow-mortals that I have more sympathy for than another on those bonnie summer mornings, it is the scholars at a country school when the harsh jangle of the bell so ruthlessly calls them from the enchantment that lies without, to the drab tasks that lie within the walls of the schoolroom. Poor, unwilling sacrifices on the altar of the Moloch of Learning!

In the city it is not so bad; from drab street to drabber classroom is merely a matter of degree of misery. But in the country . . . ! To have to file in to that depressing atmosphere of square roots, G.C.M.'s and "goes-into's," when the sun is shining gloriously and out-of-door allurements are strong . . . !

There is the wood with its carpet of wild flowers; there are the nests so cunningly hidden in the banks and bushes of the burn-side. And the trout . . . ! O! *mo thruaighe*! that the hard necessity of acquiring book-learning should tear us from the Nature's Academy that is there!

We used to spend up till the very last minute in climbing trees, in guddling for trout, in exploring—until the clanging of that thrice-cursèd bell. And if we didn't quite jump to the call, who that was ever a boy can blame us! In any case we expiated the crime of being late by a stolid acceptance of the pandies the old dominie conscientiously administered—for we had had our *quid pro quo*.

The nests of the Blackie and the Mavy and the Binkie (chaffinch) and the *Buidheag* (yellow-hammer) were fairly common, but there was a special thrill in the finding of a Jennie Wren's nursery with its wee doorie that only the hand of the littlest lassie could get into to count the eggs. Then there was the rarer nest of the "Need-lack" that was built of withered grass in a hole in the ground. There was a pair of perky Robins that built for three successive years in a discarded kettle that lay in the wood. . . .

I wonder if the boys at the old school still dig for *Corochans*? Or if they know what *Corochans* are? They are little lumps or nodules that grow on the roots of a certain purple-flowered vetch. When we came on a bed of them we carefully pulled away the grass, and then with our knives dug down into the earth until we got to the much-prized *corochan* that was believed to have the special virtue of imparting "strength," and what boy does not want to be strong?

One *corochan* would keep a boy chewing for an hour, but the great thing was to save up until you had a dozen or so to pop into your mouth at once. That was a bon-bon *de luxe*. Or, alternatively, it had a considerable barter-value in the way of marbles, transfers, knives, and skeany strings.

I am kind of ashamed to confess that I never had the moral courage to "slip" the school; not indeed because of any particular diligence in learning; it was rather because of a shrewd anticipatory instinct in regard to the parental chastisement which would follow—or pained reproach which was even worse. But how I envied those devil-may-care companions who had the pluck to "slip" for a day or two of stolen freedom! One such I can think of has for many years been an ornament in the County Constabulary. On the principle that a clever poacher makes the best gamekeeper he should be just about the most efficient member of the "force," for verily that Bobby as a boy was the impish limit. But I hope he is not another example of that numerous class of people who allow the years to blot out the recollection of their own boyish pranks; and that when he is called upon to deal with youthful delinquents a memory of the boy that once he was will cause him to temper justice with mercy.

It may be a delusion of the memory but, looking back, it does seem that in those years the winters were more decidedly seasons of frost and snow, and the summers of warmth and sunshine than they are now. In any case it was an unwritten rule amongst the schoolboys that boots were discarded on May-day, and only brought into commission again when the first snow and frost of winter compelled that literally cramping step. Should May-day prove exceptionally cold, parental authority might decree that boots must still be worn, but in that event convention and youthful *esprit de corps* demanded they should travel no farther than the nut-wood, where they were removed and hidden in rabbit-holes till evening, when it was deemed prudent to put them on again on the homeward way.

Going "barefeet" without parental leave was an offence punishable by the master; but, whether to our credit or discredit, the crime was rarely punished because it was rarely confessed. Probably we felt there was punishment enough in the cuts and sores on tender soles and toes that accompanied the first few days of pedal freedom! But by the end of a fortnight a sort of leather sole would develop that was an effective protection against thorn-stabs and sharp gravel, and we could run with the swiftness and freedom of nature until—

> "The snaw it stopped the herdin' an' the
> winter brocht him dool,
> When in spite o' hacks and chilblains
> he was shod again for school."

CHAPTER XXIV

Pigean Hoosies—Live Trains—Numbers—Hares and Hounds—
Pursuit of Learning

IN the matter of toys and games and other means of
recreation we were in the main dependent on our own
inventive resources. Amongst the girls a single doll—
of matchless complexion in its youth but sadly grimed and
maybe blind and legless, or even decapitated, by the
ravages of time—would be handed down from sister to
sister. Their "hoosies" were spacious buildings of several
rooms whose walls were pieces of broken crockery
(*pigeans*) artistically arranged on the green. The structure
was heightless and roofless, but youthful imagination
readily provided both roof and height. And the same
imagination—plus some skill in the manipulation of a
knife, and a few potatoes or turnips or pieces of wood—
soon produced the necessary internal appointments:
furniture, father, mother, cradle and baby all complete.
There was keen rivalry amongst the lassies in the building
of their "*pigean* hoosies" and it was extremely bad form
to interfere with a neighbouring lassie's hoosie—which
might lie undisturbed on the green right through the
summer.

The boys affected to despise such femininities and
leaned towards horses and dogs. Trains were also
favoured, and a string of boys, headed by their leader
emitting audible puffs and snorts, and with revolving
elbows to form crank and piston, made an impressive
train—especially when it had a hill to negotiate or a
snowdrift to "charge" and the united efforts of all were
required—including coaches, wagons, and van. But
going down a steep hill the brake van had sometimes to

sit on its bottom—much to the detriment of its trousers, and when it was wearing a kilt the damage would be even more personal.

At school a favourite game was what we (for what reason I never understood) called "Numbers." All the boys bar one, who was nominated "King," stood with backs to the wall at the north side of the playground. The King took up his position at any point he chose. On his shouting "Numbers!" all the others had to move off from the wall and do their utmost to escape capture by the King before reaching the sanctuary of the south wall. A capture was not complete until the caught one was "crowned" by the captor placing his hand on the head. Then the captured ones joined the capturers and shouted "Numbers!" to initiate another run. So from wall to wall the effort to escape and capture grew in intensity till only a few of the very fastest remained "free," and I have seen Jock-the-Hare or Dunk-the-Rabbit successfully elude a host of would-be captors for several runs. Of course numbers were bound to tell in the end and the last captured boy was the new King to start off a fresh game.

Hares and Hounds offered greater scope for individual ingenuity and stamina and took us far afield. The "Hares"—about half a dozen of them—were given a free start till they passed out of sight at the bend of the road below the mill. Then in full cry off went the "Hounds" in pursuit. No "scent" was left—the chase was much too stern for that; but in order that the run should be kept lively there was a rule that the Hares must not go "hidey" for more than a minute or two. A favourite dodge was to lie hidden in a thicket not far from the start in the hope that the Hounds would pass on. But before they passed on out of sight the Hares must show in the open again, squealing to attract the notice of their pursuers. Then back in full cry would come the Hounds, sometimes "fanning" to anticipate possible side-dodging by the Hares. But always the advantage of initiative was with the latter, so that seldom were all the Hares killed.

The best runs took us down by the mill, through the Miller's Woodie, on past the graveyard (did we stir the bones of many previous Hares and Hounds?), up by the red sandstone quarry at *Allt a' Charaiste*; then through the steeply rising wood *Coille na luib*, back through the man-high bracken on the face of *Cnoc Feirlidh*, down over the railway, and then a last burst through *Bod Ceimidh's* Wood and the Church Woodie to the sanctuary of the playground. A good six miles straight—and our course, between circling and dodging and doubling, must have been nearly twice that distance. The play hour was from one to two. A miserable hour for a job like that! Well, if they couldn't be decent to chaps, we just had either to cut the course or cut the school. Our choice usually landed us in for a severe lecture from the dominie as well as for some rather severe corrective "pandie" treatment. Fortunately, neither seriously interfered with our enjoyment—any more than our enjoyment seriously interfered with our pursuit of learning.

CHAPTER XXV

A Garden Sweet and Fair—A Bobby and a Gentleman

WRITING of the Bobby with the lurid boyhood reminds me of another arm of the law; and he was gifted with wisdom.

On our way to school we passed by the side of a garden—and such a garden! It had trees laden with apples and pears and plums; there were luscious strawberries, tart gooseberries, and fat green peas—Nyum, nyum! Between us and these there was only a stone wall with black- and red-currant bushes growing against its inner side and over the top, whose fruit just hung to our hands. At home and in school we were duly instructed in the virtue of strict honesty and had ingrained in us a highly realistic conception of the torture by fire that was the ultimate reward of thieving. But, I ask you . . .?

Anyhow, occasionally even the dread of a future roasting proved ineffectual as a deterrent. Besides we soothed our consciences with the sophistry that, even if we did resist the temptation, the chances were that most of that fruit would be left to rot where it had ripened!

The owner of the garden was an old lady, who during the last thirty years of a life-span of ninety-nine spent most of her days sitting in rigid state in an armchair in the drawing-room. I set eyes on her only once, and the sight of her in bustled skirt, lace shawl, and with long, white ringleted hair, and leaning on a gold-topped staff, remains in my memory as the picture of a being from another age—almost from another planet.

Experience soon taught us that the swiftest pace of the middle-aged maid who valeted the old lady was not quite up to the speed of the slowest of our group, and safe in that knowledge we would continue guzzling till the very last moment—till, in fact, we heard the click of the garden gate.

I have often wondered about that click. She could have opened the gate quietly—but she never did. Why? I think kindly of that woman . . . !

One evening we were well ensconced among the gooseberry bushes and the rows of peas. The gate clicked. We rose leisurely to scamper off in the usual way; and just then we got the shock! Later we learned that the usual maid had gone for a holiday, but all we saw at the time was an athletic lassie of twenty sprinting straight for us! We stood not on the order of our going. Over the wall and up the path by the side of the corn-field we streaked, with Atalanta in hot pursuit. Alas, we had no Hippomenesian golden apples to tempt her curiosity or to check her speed, and it was only a matter of moments till she had "Bumbee" by the pleats of his kilt. Poor Bumbee! That was the fright of his life. Sudden death was the least that would happen if he didn't tell her straight off the name of every raider. Bumbee had no wish to die just yet—he was only nine and in robust health—so who can blame him if he spat out the names at the double? And he took no chances, for he gave "full measure, pressed down and running over" by including in the list the names of some unfortunates who were not there that evening! For this "plus" information the wretched Bumbee was made to pay in nasal blood later on; but that is another story. . . .

There was a loud rap at the school door next forenoon. The dominie came back with a grave face and our hearts sunk lower than our boots when he called our names, ordered us to "take the floor," and then informed us that in the lobby there was "a gentleman" wishing to see us.

I shall not forget that first interview with a policeman

if I live to be as old as the owner of the garden. He was more solemn than a minister, and so concerned at our plight! ! !

"I am awfully sorry, boys," said he, in a slow, kind voice that nearly made us cry, "but of course I cannot help it. Jile is the only thing for thieving." (Pause.) "And the beds there are just boards! . . . And it will be nothing but bread and water three times a day for a fortnight!!—and not much of that!!" After a final pause to allow the awful horrors to sink well into our sickened souls he walked slowly to the door. The younger ones were now blubbering, and the older ones were just holding on.

Then he came back. "Maybe," said he—allowing just a shade of hope to creep into his voice—"Mind, I cannot promise, but maybe if I could see the Sheriff and tell him that you are really a nice lot of boys and that you are awfully sorry, and that you promise not to steal from Miss M.'s garden again, he might let you off. Will you promise me that?"

Promise? . . . Like a shot we did, and as with one voice!

"Mind you," cautioned this wise old man, "I cannot promise that the Sheriff will let you off, but I will do the best I can for you—but it will be two or three weeks before you can be sure!"

Needless to say that was the last we heard of the matter, and we never went near that garden again—at least not until that policeman retired.

Many times have I thought since then how literally true was the dominie's intimation to us on that memorable morning; "a gentleman" indeed had come to see us.

CHAPTER XXVI

School Fights

On the whole, we were a friendly lot at the old school, but occasionally something would occur that demanded the arbitrament of arms—or fisticuffs. No doubt a mother of the namby-pamby kind, then as now, would be horrified to think that her dear wee Johnnie might come in for rough treatment at the hands of the "rude, bad boys"; but the fact remains that, in the roughish, hardy training that is the lot of a lad at the average country school, there is much that is invaluable to him in after life.

Fights were mainly of three varieties. First there was the fight which the bigger boys "commanded" between two juniors. The seniors would have a difference of opinion as to whether little Jimmac could beat wee Alickie, and to settle the point nothing would do but that the two juniors—who might be the greatest of friends—must doff caps and jackets and set-to to pummel each other. There was no rancour at all in such encounters. A bleeding nose on either side usually sufficed to resolve the doubt and the interrupted friendship was immediately resumed.

Then there was the fight arising from lost tempers and heated passions. These were more serious affairs and usually resulted in a good deal of blood—bad and otherwise.

But the most serious type of fight was the one that had a moral background. Anything in the nature of bullying was by common accord condemned. Any boy who ill-treated one obviously younger and weaker than himself would be promptly advised to "chuck it"—and, if he disregarded the advice, things were likely to happen pretty quickly. That was the origin of the greatest fight at our school in my time.

We were having an exciting game of shinty in the minutes just before the two-o'clock bell. The centre-forward on one side happened to be one of a family that had for years provided a school bully. He was hated, yet feared by all. So far no one had dared question his authority. On this occasion, to the bully's chagrin, a timid little "back," but an adept with the caman, had twice prevented his scoring a hail. When this happened still a third time, the bully "lost his rag" and proceeded to make a most cowardly attack on poor wee Roddie. The game stopped. We were horrified. Then, before the rest of us could pick up courage to intervene, a voice came from the most unexpected quarter.

"Chuck that, Sparks!" commanded Dinker in a tone we had never heard from him before. Sparks was so flabbergasted at being thus addressed that he actually did "chuck it" so far as Roddie was concerned. Dinker was the quietest, most modest boy in the whole school, and nearly a year younger than Sparks. He had no particular gift for learning, but he had a gift for sympathy and friendship, and a comical sort of humorous twist of a smile and a turn for harmless mischief that made him a prime favourite amongst both boys and girls. But never once had Dinker been in a fight; and that he should be the one to pull him up was as astonishing to Sparks as it would have been to King Solomon if one of his meanest slaves had dared him to marry another wife!!

Outraged dignity shone in Sparks' eye when at last he recovered from the shock, and he was on the point of transferring his attack from Roddie to Dinker when the bell rang.

There was a tense atmosphere in school that afternoon.

Like a flash the news went round that Dinker had "cheeked" Sparks! Sparks glowered surreptitiously at the mutineer and spluttered threats of four-o'clock annihilation. Dinker said nothing; he didn't even smile. If he regretted what he had done he never let on. The great question was, would he fight?—or would he just take what was coming to him? To us the one alternative was as unthinkable as the other.

But by a quarter to four Dinker gave us the second thrill of that day when he calmly announced he would fight.

The old dominie must have wondered why the playground cleared so quickly that autumn afternoon. The scholars *en masse* repaired to the green in the Church Woodie—the recognized arena for the big fights. A ring of excited juvenile humanity was quickly formed. Sparks, true to his name, still issued threats of direst punishment. Dinker, still silent, with set face, handed cap and jacket to his young brother.

That fight was an epic. Smarting from a sense of insulted majesty, Sparks (who, to do him justice, was a real soldier) went for Dinker like a fury. No other boy I have known would have stood up against that onslaught. But Dinker stood up to it and, gradually, through the sweat and blood that soon profusely adorned his countenance, the old comical twist of a smile became discernible—but it had a grim shade in it.

From defence, Dinker went to attack. And such an attack! For good hard hitting, skill, and sheer dour, dogged pluck I have never seen his equal. Sparks fought gamely, but within half an hour his nose was battered to pulp, his two eyes were closed, three front teeth had gone, and altogether what had been his face presented literally the bloodiest mess it is possible to imagine. Twice did Dinker pause to inquire of the other if he had had enough, and it was not until the third time, when Sparks was at last thoroughly beaten and demoralized, that the answer was in the affirmative.

It was an impressive scene; we had witnessed the deposition of a tyrannical king. There was whole-hearted joy amongst boys and girls alike. But Dinker, with characteristic modesty, never made any reference to his one and only fight.

CHAPTER XXVII

Sgadan's Strategy

PRACTICAL joking may not be a very elegant form of wit; indeed there is no fun in it at all when carried to excess, and I'm not saying but some of the pranks the previous generation used to play on each other went over the score in that direction. On the other hand, when kept within bounds there was a lot of laughter and no real harm done. The victim might be the butt of the *ceilidh* or the school for the time being, but it was always open to him to retaliate; and the urge to do so had a fine sharpening effect on the wits.

On the whole we rather liked Calum Mòr, but, unfortunately for us, his idea of a grand practical joke was to steal our clothes while we were bathing, during the play hour, in a pool of the river that ran through his croft. There was a fringe of alder bushes which afforded him cover in his stealthy raids and the first thing we would hear would be a whoop of delight from Calum as he ran off with all the kilts and shirts and corduroy trousers he could hurriedly grab—for well he knew from experience that he must not wait long within range of the fusillade of stones with which we pelted him—if only we could spot him in time!

It is true our predicament was not without one streak of comfort. When Calum stole our clothes we had a very sound excuse for not going to school in the afternoon. Indeed I'm not saying but some of us would never blink an eye when, as a reason for absence, we tendered to the dominie the tale of Calum's wickedness on occasions when poor Calum was quite innocent. But that was a risky expedient which sometimes culminated in acute physical discomfort!

One summer, though, Calum was more than usually successful with his "joke." We were getting fed-up with him. There is nothing more disconcertingly humiliating for a boy than to be denuded of his conventional covering in broad ·daylight. The indignities we suffered in having, in our natal state, to implore Calum to return our garments were more than we could be expected to continue to bear.

It was the "*Sgadan's*" (Herring's) fertile brain that saw the way to revenge. Sgadan had observed Calum's tactics closely. He always approached from the west, grabbed the booty off the bank and, instead of turning back, carried on eastwards by a little path that ran parallel to the river's edge and close to the pool which was so deep and swirling that we never bathed in it. No doubt, Calum's reason for choosing this line of retreat was the fact that a big alder bush grew between it and our pool so that it afforded him a partial protection from our "fire." But there was a monotony about the plan that for ever rules Calum out of the category of great strategists —and incidentally shows Sgadan as a bright and shining light. For not only did our hero see in the enemy's tactics the opportunity for his overthrow, but with a fine dramatic instinct he never divulged his plan till our eyes beheld its greatness. We were splashing about in our pool one day when Sgadan let out the usual warning yell of "Clothes!" He must have been sharply on the look-out that day, for Calum had only time to snatch a *ciotag* (rag) or two before a barrage of stones was getting him right and left! Off he set as hard as he could leg it along the usual path. Then all of a sudden he made the finest *car a mhuiltean* (somersault) ever you saw right into the *Poll-grannda* (nasty pool).

As we ran towards the black pool Sgadan yelled a warning—"Ware! grass-snares!" We grasped the situation just in time to prevent some of ourselves sharing Calum's unfortunate fate. Sgadan, the evening before, had knotted a series of handfuls of the long tough grass so that they formed "snares" across the path; and it was one of these that had given his *congé* to Calum in his more than usually precipitate flight.

Believe me, we drove a hard bargain with our tormentor in regard to future immunity before we hauled him out of the *Poll-grannda*! And the minor tragedy of poor wee Davock's kilt—which Calum had carried with him into the pool, and which was never recovered—was forgotten in the joy of victory—and another half-holiday!

CHAPTER XXVIII

Hector and Diamond—Curing a Jibber

WHEN Dònull Og used to criticize his neighbour Rory for failing to keep his rather high-flying wife in proper subjection, his own wife Eilidh would slyly retort: "*Tha sin gle mhath, a Dhonuill, ach ceannsaichidh a h-uile fear an droch bhean ach a' fear aig am bi'i!*"—"That is all very well, Donald, but every man can discipline the bad wife but the man who has got her."

And this is as true of horses as it is of wives. It's all very well to criticize the other man's inept handling, but it must be a right awkward predicament to be landed with either a wicked horse or wife.

Take a kicker, for instance—and, by the way, it is interesting to note that horses afflicted with this particular vice are, almost without exception, of the female sex! A kicking mare is a real problem. She may be going along as meekly as a lamb the one moment, and the next it would seem that all the seven devils that are usually associated with the pig have got possession of her, for she proceeds with fiendish venom to kick your good cart to smithereens. It takes a really philosophic driver to stand that sort of thing with unruffled temper.

And look at the jibber, that coaxing or cursing or caning will not induce to move forward one step! I never see a jibber but I remember that ploy we played on *Eachann Bodhar* (Deaf Hector) and his horse, Diamond, many years ago.

Eachann used to go with his horse and cart to Dingwall once a fortnight or so. On the way home, when they came to the end of the level road and turned to face the half-mile brae, it was Diamond's invariable habit to stolidly refuse to advance another yard, for maybe an hour or more, that must have felt like a day to the impatient Eachann. Eachann might apply the whip and some shocking language as forcibly as he liked (and he did!), but Diamond would not budge. After ten minutes of this forceful but futile persuasion, Eachann would give it up as a bad job, and, sitting on a board that rested on the two sides of the cart just forward of the wheels, would proceed to fill the old clay pipe and suck such comfort as he could from it until at long last it suited Diamond's pleasure to resume the homeward way. This was a most humiliating wait for the irascible Eachann, and we youngsters never failed to exhibit our fiendish glee at his dilemma, until our bright leader conceived and executed a plan which robbed us for ever of that diversion.

The plot was carefully laid. One evening we hid behind the dyke at the corner where we knew that Eachann and Diamond would soon arrive. They duly came. Eachann turned Diamond to face the hill. As per usual, Diamond stopped, and Eachann, as per usual, stooped forward in the cart and belaboured the refractory one with the usual admixture of whip and tongue, with the usual result. Then he gave it up and sat down on the board to get the pipe agoing. It was at that moment the Bright One crept in close behind the cart, carrying in his hand an enormous "dag" that a soldier-uncle had brought home from the Crimea. This pistol had a strong and capacious barrel that we had charged to near the mouth with black blasting powder (taken from the quarrymen's bothy, I'm afraid) and packed in with a wad composed of a compressed page of a newspaper.

The explosion, right at Diamond's heels, was as terrific as it was unexpected. Diamond gave one forward spring and then set off up the brae at a gallop which never slackened till he reached home. At the first spring

Eachann lost his balance and fell backwards heels-over-head into the bottom of the cart, where he was quite safe, though rattled like a pea in a pail; and the one glance we got of his face as Diamond careered along showed on it the most amazed surprise you ever saw!

Never once in after years did Diamond try his old trick at the bottom of the brae; and at that Eachann was delighted. But the funniest part of the story is that, what between his deafness and the suddenness of the whole affair, he never knew exactly "what came at" Diamond on that memorable day—and we were too afraid to tell.

CHAPTER XXIX

Caol-an-Fhuaim or Channel of the Roaring Waters

AWAY back over a century ago, the people of a township on one of the main islands of the Hebrides were evicted by the Tacksman from the little crofts which had been theirs and their forebears for generations.

We need not enter into the rights or wrongs of the case; maybe there were faults on both sides. But it was with sore hearts the people packed up their little belongings, stowed them in boats and flitted them over the Sound to the uninhabited island which was to be their future home. It was late autumn. They expected a winter of privation, for their stores were meagre; but the storms which came that winter were unusually severe and protracted; so that to this day, on the island, it is spoken of as "the wild winter of the year of the flitting."

The surface of their new island was mainly rock and rough grazing. True, there was a belt of good *machair* land fringing the bay, round the sides of which they built the rude stone-and-turf dwellings which afforded but indifferent shelter from the storms that every now and then raged across the island and lashed the surrounding sea to fury. But it would be next September before the *machair* could be made to yield a harvest that would give them bread, and provide fodder for the few head of cattle they had managed to take with them—and the assurance of a good meal in September is poor comfort to a hungry belly the previous April! Yet manure, cultivate, and sow the *machair* they must if they were to survive another winter. So they cut seaware and carried it in creels to fertilize the land. Then they turned the earth with the *cas-chrom*, sowed with care the few pecks of seed-grain, and left the rest to the Almighty.

On a day that April half a dozen of the young men were cutting seaware. As the tide receded they followed up with their *corrans*, cutting the newly exposed ware and carrying it to safety outwith the reach of high tide. From there, in creels, it was carried by the girls to the *machair*. It was heavy work and demanded much energetic attention from all; but they were young and irresponsible enough to enjoy a little diversion each time the lassies returned to the *cladach* with empty creels for another load. Then there was some of that banter and laughter which has ever been the way with young folks, and not even the privations incidental to existence on their new island could quite smother its expression that spring day.

Late in the afternoon didn't *Mairi*, the daughter of Donald Morrison, come to the *cladach* in the capacity of nurse to her baby-brother, Colin. To guard against the bairn injuring its tender limbs on the stony beach, Mairi rolled him in blankets, and for extra safety laid him in a tub which was sometimes used for containing whelks and cockles or other shell-fish, and which now stood well clear of the tide. The child thus safely disposed of, Mairi joined in the fun with the others.

In certain circumstances time has a way of flying. It flew now with Mairi and her companions. Suddenly they realized that it was almost dark and that the tide had "made" rapidly! The bairn . . .! Swiftly they ran over the intervening rocks to where the child had been left in the tub—but, to their horror, no trace of child or tub could be seen. Distractedly they ran, this way and that, shouting and scanning, but to no avail. . . .

It was when the panic was at its height that Angus *Og*

—a lad wise for his years—said in that quiet compelling way of his: "This is not the time for useless wailing. This is a case for *Calum Glic*" (Wise Malcolm). And like the wind he set off for the earthen hut which was Calum's dwelling.

"Calum," gasped Angus, "Donald Morrison's bairn is carried off with the tide. He was in the cockle-tub at the *cladach* and we forgot about him!"

Calum, a man of uncanny insight and little speech—except on occasion when he could be eloquent enough—went without a word to the shore. There the jollity of but an hour before had changed into the gloom of dread. Calum demanded information—exact information—as to the spot where the tub had stood. Did it contain any cockles?—or was it just weighted with the child? —The wind?—its strength—when did it change? He asked for the information jerkily, but with command in his voice. The youths gave him to the best of their recollection.

Then Calum appeared for some minutes to go into a trance. He stared at the stars and could be heard muttering. Well the young folks knew his problem. He was trying to read the riddle of the tides, making due allowance for the effect of varying winds. Round to the east of their new island, in the channel which separated it from the neighbouring land, there is the rather rare phenomenon—contending tides. There, twice daily, the tide from the Minch rushes westwards while the tide from the Atlantic rushes eastwards, both with the speed of a fast river. They meet in mid-channel and wild is the resulting commotion. That channel is known locally as *Caol-an-fhuaim* (The Channel of the Noisy Waters). That night the tub containing Donald Morrison's youngest-born would be wafted gently by the south-west wind that blew an hour ago, until it got caught in the swift flow of the current from the Minch.   Then nothing could save it from being engulfed in the dreaded waters of *Caol-an-fhuaim*.   True, the wind had changed and now blew freshly from the west; but no! no!   Not even the wisdom and skill of *Calum Glic* could give them a glint of hope!

Calum was now coming out of his trance.   He was quite calm, but under great strain.   Then he thundered in a voice that made the lads jump to obey, "Put out the big boat."

In a trice the boat was ready.

"*Athainne!*" (A torch) was Calum's next command; and in a twinkling black peats with one glowing end were brought from the big fire they had kindled at midday in the shelter of a rock.   They also put some unkindled peats in the boat.

Four men went to the oars.   Each of other four held in his hand, by the cold end, a peat with lighted end to the wind so that it glowed, and a considerable halo of light shone on the waters round the boat.

"Steer on that blue star to the south of east," Calum commanded.

For an hour they pulled, with never a word spoken except for an occasional brief command from Calum. Right out they went over the dark and now stormy waters of the Minch.   As one peat nearly burnt itself out another was set to its glow till it also took fire; and so the torch-light was continuous.   But the wind was growing stronger. Peat after peat got more quickly finished.

"Dip them in the sea," ordered Calum.   This was done, and the damped peat lasted a little longer.   But soon even this plan would not suffice.   The peats were nearly finished. . . .   Soon they would be in darkness and without a vestige of hope. . . .

But Calum for the past few minutes had been keenly scanning the sea.   His eyes, though old, seemed to cut into the darkness. Suddenly, and with the first touch of emotion his voice had shown, he shouted to Angus *Og* who was holding the last glowing ember of the last peat in fingers that were burning with the heat of it: "*Tog suas an t-athainne!* (Lift up the torch)."

Up went the torch to the full stretch of Angus *Og's* arm, and there, within the halo cast by the burning peat, was the cockle-tub, smoothly riding the waves! And inside it, with uplifted arms and cherubic smile, the newly awakened child of Donald Morrison.

Then, in the middle of the marvel of it, Calum removed the bonnet from his white head, that shone in the light of the peat, and reverently thanked his Maker for the guidance He had vouchsafed to His unworthy servant.

CHAPTER XXX

The Trysting Place

No, this is not a love story. It's a story of another sort of trysting place altogether, and of a shepherd and his dog connected therewith, and some other things.

As you leave the town of Inverness and travel up by the Great North Road you pass through a country of rare beauty and interest. Inverness itself is definitely left behind when you rumble over the narrow bridge that spans the Caledonian Canal. A new modern bridge is now in course of erection. To the left of the road the ground rises steeply to Clachnaharry, a rocky height from which, in the old days, watch was kept against the approach of enemies.

Close by the road, on the right, the Beauly Firth lies like a burnished sword, bending and sharpening to a point that stabs the heart of the hills. Across the Firth lies the Black Isle. The name does it a rank injustice, for its wide fringes round the shores of the Beauly and Cromarty Firths present a pleasing picture of green trees and fertile, well-tilled farms.

In the far distance Ben Wyvis rears its solemn massive bulk bathing in the sunlight, but with a few spots of snow still showing in its deeper corries. Or it may be that you can only catch a shadowy glimpse of the Ben itself as the clouds and mist scud across, or enshroud it in calm white mystery. But whatever its guise, and whether under summer's sun or winter's snow, it is one of those sublime things in nature which never fails to stir the finer emotions of the human mind.

Some four miles from Inverness is Bunchrew, with its narrow belt of fertile fields and its lovely woods where

Neil Munro's *Beachdair* slept in the cave by the side of the burn and guddled for trout for his breakfast.

Another few miles and you pass the old Bog Roy Inn, where in bygone days the smugglers outwitted the gaugers. The gaugers had captured a cask of whisky in a smugglers' bothy near by, and had it taken into a room in the inn pending its removal to Inverness. To make doubly sure of its safety (they had been outwitted before) two gaugers sat on top of the cask while a third walked back to Inverness for a horse and cart. But the smugglers, reluctant to part with the potent fruit of their labour (and helped by the hints of a friendly servant-lassie), quietly entered a room immediately below the one in which the cask and the gaugers sat, placed another cask "plumb below," and bored a hole with an auger through the floor and the cask above. The spirit obeyed the ordinary law of gravity, and when the horse and cart, etc., arrived from Inverness the gaugers soon discovered to their chagrin that their prize now consisted of an empty cask!

Soon you are passing through the Lovat country and the rich alluvial lands that once belonged to the Monastery. You cross the River Beauly by the bridge of that name—there is always a chance of seeing a salmon leap in the pool below—and then turn sharply to the right for the village. On the left, about two miles distant, and just discernible over a wealth of tree-tops, stands Beaufort Castle, the ancestral home of the Lovat family, and near by there are the ruins of Castle Dounie, closely associated with many stirring episodes in Scottish history.

The village of Beauly itself, with its quaint wide square, its shops and trim villas, and its ruins of the Old Priory, makes a pleasant and restful picture. It is true that nowadays many buses pass through the village—indeed they stop there for a few minutes—but, as they are smoothly designed and tastefully coloured buses, and as their passengers are usually quiet and reflective people, even these modern transport vehicles do not seem out of place in this charming Highland hamlet.

Still another mile farther north and the road for some two hundred yards winds gracefully up a brae. At the top of the brae a new picture is, as it were, thrown on the screen. You are now on an old raised beach as flat as a table for two miles in front and for half a mile on either side. The soil is light and shingly and there is a profusion of whin and broom which—if it happens to be June or July—looks like a carpet of gold.

There is plenty of variety dimly discernible in the far distance, and I should like to carry you with me to the farther north where there is breath-catching beauty round every bend of the road. But for the present at least we can go no farther, for we have arrived at our Trysting Place—the Muir-of-Ord.

The Muir-of-Ord is now a golf course—shade of Corry-choillie! (a noted worthy of the Market). It that was once the Falkirk Tryst of the north! Here in the old days, once every month, met farmers and flockmasters, crofters and shepherds, bringing with them thousands of sheep and hundreds of cattle for the purpose of selling to each other and to the farmers and dealers and drovers that came from the south.

As a small boy I attended the Market for the first time well over forty years ago. Even then it was past its best, for the auction mart had carried its invasion to the north some years previously. But there was still a great gathering of men and dogs and beasts, and that first day stands out a landmark in the memory.

There were fair-haired Scandinavians from the plains of Caithness with never a word of Gaelic in their heads; they and their beasts had been on the road for ten days. Then there were the big flockmasters from Ross-shire and

Sutherland, of whom not a few were the descendants of Border men who had migrated north some decades previously, and, in conclave with impecunious proprietors, appropriated extensive grazings that had previously belonged to the native peasantry. And there were big, bearded, picturesque men from Skye and the Hebrides, with their equally picturesque Highland cattle whose horns spanned six feet and more. There were also hundreds of small farmers and crofters from far and near. Men from north and south of the Border were there in plenty, mostly with clean or partly shaven faces, coloured by a sun-cum-whisky admixture to various tints of red and brown.

No two men were dressed alike; each man seemed to have a distinctive garb of his own. One gentleman I particularly noticed wore elastic-sided boots, trousers of the shepherd-tartan pattern, a blue-green coat with tails, a flaming red gravat, and a tall, tapered, flat-topped hat; and all over, there was a picturesque display of colour and individuality in dress and character that is woefully lacking at the ringside of the modern auction mart.

And what a confusion of sheep and cattle and dogs and shepherds and shouting! To the uninitiated it seemed that never could order come out of that chaos. But order did come eventually; each lot was stanced and the battle of buying and selling began. It was a hard school and it was intensely interesting to watch and listen to the experts at work. With what withering scorn Alastair Breac could point out the defects in a lot of beasts he wanted to buy! And then the convincing manner in which he revealed to prospective purchasers the admirable qualities of that same lot later in the day when he wanted to sell them! A day at the Muir was a liberal lesson in tact, diplomacy, guile, and a hundred other arts useful to existence in this hard world! There

every man had better have a shrewd idea of the value of
what he wanted to sell or buy, and he required to have
the courage of his convictions; for indeed the Market
was no place for fools. One wonders how the rising
generation of farmers would fare in a battle of wits with
Alastair Breac and his kind. Badly, I fear; for open,
competitive bidding and the weigh-bridge of the auction
mart have deprived them of the opportunity of exercising
their personal skill and judgment.

As lots changed ownership, so did wads of notes—or,
better still, solid golden sovereigns—and soon the refreshment tent was doing a roaring trade. The bar-tender's
job was simple in those days, for he had practically one
drink to serve—the wine of the country, at fourpence per
half-gill, and nobody thought of taking a smaller measure
than that at a time. They were hard drinkers then, and
could carry an amazing quantity with impunity, or at
any rate without detriment to their bargaining acumen.

It was to this Market that Bob Cairns came every
autumn in charge of his master's ewes. Bob was shepherd
on an outlying hirsel of a farm situated some fifteen miles
from the Muir. He was one of those Border shepherds
who moved north with the Cheviot sheep, and these men
were in a class by themselves at that time. They were
artists in their profession, and the main object in their
lives was to present to their employers when Market day
arrived the finest lot of sheep that hard work and care
and skill could possibly produce. Rivalry in the matter
of prices was keen, and the shepherd took a keener pride
than his master in overtaking or beating a neighbouring
lot in the Market.

(It is but fair to interject here that that spirit and
tradition are still to be met with amongst that very
superior class of men, and that the natives of the north
have not been slow in learning the craft; so that now men

with names like Sutherland or MacKay may hold their own with Scotts or Waughs or Armstrongs.)

But Bob's strongest point was his training of dogs. He had a gift for that. No floggings nor senseless shouting were part of Bob's method, but that quiet voice, even temper, gentle but firm reproof, and judicious encouragement—in fact it was as one gentleman to another; and the result was superb, for Bob and his dogs were noted over a wide district.

One of the very best dogs he ever had was Risp, a beautiful black collie with a white ruff and white-tipped nose and tail. Risp was reputed to be able to do anything but speak. To those who have witnessed a sheep-dog trial, the collie's almost incredible intelligence and sagacity are known. The dogs at those trials have been specially trained to become expert in controlling a certain limited number of "situations," but the problems which confront the ordinary shepherd's working dog in the course of a heavy day—problems demanding instant solution—are innumerable; and Risp was master of his calling. Moreover—what is rather rare in a good working dog—he would frolic with the bairns like a puppy. He and Bob Junior, four years old, and second-youngest of a family of ten, were boon companions in fun when Risp had an hour to spare.

When Mrs Cairns' tenth child arrived on the scene, wee Bobbie and Risp felt rather uncomfortable about it, and gave that squalling youngster a wide berth. But soon he was the unconscious cause of great grief to both.

A sort of double-faced problem confronted Bob Cairns: the baby had to be baptized and he (Bob) had to go to the Muir-of-Ord Market. One might think that that problem shouldn't present any great difficulty; but it did, and it's just as well to make the confession here. Bob had one weakness—if indeed it amounted to that.

Anyhow, like many a good shepherd living a lonely hard-working life in a remote glen, he rejoiced to meet his fellows, and the Market was his one opportunity. There the pent-up austerity of a long year would be effectively drowned in the social bowl. There would be a few glorious hours of "kindled wit and waukened lair" and utterly happy companionship with half a dozen good fellows whom he hadn't seen, and wouldn't see again, for twelve long months; and they would make a night of it— and in short they would have a glorious spree. That had happened to Bob with unfailing regularity—once a year —and who dare say, in all the circumstances, that it did not do him a lot of good?

But the new minister was very strict in the administration of the baptismal sacrament, and he, unfortunately, late on the night of the previous Market had come across Bob and two friends lying in the bottom of a peat-hag— fortunately a dry one—into which they had stumbled, singing at the top of their voices with the enthusiasm that is spirituously inspired, each with a bottle in his hand and another in his pocket. Nor did the advent of the minister appreciably damp their enthusiasm, for they had attained victory over the ills of life.

His Reverence lacked that sympathetic understanding which Bob's wife displayed on these occasions; he was shocked and angry.

As the date of the Market drew near, therefore, Bob became uneasy in his mind at the thought of the visit to the manse. He looked so glum at breakfast one morning that his wife remarked in her cheeriest voice, "What's the matter with you this morning, Bob? You haven't eaten half your porridge!—and your face is no' just beaming!" And then in that sympathetic, understanding way she had she added, "It's no' the minister and the baptism that's bothering you, is it?"

"You've struck it first time, Meg," said Bob in a rueful tone, "that's just what is bothering me."

"Bob," said Meg, coming over to her husband's chair and placing a sympathetic hand on his head, "you shouldn't let that bother you, lad. You have nothing to be ashamed of, and surely Mr MacLeod must know by this time what sort of man Bob Cairns really is."

Bob caught her hand in a grip that hurt. "It's just like you to say that, Meg," he replied, "but you see Mr MacLeod does not look at me with your eyes; and I'll admit that that night he found Davie Scott and Jock Elliot and myself singing and drinking in the peat-hag we were pretty bad. Indeed I can't mind much of what happened, but I'm sure that Davie offered him a dram and I think I wanted to argue with him about religion! Oh! he was very angry, and there was no fun in him at all; and I didn't like his look when I met him in Garvalt last month!"

"Never mind, Bob," consoled his wife. "It's your only day off in the year, and he might have more sense than to take any notice; and besides," she added, with a daring in advance of her generation, "I sometimes think it would do him a world of good if he took an occasional spree and sang in a peat-hag himself!"

"Wheesht, Meg! Wheesht!" exclaimed Bob, rather alarmed at this outspokenness. "It won't do to *say* that anyway. But I'll try to finish early the night and then I'll go down to the manse and face the music."

That evening Bob, with Risp at his heel, set off on his joyless errand with a heavy heart, but with such long swinging strides that he covered the four miles in under an hour. The minister had been expecting him one of these evenings, and when, through the study window, he saw the shepherd walk up the garden path he assumed his most relentless, uncharitable expression, for—according to his lights—he had a duty to perform.

Bob was ushered into the study, cap in hand—Risp had been ordered to lie at the outer door—and the two men looked each other straight in the eyes. The minister's hands were under his coat-tails and he did not offer to shake hands—that would have been a weak start which would make his duty all the more difficult.

"Good evening, Mr MacLeod," began Bob, going straight to the point. "I have come down to ask when will it be convenient for you to baptize our little boy."

"I'm sorry, Bob," said the minister in a stern voice, "but I am afraid I cannot baptize your child."

Bob's heart seemed to drop a foot inside his body but he still looked straight at the minister and asked, "And why not, sir?"

"Why not!" repeated Mr MacLeod with rising wrath. "Need you ask why not? You should know, Mr Cairns, that baptism is a sacrament that is not to be lightly administered. A father of a family has responsibilities, and in my parish no baptism will be administered to the children of drunkards; and you cannot deny that you were shamefully drunk in my presence less than a year ago. I admit that your conduct has been good since then, but the Muir-of-Ord Market will be next week and you know what that means for you!" Then in kindlier tones he continued, "But I'll tell you what I'll do; if you come home sober from the Market I'll baptize your child."

Bob's face flushed. He knew well that he did not neglect his responsibilities as a father, and that he was no drunkard. The condition imposed by the minister was cruel; but the choice before the shepherd was critical, for in those days an unbaptized child was in a precarious position *in* this world, and *for* the next. Bob considered a few moments, and then spoke in his usual quiet way. "I do not admit, Mr MacLeod, that I am a drunkard or that I forget my duties as a father; but I see your point of view and I will do my best to come home sober from the Market." The minister and the shepherd shook hands in silence, and Bob and Risp set off for home.

"How did you get on with His Reverence?" inquired his wife as she met him at the door.

"Oh, right enough," replied Bob vaguely.

"Good," said Meg. "And when is the bairn going to be baptized?"

"Oh! some day after the Market," evaded Bob. "We didn't just fix an exact day," and he did not disclose anything further.

Market day duly arrived and Bob and Risp were there with the ewes; so were Davie Scott and Jock Elliot and half a dozen other boon companions. The drinking started as soon as the main responsibilities of the day were over, but to the amazement of the others Bob would not join in. At first they were incredulous and regarded his refusal as a great joke. But soon it became quite clear that Bob was taking no drink that day; and he looked very miserable—and no doubt felt even more miserable than he looked. Davie Scott was really perturbed about it; he left his companions and came over to Bob, who had just delivered his last lot of ewes to the buyer.

"Bob," said Davie, in that solemn sympathetic way of a friend who is half-drunk. "Bob! For God's sake, what's the matter with you?" And then in an anxious whisper, "You haven't got the cancer?"

"I'm all right, Davie," replied Bob, "but I'm no' drinking any the day." But how he longed to join them! Only he knew the full misery of that day. Davie went back to the crowd, sorely perplexed, and informed them that he couldn't make anything of Bob. "It's just fair puzzling," he mourned; and, no doubt with the idea of getting some light on the mystery, they all took several more drams.

By four o'clock Bob was ready to start off on the fifteen-mile road for home. But where was Risp? He couldn't just remember when it was he had last noticed the dog. But there never had been any occasion for Bob to look after Risp on the Market. Indeed it was the other way about! For, the higher Bob attained to heights of earthly bliss and freedom from the world's cares, the more closely did the faithful dog stand by. Bob gave the special two-toned finger-whistle that Risp knew so well, but no Risp appeared.

"Risp saw you were sober," said Davie very solemnly, "and he'll be off on a dander of his own." Davie's remark brought the only smile of that dreary day to Bob's lips, for the ironical thought had flitted through his own mind that Risp, seeing his master sober, must have concluded that there was no need for his watchful care and had gone on some intriguing canine adventure of his own! For a moment the hurting thought came to him that Risp might have been stolen by some scoundrel who had admired the dog's work and that he might never see his dog again—such things had happened before—but he thrust that aside and comforted himself with the reflection that Risp would turn up all right—indeed the dog might be home in front of him and give him a welcome on arrival.

Anyhow, there was no help for it, and Bob, sober, and with a sorry heart, set off on his journey.

When he came to the path that led to the footbridge which crossed the burn near his house he stopped, put his first and third fingers in his mouth and whistled in the way that never failed to bring Risp to his side if he were within hearing. No Risp appeared. Bob whistled once again. This time his wife appeared at the door and came towards the bridge.

"Is that you home already, Bob?" she asked, inwardly amazed, but casual without.

"Yes, I'm home early," said Bob.

And then Meg inquired, "But where is Risp?"

"He is not in the house, then?" countered Bob.

"No; he is not here," Meg assured him; "but when did you miss him?"

"I couldn't find him when I was ready to leave the Market," explained Bob. "I was hoping he might be home in front of me, but no doubt he'll turn up soon."

But next day there was no sign of Risp and there was a heart-breaking scene with wee Bobbie when he learned that his playmate had not come home. The father tried to assure him that Risp would be to-morrow, but indeed his own heart was heavy too, for well he knew that if Risp were a free agent he would have been home that day.

Two days later wee Johnnie Cairns was duly baptized.

Day after day and week after week went by and ultimately all hope of his ever returning was given up. Bob missed his faithful assistant on the hill tremendously. The superannuated Glen—to his intense joy and subsequent pain, for he was stiff and old—was invited to accompany his master at his work; but soon another dog had to be trained, for the work was very trying.

Bob's next yearly Market came round and he was there with his new dog. There was no ecclesiastical restraint on the shepherd this time, and Davie Scott and all the rest of them were there, and delighted to see that Bob was himself again. The old crowd were talking at the refreshment-tent door when suddenly Bob bit his clay pipe so hard that the stem broke and the head fell to the ground. He was staring at a dog which was "weaving" sweetly at the far side of a lot of sheep. The dog was being directed by a big, florid-faced drover from somewhere in the far south.

"What on earth are you staring at, Bob?" asked Jock Elliot.

"Wait a minute," said Bob. And then, as the dog started to run again in response to a command from the drover, Bob whistled. The dog "clapped" as if shot, and then raised his head and looked eagerly around. The drover yelled some other command at him which the puzzled dog proceeded to obey. Bob whistled again! Down went the dog, and again that questioning look! This second interference with his dog was so marked that the drover came over to the group at the tent door, his red face redder with anger. "Who is interfering with my dog?" he demanded. Bob stepped out. "I interfered," he said, very quietly, "that dog is mine."

The language that followed is not to be printed in any respectable book, and the threats . . . ! But Bob's friends rallied round him and it was not going to be a one-sided affair. Two policemen were called and the cause of the dispute explained to them. The officers of the law were rather perplexed, but Bob, who seldom lost his head or his temper, came to their assistance. "That dog is mine," said he, pointing to the dog who was still on the far side of the lot of sheep. "I lost him, or he was stolen from me, on this Market last year. This man" (pointing to the drover) "claims him, and for all I know he may have come by him honestly; but the dog is mine, as I will prove to you. If you," continued Bob, turning to the drover, "will walk round to the dog and stand beside him I will whistle and call him by the name of 'Risp,' and if the dog starts to come to me you can call him back, but I can call again, and if the dog leaves you and comes to me that should prove that I am telling the truth when I say the dog is mine."

All but the drover were agreed that that was a fair and even generous line for Bob to take, but the drover realized that he could not afford to refuse the test. He walked over to the dog and spoke kindly to him. Then Bob whistled. The dog sprang to his feet and gazed. Then Bob called "Risp!" The dog started to move in the direction of the group at the tent; the drover spoke commandingly to him. "Risp!" called Bob again, and this time there was no hesitation. Risp—for Risp it was —came tearing round in the direction of the voice he would never forget, and when he scented and saw his beloved master his expressions of joy were simply indecorous for so staid a gentleman.

The proof of ownership was overwhelming, but Bob, ever considerate of others, suggested to the now dogless drover that he (Bob) and Risp would drive the sheep for a couple of miles down the road where they were to join up with a bigger lot in charge of other shepherds and dogs. The drover gladly accepted and there was no happier dog on the Muir-of-Ord Market that day than our friend Risp as he "kepped" and "clapped" and "checked" at a word from the master he adored.

The gathering at the refreshment tent that evening is historic; Risp had a well-remembered duty to perform, and the light of canine love beamed from his eyes.

CHAPTER XXXI

The Charmed Thread, or *Snàth Sgochadh Fèithe*

"MAN, it's fine to see them all again, Sandy!" said the Right Honourable Hector MacLean, statesman and banking magnate of the Far East, as he sat with his brother Sandy on the rustic seat under the gean-tree in the old home garden at Strathulladale and looked across the valley and over to the hundred hills whose tops mingled with the clouds in the far distance—"*Cnoc-na-h-eaglais!—Beinn a' Bhàthaichard!—Sgurr a' Mhuilinn!* and all the rest of them, so cool and yet so warm and friendly. God, how often in the scorching sun out yonder did I think of them! I sometimes dreamed of them too!— and now after thirty years——" Here, with true Celtic instinct, the speaker helped himself to a dram to hide his emotion.

"Yes, I suppose they are fine, and very likely I would miss them too if I didn't see them every day," replied Sandy, who was the one of the family who had had "to stand by the old folks" in the croft while the rest, one by one, went out into the world; and to make believe that he hadn't noticed his brother's emotion Sandy poured himself out a dram too.

In spite of their divergent paths through life the brothers were remarkably alike, for though Hector's hands looked soft beside Sandy's gnarled fists, and the London suit was somewhat better cut than the home-spun, the strong massive features were the same, and the clear grey eyes were ridiculously alike—as were the generous mouths that flickered into humour so readily at the corners.

"Aye," continued Hector, "the hills at least have not

148

changed, although, I suppose, nearly everything else is different. There won't be any of the old folks left, and the old customs and superstitions will have died with them."

"Indeed there's not many of the old folks of your day left," agreed Sandy, "and some of the old beliefs have died too. But I'm not so sure that what we used to regard as the superstitions of the older generation may not have a natural enough explanation after all."

"But surely, Sandy," objected the banker, "nobody believes nowadays in *buidseachd* (witchcraft) and the evil eye, and cures like *bùrn-airgid* (silver water), and all that sort of nonsense!"

"Well, anyhow," argued Sandy, "I try to keep an open mind on these things. What would you have said thirty years ago if someone had told you that in a few years' time I could hear you speaking in India as well as I hear you now speaking in that seat? And look at Conan Doyle and Stead and Oliver Lodge? You can hardly call these men cranks or think that they would want to make fools of the rest of us, eh? No, no. I'm thinking that after all there may be more things on this earth than are dreamt of in our philosophy." Sandy was now on a favourite topic and proceeded to enlarge on it.

"Poor Sandy," thought Hector, but he did not say it, "you are as old-fashioned as ever—— Hullo," he broke in, "who is the budding piper?"

Sandy stopped to listen.

"That will be *Seorus Caol's* boy Calum," he said. "He is daft for the pipes and is always whistling like that and practising the notes."

The whistler was not yet in sight but the notes of *The Atholl Highlanders* came to the ears of the listeners with a lilt and a swing that only one with martial music in his soul could impart. Then the lad came into view at the end of the garden hedge, stepping grandly to the twirling music of his lips and tongue, while at each step the mud of the soft path squeezed up between the toes of his bare feet. On seeing the two men Calum brought strut and tune to a sudden stop and pretended he had only been whistling to his collie.

"Good evening, Calum," Sandy greeted him. "Man, you can fairly get the dirls into that one." Calum blushed. "And how are they all with you at home?"

"Fine, thank you," replied Calum; "but the red heifer is lame and I'm just going east to get a *snàth sgochadh fèithe* from *Iain Dearg*'s wife."

"*Dhia gleidh mi!*" exclaimed Hector, turning to his brother. "Is Iain Dearg's wife still alive and does she still make the *snàth sgochadh fèithe*?"

"That she is and that she does," replied Sandy. Then he politely introduced his brother to the boy. "This is my brother Hector from India, Calum."

They shook hands, Calum remarking shyly, "I have often heard about you."

"Well, here I am in the flesh," said the banker kindly; "and maybe some day you will be going out to India or Australia yourself, Calum; they could do with your kind out there. But what happened to the red heifer?"

"Indeed, I'm not sure," said Calum. "My father thinks it was the black cow that pushed her down the river-bank, but my mother says she is sure it was the *ban'-cheard* (tinker-wife) with her evil eye."

"But I thought your people were quite friendly with the tinkers?" said Sandy.

"And so we were till the other day when my father took a rise out of old Kirsty," explained Calum. "When father was raking the stubble-field Kirsty came along and begged for a windling of rakings. 'There's the rake, and rake a windling for yourself,' said he. Kirsty was very insulted at being asked to work like that. She refused, and went away cursing like anything. Father was delighted with the joke, but this morning when my mother was going to milk the cows she is sure she saw Kirsty disappearing in the broom bushes, and when mother got to the byre there was the door off the sneck and the red heifer very excited and quite lame on her near hind-leg."

"But the *snàth* is only good for accidents," said Hector, the lore of his youth coming back to him. "If it's the evil eye that did it, it's to the wood you should be going for a bit of walnut or elm to carry in the pocket."

"Yes, I know; but I did that to-day already," explained Calum, "and my mother has the bit elm in her pocket now; but father is not satisfied and that is why I am going for a thread from Iain Dearg's wife."

"It's many a day since I got my first *snàth* from her," said Hector reminiscently. "It was for that," extending his left wrist—"and I mind fine how soothed I felt when the thread was tied loosely round it! Calum," he asked, "will you let me do your message for you? Sandy tells me that *Peggi Ruadh's* daughter is now in the shoppie at the bridge and that she sells grand chocolates instead of the 'caravies' and conversation 'lozengers' we used to get from her mother. You run down and get some chocolates and I'll go over to Iain Dearg's for the thread."

The boy demurred at taking the proffered money, but it was pressed tactfully, and *Mairi Peggi Ruadh's* chocolates were tempting—and so he agreed. "But you will not be long in coming back?" he stipulated with a sense of responsibility, and the banker assured him he would start off immediately.

In a matter of twenty minutes he was approaching Iain Dearg's house. The old woman stood in the door shading her eyes from the sun and scanning the stranger keenly.

Soon she recognized him and stepped slowly out to give him greeting. But it was no old country woman giving humble greeting to one of the great ones of the earth. It was a queenly old lady giving welcome and a blessing to the boy Hector on his return to the home of his fathers; nor did Hector ever dream that it should be otherwise. Both fell into the Gaelic tongue as naturally as flowers expand in the sun, and the past thirty years were as nothing to the banker who was a boy again; and indeed the delusion was not difficult, for the years had left scarce a trace of their passing on this mysterious, kindly woman. The long black frock, the white apron, and frilled mutch were just the same, and the dark eyes that scorned artificial aid were keen and all-comprehending as ever. Only the hearing was somewhat dulled, Hector noticed.

For a few minutes there was kindly talk of old friends and memories, but soon Hector had to explain the particular urgency of his errand. It seemed quite natural too that this boy should ask Iain Dearg's wife for a *snàth* for the leg of Seorus Caol's red heifer.

"Indeed and that I will," the wife assured him, "it is our duty to help a neighbour if we can"; and straightway she went to an old wicker-workbasket from which she selected a pirn of white linen thread. She unwound and broke off about a yard of the thread; this she doubled, and, holding the doubled end between the thumb and fore-finger of her left hand, she laid the thread on her right knee with the single ends hanging down. Then she spat on the palm of her right hand and with it "rolled" the double thread on her knee. This had the effect of "twining" the threads for an inch or two of their length, and there a knot was tied; then another spit, another "twine," and another knot, and the process was repeated until the thread was all twined, and it had about a dozen knots on the length of it. But all the time that the thread had been manipulated Iain Dearg's wife half-muttered, half-chanted a *duan* (rhyme). Many a time had suppliant boys and girls tried to catch the words of that *duan*, but the old woman took good care they did not hear much. Now, however, her deafness deceived her, and Hector heard almost every word of it. Freely translated it ran something like this:

> Powers from East and Powers from West,
> Powers Above and Powers Below,
> Listen to my heart's request;
> Join in one and favour show,
>
> To those buffeted by Scathe,
> In their flesh or bones or blood,
> Give calm courage, give strong faith
> To resist Fate's swiftest flood.

And then there followed a third verse which must not be quoted here.

As the words were chanted earnestly again and again the listener became embarrassed, for well he knew that the *duan* should not be "stolen" like this: that the secret could only be imparted voluntarily by a woman to a man or *vice versa*.

"'*Bhean Iain Dearg*," he said apologetically, "I am sorry, but I could not help hearing the words of the *duan*."

For a moment she flushed with vexation. Then she smiled resignedly. "Well, well, Hector; maybe it's the hand of Providence. I am now an old woman and it's high time I was handing on the secret. You were always a clever, understanding lad, and I have no son living of my own; now listen and be sure you get it right. I got it from my grandfather, *Alastair a' Bhreabadair* (Sandy the Weaver), fifty-two years ago, when I was only forty years of age, and if it has not always done good, it has often helped, and it never did any harm."

And so it was that Iain Dearg's wife, the granddaughter of *Alastair a'Bhreabadair,* handed down to the Right Honourable Hector MacLean the secret of the *snàth sgochadh fèithe* at the same time as she handed him the last *snàth* she would ever make; for, once disclosed, the "gift" was hers no longer.

CHAPTER XXXII

Memories, or *An Gleann' San Robh Mi Og*

ONCE every year, for a few fleeting days, I return to the place of my birth—*an gleann' san robh mi og*. Just why, it would be hard to explain. For the chairs by the old fireside have now new tenants; the dear old friends who filled them are gone. It is the same throughout the Glen, too. One by one the old folks have been gathered to their fathers. A new brood has arisen that to me is alien. Only an old school-comrade here and there. But to meet these—to look into their eyes again—to feel the firm hand-grip—to hear the warmth in their voices, is one of the deepest joys in life. As we move about the world we are ever forming new friendships. But new friends can never be quite like these. We see new friends as through a glass, darkly, but into and through the friends of our childhood days we see with eyes of utter understanding.

So that the annual sojourn in the Glen brings a mixture of emotions. Frankly, the holiday never comes quite up to anticipations. But the anticipation itself is grand!— and so is the retrospect.

Weeks before the great day, thoughts of it intrude themselves and give a lightsome lift to the daily darg. The process accumulates as the day approaches. Plans are discussed; programmes mapped out for filling in the rosy hours. Quite likely most of the plans will never materialize. But look at the joy of making them!

Then on the day itself there is the bustle of getting to the station and scrambling for seats in the train. By the time we recover our breath we are well away from the smoke, and the sordid surroundings of the city, and racing up the Great North Road. Past Blair Atholl we climb into the heather. And now with every mile there is a subtle change. It is as if a weight on your chest had been removed. You can fill your lungs with the honey-scented air of the hills. You are like a horse trotting homewards. Not an old horse either, but a young high-stepper with ears aprick. And when you reach the *druim* (ridge) between Carrbridge and Culloden, that affords you the first distant view of the hills and Bens of Ross . . . ! Confound those splashes! I had to use my hankie—and the bairns wondered if Dad were catching a cold. . . .

One evening last autumn I indulged in sadly pleasant retrospect—the sort of emotional ecstasy one sometimes achieves on a visit to the old churchyard. But this was not in the churchyard. I walked along the braes, and in less than a mile I passed where nine houses had been— the homes of people I remember—but of which now only ruins, or less, remain.

Beside that rowan-tree there stood old Ciorsti's cottage. Not one trace is left; there is a rabbit-burrow just about the spot where the old lady used to sit and spin.

Beneath those lumpy mounds covered with green grass are the stones that used to form the walls of Rory the shoemaker's workshop. It would be just here by the ingleneuk where Rory used to sit on a backless oak chair cutting out the uppers for the eight shoemakers that sat in two rows down the room, each intent on turning out an article that would be a masterpiece. As I gazed at the spot it seemed to me that Rory was there again. I seemed to see him straighten his back as he used to do, and inhale a copious *snaoisean* (snuff) from yon queer old *scrogag* he had.

Not even the *larach* (site) of the old *breabadair's* house is left, where in other days the shuttle flew swiftly this way and that to build the homely web.

Twice this autumn did I climb to the top of the Ben. She is the only thing that is changeless; even her mists are the same. On the way to the Fuaran Mòr we startled coveys of grouse. There was a water-ouzel fishing in the pool at the Falls and we saw the brown trout like dark shadows flitting in the pools of the burn; while on its banks we had a rare feast of *Oighreagan* (cloud-berries).

The mountain was in frowning mood both days. From the Big Well to the summit there was a rolling mist that made the sheep as big as deer and the hares as big as sheep. The few ptarmigan we saw, too, were magnified to the size of geese. Not one blink of distant view did the fickle jade vouchsafe. But once—just a matter of moments—there was a rift in the rolling canopy, and (like part of a film projected on a gigantic screen) we got a perfect view of the Corrie with the sun blazing down from above and a herd of deer streaking up the eastern slope.

1   Colin MacDonald at Tigh-na-Gaoith.

2   Plus-fours into instant shorts: Colin climbing Ben Wyvis about 1935.

3 MacDonald family group. *c.* 1911, in front of the croft: (left to right) Blackie, the dog; Elsie, née Mackenzie and Donald MacDonald, Colin's parents; Thomas Young from Crieff (Colin's future father-in-law); Belle Foubister, (Colin's sister with her sons David and Donald); Alec MacDonald, (Colin's brother); Margaret Stewart Young (Colin's future wife).

4 MacDonald family group with neighbours about 1911.

5 Margaret MacDonald, gutting herrings on the doorstep of the croft, 1937.

6   Primitive ablutions, Colin Tom MacDonald.

7   Strathpeffer from the Heights. Sandy MacDonald sighting a shot on the Territorial Army camp below.

8   Colin's work took him to Stornoway Market in 1911.

9   Neighbouring crofters, Mr and Mrs Hugh Rose, Redbank, Heights of Keppoch.

10 Reaping and binding oats on the Heights.

11   Jock Richmond and Mary MacLaren, Balnaird Farm, *c.* 1932.

12 'The Shoppie' at the bridge above Achterneed, early 1920s. It sold 'everything' and was a great meeting place.

13   Jimac o'Davie—James Mackay of Davidson Croft—driving a pony trap, about 1918.

14 Mairi à Claidheamh, aged about 85 in 1937, at the end of her two mile walk each way to Strathpeffer, with her weekly 'messages'.

15 Bob Aird, Heights of Inchvannie: ex-gamekeeper and crofting
mentor to the young MacDonalds, 1938.

Part Two

HIGHLAND JOURNEY

OR

SUIL AIR AIS

CONTENTS

PART I

5

PART II

NOTE TO THIRD EDITION

I AM somewhat surprised and altogether delighted by the reception which a varied public has given to *Highland Journey*. In these days of "quotaed" paper it has been found quite impossible to keep up with the demand for it. No doubt there is an element of the truth in what a bookstall friend of mine said when, just prior to the publication of the first edition, she assured me she would order a large number straight away.

"Better not order *too* many," said I. "I wouldn't like to see a pile of unsold copies going stale on your stand."

"Oh," said she, "you needn't be afraid of that. We can sell *anything* these days!"

But indeed—as my lady friend readily admits, and scores of most complimentary letters from readers allege—it would appear that it has sold partly on merit.

Ordinary readers may not notice any alterations in the Gaelic bits in this edition, but Gaelic "purists" no doubt will; and I would have such know that the master hand of my friend Mr Angus MacDonald, Inverness, is responsible. So what? But in any case the main idea is to easily convey the right atmosphere rather than to give a display of irreproachable Gaelic—if such there be!

I have been repeatedly complimented on the Gaelic title "Sùil air Ais (pronounced Sool er ash and meaning "Looking Back"). Now the credit for that really belongs to my friend Dr D. J. MacLeod, O.B.E., to whom, and to Mr MacDonald, I am greatly indebted.

C. M.

PART I

INTRODUCTION

Let me be honest about this book-writing business. Why do I attempt it? For a great statesman, soldier, scientist, scholar, or criminal, writing a book should be an easy matter and a safe venture for his publisher. Such may rest assured of a public intensely interested in his sayings and doings; especially the criminal—if he is a sufficiently notorious criminal. But that a very ordinary fellow like myself should venture to write a book displays a degree of self-assurance, if not of sheer impudence, which—because really I am somewhat of a modest disposition—requires some explanation. Well, in a word, the explanation is the "kick" I get out of it.

Some eight years ago I was—or imagined I was, which is nearly as bad—in a miserable state of health. Work, wife, family, friends, food—all for me had lost flavour. I went about in a state of physical misery and mental perturbation and depression. A serene philosophy which, when in robust health, I had evolved for my guidance and conduct, in whatever circumstances of prosperity or adversity Fate might bring my way, fell to sorry bits at this first test of trouble. That was intensely humiliating. I who had so often in a superior, strong-man sort of way advised others—how they must have hated me!—how to comport themselves under the buffets of Fate, to be so utterly found out. And when it came to the stage that I couldn't laugh at myself I knew the case was serious; that something had to be done about it. I must put a compulsitor on myself: must force myself to take an interest in something.

So I wrote to my friend David Watt, of the *Ross-shire Journal*—who indeed *is* the *Ross-shire Journal*—suggesting I should write an article for his paper for each week of 1932. I couldn't give him the foggiest indication of "How the subject theme might gang," but he generously agreed. During that year there appeared each week in the *Ross-shire* an article under the heading *Beachdaireachd* and signed *Beachdair*. These are Gaelic words, the first roughly equivalent to "Stock-taking" and the second meaning "The Fellow who takes Stock." For the first six months the authorship of *Beachdaireachd* was a well-kept secret, and many a time when passing through Dingwall, and some other places in the north, did I join eagerly in local conjecture as to who on earth the author of such interesting articles could be.

Soon a certain tendency in the articles developed. They were prone to browse among my own recollections of early life in a Highland glen; and, as soon appeared, they evoked a keen interest not only locally but in far corners of the world where the *Ross-shire* finds its way to exiled natives of the north. It was then I began to get the "kick" aforementioned. When you are told by an old lady in London—or Australia—of how she cried for joy over some memory-stirring passages you have written, or by an exiled Scot from many places of how he chuckled over certain bits and read them over and over again; and when you get scores of letters in similar strain from a great variety of people at home and abroad, it gives you a grand glow of satisfaction. That was my happy experience, and I who had but a few months before imagined myself past and dead to all human vanity found myself as vain as a peacock: my chest swelling like a pouter pigeon at such tributes to my cleverness. Oh! it was a grand feeling, and more effective than tonics from a dozen doctors.

In 1936 a good deal of *Beachdaireachd* was incorporated

in my *Echoes of the Glen*, whose kindly reception by the Press and public gave me renewed and deeper thrills of that self-conceit a modicum of which, I am convinced, is a most useful, necessary, human attribute. But, mind you, it takes some courage to let a book that you have written go out into the world. For, inevitably, a book is more or less a reflection of its author. To a greater or less degree it lets the critical eye of his friends and fellows penetrate his inmost thoughts and being. Spiritually it is somewhat analogous to what walking along Princes Street without his trousers would be physically. But indeed I was needlessly apprehensive about that, as you will see.

On the morning of the day on which *Echoes of the Glen* was timed to appear in public I was in a fever of self-consciousness. What an ass I had been to write a book at all! It wouldn't catch on! And there was that horrible publicity! I sneaked down in a street car to the Caledonian Station, and in by the side entrance, in agony at the thought of the blatant placards. Timidly I glanced towards the near end of the bookstall, but was surprised and relieved to see no placards there.

"They'll be round at the front," I thought with dismay. So, bravely to the front I went. Not a sign of me or my *Echoes*. I scanned the myriad books on the shelves but nary an *Echo* could I see, nor any reference to it or me. Half-relieved, half-disappointed, I went along Princes Street and glanced at the bookshop windows. Blank again! If it was there I didn't see it.

Somewhat resentful now I made for the Waverley bookstall. "That's where the show will be," thought I.

But the Waverley bookstall was like the other one—oblivious of my existence.

Chuckling now at my previous apprehensions I went to the small bookstall at the east end of the Waverley Station to make sure my child wasn't there. It wasn't in sight, but by bending down and forward and then creaking my neck for an upward glance behind an obscuring shelf I got a shock! There, in its artistic blue-toned cover, was a copy of *Echoes of the Glen*! My heart raced, but I pulled myself together.

With the steadiest voice I could muster, and in most casual manner, I said to the bookstall lady: "I'll take a copy of *Echoes of the Glen*, please," and waited for the brightening of her eye. But there was no brightening: the magic name conveyed nothing to her.

"I beg your pardon?" said the lady.

"*ECHOES of the GLEN*," I repeated distinctly, and in a hopefully suggestive tone.

"Is it a sixpenny one?" the lady brightly inquired.

"No!" I now bawled; "it is a five-shilling one, and it was published this morning."

"Oh, sorry! I haven't got it yet," said the lady, "but maybe you will get a copy at the big bookstall."

"Thank you," I said quite nicely, and I hadn't the heart to tell her that on her shelf there was a copy which she must have put there that morning.

Then and since my experience not only of bookstall assistants, but of booksellers generally—with very rare exceptions—has led me to believe that they take about as much interest in an individual book as a potato merchant takes in an individual potato.

Of the many compliments paid to my initial effort in the book line the one I like perhaps best of all came unconsciously from a Sutherland crofter. Donald was in our Thurso office paying his rent. That formality over, he sat with my colleague, George Stewart, enjoying a pipe and a crack. All of a sudden Donald "remembered" and the following conversation took place:

DONALD. Man, Mister Stewart, did you see that Colin MacDonald has written a book?

G.S. Yes, have you read it?

DONALD. Yes, man, and it's a *grand* book!—there's *nothing* in it!—*anyone* could write a book like yon!—if he could *write* it!

Well, equally there may be "nothing" in this one. I am not even sure that I can write it, but I do venture to hope that of a winter's evening it may give a little entertainment to some of my fellows on the Journey.

CHAPTER I

THE Journey began on 28th January 1882. I was
serenely unconscious of its course for the first year or two.
After that just a spotlight here and there, dimmed almost
immediately to leave but a shadowy memory.   There was,
for instance, that day I saw at the foot of the bed a strange
man, wearing black whiskers and a black suit, carrying a
black bag in his hand.   I saw him shake his head and
heard him speak to my mother, who looked unhappy.
Years later I learned that he told her there was only a
faint hope of my pulling through.   I also learned that
within ten days I was doing full justice to porridge and
potatoes and herrings again.

Then a little later there was the time my father surprised
us.   Like every self-respecting Highland crofter of his day
he left the performance of all domestic duties to his women-
folk.   I had never seen him sweep the house floor, cook a
meal (other than stir his own brose), milk a cow, or "wait"
on us children in his life.   Imagine my surprise then when
one morning he came to the kitchen bed, where three of us
were lying, carrying a tray with plates of porridge for us!
The reason for this astounding phenomenon was a double
one: we three were recovering from measles, and the
previous night my youngest sister had been born.   But I
cannot remember him lapsing to that extent on any future
occasion.

About the age of three I remember sitting on a stool on
a table near the window of a maiden aunt's house trying
to catch flies, that crawled across the panes, and hoping to
put them into a *pocan-ordaig* (a thumb-screwed paper bag).

It was a day of disappointments: the flies just slid away before my fingers could get them.

Four or so saw—and heard—me exchanging greetings by shouting to the wife of our nearest neighbour two hundred yards away. I have frequently seen townspeople amazed at the facility with which country folks can carry on a conversation with neighbours at anything up to a mile. In this art, as in most others, early training counts for much. The star performer in our district was the Griasaich Mòr (Big Shoemaker). Once on a still, frosty May morning, while an uncle and myself were metalling the road at Contin Bridge, we heard the Griasaich as clear as a bell calling on his dog "Curly." The distance by bee-line from the Griasaich's house to Contin Bridge is just over three miles.

In 1887 came Queen Victoria's Jubilee celebrations. There is more substance in this memory. Every bairn in the district went, with a mug, to the Castle Park. There were races, in which all competitors were prize-winners, some dancing, and—the first I had ever seen—a gigantic piper majestically arrayed in all the gaudy trappings of his trade. That piper fascinated me and my coevals, and soon after some of the older boys got practising chanters. In the afternoon we all marched into the Castle, to be regaled on pie and lemonade—another novelty to most of us. Not even champagne in after years quite touched the glory of that first lemonade—which was contained in yon old bottles with rounded bottoms like Indian clubs.

The Castle was awesome, as were the folks who lived in it. Its high, grim, six-foot-thick walls, its richly furnished wood-floored rooms, were such a contrast to our own thatch-roofed, earth-floored little houses. Seeing the Castle at close quarters for the first time gave me my first twinge of inferiority. Later in life, a fairly extensive familiarity with castles and those who live in them led me to the knowledge that the latter, in the things that really matter, are not so different or superior after all. I have quite ceased either to fear or envy them. If anything, I rather pity them. Of this I am certain: that if freedom from worry and debts and pretence—that awful blight on human life—and the possession of robust health and loving, happy, family unity be applied as the measure of a desirable existence, then the average inhabitant of the crofter's cottage leaves the average inhabitant of the castle far behind.

CHAPTER II

SCHOOL came at five. In *Echoes of the Glen* I tried to give
a few glimpses of our doings there, so I must avoid repeti-
tion, but will venture a few further references to our rural
academy. The school lay in the flat of the valley, some
five hundred feet lower than our home. Of my first day
of book-learning I retain only one, but most vivid memory.
All the bairns from higher up "The Heights" called for
us on their way to school that morning to give convoy to
the new scholar. There were three of the gamekeeper's
family from far up the hill-side, two cousins from just
above us, and three of our nearest neighbour's bairns.
Lower down we collected the MacKays, and when we
came to the railway crossing we were joined by a bigger
contingent from the Bottacks. Of course, I was the show-
piece, and very shy and embarrassed I felt by the crowd's
attentions. Instead of crying—as I very nearly did—I
picked up a stone from the railway and threw it as far as
I could along the line. It was a sort of gesture of independent manliness which I was far from feeling. Speak
of "shots at random sent"! That stone happened to
come bang down on the steel rail, about ten yards away,
a fraction of a second after a young linnet had alighted at
that identical spot. It was instant death to the linnet.
The bigger boys were impressed by such marksmanship:
what an eye! what an aim! I felt momentarily proud of
a feat which—quite undeservedly—jumped my stock
in the market of that somewhat callous lot of hooligans'
esteem; but indeed my triumph held a cankerous seed,
for, as I looked at that pathetic fluffy little heap, still

warm and trembling, which but moments before had been the incarnation of joy and gladness, a tear rolled down my nose and I had to laugh in raucous bravado to avoid disgrace. That little linnet remains the only song-bird I have injured in my life; and when at the last bar of judgment I shall be asked, as I still dread—"Why did you do it?"—the only plea I can tender is that I didn't mean it and that it has been a lifelong regret.

There were over a hundred scholars all told, with a headmaster, a headmistress, and two pupil teachers to instruct them. The scholars came from four main social strata. An outsider might well fail to see reason for differentiation, but he would be wrong. In numerical order we derived from:

1. *The farm-servant class.*—A prolific breed: I remember one family of fourteen, two of twelve each, two of nine, one of eight, and one of seven—a total of seventy-one, which assured an average school contingent of about two dozen—at one farm alone. With the individual family wage totalling not more than from twenty-five to thirty pounds per annum, plus an allowance of meal, milk, potatoes, and coal, one may assume that pampering in their early years did not spoil the family of the farm servant. Only God and their mothers knew how they were clothed and fed. But they were a tough and hardy race, who in the main took to hard manual labour—what other choice had they?—as soon as the attainment of their fourteenth birthday freed them from compulsory attendance at school. With few exceptions—but I can think of some bright ones—they were below the average in scholastic attainments; but that was probably largely due to their parents' nomadic propensity, which gave them little opportunity of a continuous course of education at one school.

2. *The crofting community.*—The "Heighters," as we

were called, lived up on the braes, where their progenitors had lived in the same croft for generations—in some cases centuries. Here was greater solidity and permanence; also a good deal more of material and cultural advantages which such permanence engenders. But we were still far, far, from being pampered! Almost invariably it was from this section the school's best scholars came. There was a second crofter contingent who came from the adjacent parallel valley, where their parents or grand-parents, on being evicted from the estate of another land-lord, had been permitted by our landlord to settle on small areas of unreclaimed land, which they industriously brought into cultivation. These still lacked the homo-geneity of the older community; but they were a friendly, hospitable people, known—a reference to their original home—as the *Cononachs*.

3. *Villagers' families.* — Shopkeepers, feuars, estate officials, etc., a comparatively well-to-do class. These youngsters esteemed themselves no small beer, and infinitely superior to the "Heighters" and the farm "Sgalags," whom they held in supreme contempt. It is only fair to say, though, that we returned this unchar-itable sentiment with interest. There was a satisfying savour of opprobrium in the nickname of "Strath Scraabs" which we used to hurl at them in our after-school-hours battles.

4. *Farmers' families.*—A very small contingent indeed: mostly such didn't come to our school at all. Their parents had more ambitious and (?) better views in regard to the education of their offspring.

The school classes were simple and obvious in their progression:

The First Book, Penny Book, or A, B, C.
The Second Book (2*d.*).
The Third Book (3*d.*).

Standard I.
Standard II.
Standard III.
Standard IV.
Standard V.
Standard VI.
Ex-VI Standard.

Even if you waited at school to take the "Ex-sixth" you should finish at fourteen: but if you were unfortunate enough to finish with the Ex-sixth at twelve—as some of us did—unless your parents could afford to send you to another school you had no alternative but go on, like a repeating decimal, on that same standard till at fourteen you earned emancipation. This repeating business was, I am sure, largely responsible for the reign of rebellion against discipline which for years was rank in our school. The older boys *had* to do something interesting. As they couldn't very well continue to be interested in the same dry lessons year after year they resorted to many ingenious trouble-making devices, which gave spice and variety to their period of compulsory detention—and incidentally did much to whiten the beard of the headmaster.

The assortment of natural-history specimens which a group of industrious country boys could collect during the midday play-hour was surprising. Half a dozen paddocks from the marsh near the mill-dam, a dozen eels from the mill-lade, a match-box full of bees—bumbees, *boddach ruadhs*, and *ton-deargans*—mice, *fiolagans*, and an occasional rat were a reasonable expectation. And you have no idea how this menagerie, stealthily liberated at various places on the classroom floor, could make the dominie hop and splutter with rage. And when, as sometimes happened, in process of shooing the creatures out of doors or windows, "himself" was well stung by a wasp, did we howl! Of course, it was fiendishly wicked! But there you were! We enjoyed it, and if some of us— often the wrong ones—paid the penalty in pandies and by being "kept in" it was still worth it.

That poor man! Yet looking back I am convinced it was largely his own fault. No one who cannot control his—or her—own temper need ever hope to control a class of boys. Neither can he hope to win their confidence or respect. The opposite was strikingly proved in this small school some years after my time. The old dominie was followed by a succession of female "heads," who took the very earliest opportunity of resigning. At last a man was appointed. He was rumoured to be one who would soon have the rebels (now riotously triumphant) in subjection. The big boys held an anxious conclave to decide on measures adequate for putting the new master in his place and so ensure continuance of "freedom." "Fireworks" were timed to begin in the forenoon of the very first day. But the new master forestalled them. He made an opening speech to the rebels—something to this effect—and he spoke throughout in a friendly, chummy tone, but with a deadly disconcerting ring at the back of it:

"Well, lads, here I am, the new master of this school. I hear that you have your own views about that: that *you* have been in the habit of bossing the school and that you mean to continue to do so. Well, as I mean to be boss—that's partly what I'm paid for—it looks as if there might be a spot of trouble unless—and I'll make a sporting offer—unless we can come to a friendly understanding. I have here" (he produced a vicious-looking belt) "a strap which, if I must, I will use freely and forcefully to get that discipline without which no school can be of much use. On the other hand, if you give me your word of honour that you will obey my orders—and I promise they will be fair and reasonable—that strap goes into this drawer, and will remain there while I am headmaster here. The choice is yours. You can now go to the playground for half an hour to talk the matter over amongst yourselves. At the end of the half-hour I will ring you in and get your decision as to whether it is to be peace or war."

They went out. This method of challenge was highly disconcerting. Even "Fraochie," who was one of the riot ringleaders, counselled peace.

"Ach! Shut up! Who's going to be a softie," insisted "Binks," "doing everything you're told like a baby!"

Each got some backing, but the weight of opinion was with Fraochie. The bell summoned them in with the great question still undecided.

"Well," said the new dominie, "what is the verdict?"

No answer: only an embarrassed silence.

"In that case," the head announced, "we will just go on with the day's work and see what happens."

He hadn't long to wait. Binks the bellicose would not be disgraced: he had a reputation to maintain. He shouted to someone in the front seat inquiring if his mother knew he was out, or some such witticism.

"Binks," said the new master quietly, and without a trace of anger (and fancy him knowing the nickname, and using it!), "if you do that sort of thing again I shall punish you good and hard."

A direct challenge! That was enough: Binks bawled some other inanity at a front-bencher. But he had no intention of being caught. In former days when he wanted to elude a walloping one stratagem was to run along the back seat away from the centre corridor, thereby encouraging pursuit, and when he got the old dominie well messed up among the desks he made a bee-line over the top of them for the door and freedom. It nearly succeeded this time. But the new dominie had played

Rugby. With a low tackle he downed Binks near the door. The mutineer's strength was as straw to the steel of this man's muscles. The next few minutes for Binks were a painful experience. It was an all-in devastating loundering that not even Binks—and I would never decry his pluck—could continue to stand up to. At the first howl for mercy the dominie stopped, still smiling if somewhat grim.

"Sorry, Binks! I had to keep my promise," he said really quite kindly. "Will we shake hands and be friends for the future?"

It was a bitter pill, but Binks had savvy to see in which way lay wisdom. They shook hands, and to Binks' credit he scrupulously observed the compact. Ceremoniously, the belt was consigned to the drawer, where it lay undisturbed and unrequired throughout the years of that dominie's reign.

CHAPTER III

First Love—Timing the Tank—Blasted Romance

THERE was a lassie who came to school the same year as myself. Right through the school years we had sat side by side in class. Her hair was abundant and wavy and brown. Her grey-blue eyes were so warm and kind. Her cheeks were suffused with that so adorable rosy blush of rural health. And her lovely rounded soft-firm throat and neck disappeared so intriguingly beneath a white blouse! And she was so quiet and kind in her voice and ways. She usually sat on my left, so that, when the afternoon sun shone in at the window—as it often did—it glorified her hair and face and whole expression in a way that thrilled to my inmost being. This my first was a lustless love: a pure, tender emotion. Old folks should never laugh at calf-love. It is indeed something pure and sacred, which usually finds its only expression in little acts of service. On one occasion it inspired me to real heights of altruism. It was during the annual competition for the dux medal. All forenoon the competitors had wrestled with history, geography, and "sums," as we called arithmetic. There was one of those tricky problems where a tank of given length, depth, and breadth is being fed by water from a tap of certain diameter and emptied through another tap of lesser calibre. Given an empty tank and the two taps set to functioning at full bore you have to calculate how long it will take the tank to reach the overflow point. I have often thought how much more easily and pleasantly most youngsters could solve such problems with actual tanks and taps and a watch. But of course that would eliminate those exercises in mental gymnastics which arithmetic is designed to provide.

24

Anyhow, to some at our school the elucidation of such problems via slate and pencil processes remained for ever a profound mystery. You are just born with a gift that way, or without. I happened to be in the former category. Mary—that wasn't her name, but it will serve—wasn't. At the play-hour I asked her how she had got on with the tank sum. She hadn't. She hadn't been able even to make a shape at it. Tear-drops trembled in those kind eyes. I just couldn't stand it.

"Go," I said, "round to the back of the west dyke and wait there till I come."

She went. I collected a bit of broken slate, hid it under my jacket, and stole round to where she was waiting. In five minutes I had figured out on the slate the solution of the mystery of the tank. In less than other five minutes she had copied it out on a piece of paper for afternoon use—thereby jeopardising my chance of winning the medal. I still rate that as the most gallant action of my life.

School finished, Mary went her way; I went mine. For over forty years we never met. Indeed, we lost all trace of each other. But even to an oldish family man there sometimes came a tender memory of a schoolgirl sweetheart.

A few years ago, back in the homeland I entered a local ladies' emporium to exchange greetings with the proprietrix. I found her engaged with a customer and offered to withdraw.

"Don't go," said the lady of the shop; "you two surely know each other? Why, you must have been at school together!"

I looked at a *cailleach* of ample form and white hair and many wrinkles—an utter stranger. She looked at my waistless form and hairless dome. Not a jot of recognition on either side.

"Goodness me! Weren't you in school with Mary ——, and weren't you in school with Colin MacDonald?" inquired the shopkeeper.

"Mary!" I gasped; but believe me there was tender emotion in my voice and a warm feeling at the heart of me. For me, as by magic, the *cailleach* was transformed into a lassie of twelve with sunlit hair and grey kind eyes. Indeed, I was deeply moved, and I looked for similar glad response. But I looked in vain! Not a vestige of recollection: not even of my name!

"But surely, surely, you can't have forgotten *me*?" I said, incredulous.

But no! At first I thought so utter a memory-blank could not be possible. But soon I knew it was no pretence. She just couldn't place me, or at least but vaguely. It was indeed a tragi-comical ending to an exquisite memory that had remained with me off and on for nearly half a century.

But, still, I repeat: old folks should not ridicule a thing so pure and sacred as the first love of a laddie.

CHAPTER IV

The Whupper-in—Storks and Angels—First Earnings—Rory's
"Rosie"—*A' Bhò Ruadh* (Red Cow)

WHILE there was never any suggestion of lack of the essentials of life in our circles, coin of the realm was a rarity. Augmentation of the family funds, therefore, was the concern of everyone, including youngsters down to seven or so. In this connection, compulsory attendance at school—a recent innovation—was somewhat of a trouble. But there was a sensible leniency in regard to the matter during summer and autumn, when most opportunities of getting a money-making job occurred. Then old Daanie the "Whupper-in" postponed his admonitory visit as long as his fairly accommodating conscience permitted. Considerable reflection on this point has led me to the conclusion that those latter-day educationists who make a fetish of "regular attendance" and regard "child labour" as a crime might well take a leaf out of Daanie's book—with advantage to all concerned.

At a very early age most of us were skilled in a variety of jobs. The boys knew exactly how much straw or hay or turnips should be given to the different beasts—including variations near foaling or calving—and were trusted to feed them accordingly; and there is much more in that than most people who don't know imagine.

Because of our smaller hands we could in difficult cases give more effective help than our parents to a lambing ewe or calving cow—and were occasionally called upon to do so. For us there were no storks or angels about births or deaths: just an intelligent understanding and sensible acceptance of natural happenings.

Singling turnips; turning, gathering, and coling hay;

planting and lifting potatoes; lifting and binding corn, and setting it up in stooks ("Set end-wise to twelve o'clock of the sun and don't you forget it!"); forking, building cart-loads of sheaves; threshing and winnowing grain, and many other operations requiring a surprising degree of skill were all well within the compass of boys— ay, and most girls too—before they reached their teens; and already the boys would be ambitious to try their hand at ploughing, sowing, drilling, building stacks ("Keep your stack well hearted-up in the centre, man, or your sheaves will take in the rain instead of throwing it out!"), and some of the more highly skilled—almost sacred— agricultural arts.

One of my first wage-earning jobs did not encroach on school hours. It started when I was eight, and I had three seasons of it. Certain crofts were too small to provide summer grazing for the family cow. In such cases the cows were sent to graze on the cow-park near the Castle. They had to be driven there each morning and home each night. I took on the contract of driving three. A neighbouring lassie aged eleven was responsible for another couple of cows, and we made one drove of the lot. At seven-thirty each morning for four months (bar Sundays, when the cows were tethered at home) I called for Rory Ruadh's cow "Rosie," then for Aunty Maggie's "Daisy," and finally for Anna Nic Aoinish's nameless old brown cow.

In addition to cash wages (five shillings per cow per season) there were unspecified but never-failing perquisites to the drover. From Rory's grown-up daughter there was a "piece" of loaf bread with butter and honey. Aunty Maggie (who had a shoppie) gave a handful of "lozengers" or "bachelor-buttons" or a caraway-seed biscuit. Anna was old, and went back to bed after doing the morning milking, but never failed to leave a *ceapaire*

—oatcake, butter, crowdie, *and* jam—on top of the garden gate-post. All was grist to my anatomical mill, and went the same road as did my regular breakfast of porridge and cream on my return home at nine o'clock preparatory to starting off for school.

Driving the "empty" cows in the morning was a short and simple job. Driving them home at night with their bellies blown to bursting-point compelled a canny, stately pace calling for philosophic patience, and woe betide if Rory's Rosie arrived in a state of distressful peching!

Was I proud that late September day going home with my first fifteen shillings? And did my health or education suffer?

We of the crofts did not regard our live stock merely as commercial possessions to be ruthlessly bartered for gain. True, we did sell off each year the lambs and stirks and an occasional foal; but these had not yet attained to that degree of warm affection with which we regarded the permanent stock. *Bhò Ruadh* (Red Cow) and *Bhò Bhan* (White Cow) and Maggie-the-Mare were more or less members of the family, all doing their utmost for the common good. Consequently, when Anno Domini did at last compel a severance with one of these, there was gloom in the household for several days. In the case of *Bhò Ruadh* this distress was intensified, as you will see.

Bhò Ruadh had been on the place years before I was born. She was a strawberry-red, always as lean as one of Pharaoh's dream cows, but with the silken skin which denotes good health and the heavy milker. Not once in her fifteen years of maturity had she failed to contribute a calf to the family wealth each spring. But alas! though she still retained much of youthful appearance, prudence advised getting rid of her. One day I overheard my father say to my mother he was afraid *Bhò Ruadh* would have to be sold.

They were speaking in the Gaelic, but fine I understood what they were saying, and I think that was the first big sadness in my life. *Bhò Ruadh* to be sold! *Bhò Ruadh* that was there before I could remember! The cow I had so often herded on the good belts of grass that grew at the edges of the corn and turnip fields! Truth to tell, I didn't like the herding. What a wearisome job it was to have to stand by for hours and hours watching that the beasts didn't steal a turnip or a mouthful of oats. Herding was the bane of my young life. Even now I protest herding is a job for old, old men—not for active boys.

Yet herding had some compensations too. There was ample time for observing the queer ways of the bird and insect life that swarmed around. Blackies, Mavies, *Buidheags*, Binkies; grasshoppers with their ticking noises but so difficult to locate; *Corra-chòsags* (Slaters) that lay under flat stones, and *Sneamhans* and *Gobhlachans* (ants and forky-tails) and Jennies-with-the-hundred-feet, and a thousand other queer and interesting creatures.

Often indeed, on beasties bent, the main job was forgotten until a warning shout from a watchful parent brought us sharply to earth, and the knowledge that the cows, like those of Boy Blue, were in the corn!

There was also the fascination of watching the cows feeding. Yon long tongue would come out and coil itself round a bit of grass to be cut against the upper lip and taken into the mouth and swallowed without chewing at all!

And when the cows had taken so much that their sides bulged like balloons I would drive them in the gloaming back into the byre. Then Mother would come with a *creaban* (milking-stool) and pail, and hum a Gaelic air that set *Bhò Ruadh* to chewing her cud, as with strong and practised fingers the jets of milk were squirted into the pail so that a crown of froth was formed that rose and rose and looked like spilling over, but never did.

Near the end of the milking Mother would take from me my jug. This she filled with the last jets of milk—"strippings"—that were so rich in cream, and I would drink it off at one go. That was the stuff to make a man of a fellow!

These—or something like these—were ·the thoughts which went vaguely through my mind as I thought with sorrow in my heart of *Bhò Ruadh* being taken to the market and sold to a stranger!

When the dreadful day arrived, Mother and myself went down with Father and *Bhò Ruadh* as far as the county road. They went on. We came back, and indeed there was a load of sorrow on the heart of both.

"Och! *Bhò Ruadh* was getting old anyway," said Mother, trying to comfort herself as well as me. "And *Seonaid* will make a fine cow. Besides," she added, "Father will not sell *Bhò Ruadh* to any drover that comes along. He will try to get her a good home even if he has to take less money for her."

But indeed it was sore hearts we had all the same.

We had a busy day though. We shifted *Seonaid* into *Bhò Ruadh's* stall. We also shifted *Mairi*—that was a young sister of *Seonaid*—from the calf-pen into *Seonaid's* old stall, so that when *Seonaid's* calf came there would be a place for it in the pen.

Then when my father came home from the market and showed us the eight golden sovereigns he had got for *Bhò Ruadh*, and we thought of the many useful things these would buy, we nearly forgot our grief. We were delighted to learn, too, that *Bhò Ruadh* had been sold to a gamekeeper, who lived in a glen over twenty miles away, where she was sure to be well fed and well treated.

To get to her new home *Bhò Ruadh* had to travel

some fifteen miles by train and thence some ten miles by road up the glen.

"She will be arriving at her new home just about now," said Father, looking at the old wag-at-the-wa' before we went to bed about ten o'clock.

But it was some time before I slept. *Bhò Ruadh* and recollections of her would come into my mind, and I'm not saying but there was a damp spot on my pillow that night.

Moreover, when sleep did come it was disturbed by crazy dreams in which *Bhò Ruadh* shed copious tears and then howled like a dog.

Suddenly I realised that it was morning and that there *were* some queer noises going on. The first distinct noise I heard was Rover barking furiously.

"Quiet! Rover," commanded my father from his bed. But not a quiet would Rover. He barked and louder barked in the kitchen.

"What on earth is the matter with that dog?" I could hear my mother say.

Then the strangest thing happened.

"Moo—amoo—amoo!" bellowed a cow outside.

"Gracious me!" exclaimed Mother. "If *Bhò Ruadh* wasn't in Fannich I would say that was her *geimnich* (lowing). But of course it can't be her."

"No, of course it can't," said Father. "*Bhò Ruadh* was never a mile away from here in her life until yesterday, when she was carried fifteen miles away in a train and then walked a further ten miles to Fannich. It can't possibly be *Bhò Ruadh*. It will be one of the shoemaker's cows broken loose."

"Moo—amoo—amoo!" came the strident call again. In a moment I was at the door in my bare feet.

"It's *Bhò Ruadh* right enough!" I yelled. "And there she is standing at the byre door waiting to be milked!"

And sure enough *Bhò Ruadh* it was, footsore and weary with her twenty-five-mile overnight tramp. There was a look half of bovine content and half of reproach in her large brown eyes.

But och! she was glad to be home!

CHAPTER V

Down at the Castle grounds a wealthy shooting tenant would spend in five months in rearing pheasants more money than was required to feed and clothe the whole of the bairns in the neighbourhood for five years. The process involved the importation of bags of ants—a great big black crawly variety—that kept together in a heap round the base of the trunk of a tree until gradually removed in pailfuls to feed the pheasant chicks. The aim and purpose of the whole thing was to provide maybe a· fortnight's sport to half a dozen "gents." It seemed—and seems—a frightful waste of money; yet it is mightily difficult to say just when money is wasted. Anyhow even the pheasant-rearing had its compensations for us:

(1) We supplied the clocken hens—at twice the price we could have got otherwise—and got them back for nothing at the end of the season if they still survived.

(2) One or two boys from the crofts got a job assisting at the rearing.

(3) Every man and lad in the district who could go got a few days at the "beating" at good pay.

(4) There was a goodish remnant of the pheasants which spread over the crofts, and if occasionally a cock put his foot in a snare meant for a rabbit, how could we help that?

My brother at the age of twelve was one of the assistants at the rearing, earning ten shillings per week. One memorable week, when for some reason he was off duty, I deputised and got seven-and-sixpence for myself. I felt oppressed with affluence.

34

In November and December, in the year of a late harvest, the grouse if left undisturbed would play havoc with the stooks on the higher lying crofts. One such year they came to Kenny Fair's and Rory Choinnich's stooks in hundreds, and I earned a whole pound in one month scaring them off. "Earned" is the right word too. I had to be on the spot before the streak of dawn, wait there for a couple of hours till the people of the croft were themselves free to shoo them away, and then back again from early gloaming till dark. The tedium of this job was greatly relieved by an old muzzle-loading gun into which I packed powder to blaze away with terrific noise.

One winter my brother had a rabbit-killing contract on the estate—threepence per couple. It wasn't too bad either, on the whole. Ten couples per day meant half-a-crown—then big pay for a lad of fourteen. Snares, traps, ferrets, and nets were the stock-in-trade. Occasionally, on a Saturday, I went to give a hand. One such day in December I won't soon forget. It was one of those hard frosty days with a biting north-east wind and feathering snow. The hard ground put traps and snares out of the question; so off we set with two ferrets — one borrowed from a neighbour whose most cherished possession it was.

We decided to try the holes above Glen Sgaich, some two miles from home. Within seconds of putting a ferret in the first hole a grand bunny was in the bag. A good start. It was going to be a record day! But then things began to go wrong. The ferret "stuck." We could hear unmistakable sounds of a kill inside. Botheration! The brute would drink his fill of his victim's blood and then sleep for hours in the warmth of its body; and it was Duncan's precious ferret, that we must not lose nor leave!

We resorted to all the known expedients: we thudded the earth with our feet; we made mouth-noises like a squealing rabbit; we rattled the dead rabbit in the mouth of the hole; we gutted it and proffered the entrails as an enticement; we put in the other ferret (muzzled), but divil a nose did that precious ferret of Duncan's show.

Snow had started to fall at midday. It was already forming considerable drifts. The cold penetrated to our very hearts. We rubbed our ears, we slapped our arms, we danced; but there was a deadly persistence in the increasing cold. Finally, with darkness coming on, we built the ferret-box into the mouth of the hole so that (we hoped) the ferret could not escape, and when his orgy was over would probably sleep in the box, where he might be found next morning. The last bite of our "piece" had been consumed by three o'clock. We were terribly hungry. By now the snowdrifts were so deep that the direct line across the moor was dangerous. The long way round was the quick way home, so we trudged down to the railway and along its weary length. The final lap was up a steep brae through fields, and snow that in places lay ten feet deep. But for Alick's example of sheer pluck I would have lain down and perished. As it was, of the last half-mile I never had but a vague recollection, but I did remember falling in at the door and thinking grimly that that one rabbit represented a hard-earned three-halfpence.

Johnnie MacLeod was one of the drovers who visited the crofts periodically to try to buy stirks, pigs, calves, or other live stock on which to turn a profit. Johnnie was rather a favourite. He never tried to do us down too badly and sometimes, when old women were the sellers, he was known to give more than market value. One week in July Johnnie bought seven pigs in the neighbour-hood. He asked Jockie (my cousin) and myself if we would drive the pigs to Dingwall—to arrive at eleven o'clock on the Wednesday forenoon—for which service he offered us two shillings apiece. That was good going! We agreed. But we could not claim much experience in driving pigs. Johnnie said we would learn. He was right. Our deficiency was to be amply remedied on the Wednesday!

First, there were the contests with individual pigs while we were in process of getting them together. When at last they were in one lot it was soon obvious they were not of one mind. Certain bitter animosities were immediately discernible. For example, the tailor's pig—a cannon-snouted ugly enough looking brute himself—conceived a violent dislike—nay, hatred—for "Bogaran's" snub-nosed inoffensive-looking little porker. Straightway Cannon-snout bit a gash out of Snub-nose's neck. The latter emitted a piercing squeal which might have satisfied the former as to which was the boss. But it only encouraged him. He next attacked in flank, then in the rear, and then all round, till his poor victim was streaming gore on all sides. We did our best with admonitory hazel switches, but a pig bent on bullying is not easily dissuaded. We had just decided we must separate the two if Bogaran's pig was to reach Dingwall alive—when there was a dramatic change. Presumably Snub-nose decided if he were to die anyway he would die game. A red light showed in his beady eye. The worm turned. With the courage of despair he made a grab at the tender area beneath his tormentor's tail and hung on. For a moment the bully didn't believe; but soon the reality of the situation was painfully borne in on him. Bully that he was, he squealed at the first hurt. He set off full gallop down the road—fortunately in the right direction—with Bogaran's little hero clinging to his rear. We laughed till we nearly cried.

There were several minor conflicts between other members of our drove, and between them all and us as to the road to be travelled; but Cannon-snout *v.* Snub-nose remained the star turn till we reached the railway bridge. There, right below the bridge, there was a dark shadow due to the brightly shining sun. As by one accord the pigs came to a dead halt. We shooed them and shoved them and switched them in vain. Divil a pig would set foot on the black shadow. While we were still arguing the matter out what should come along but a goods train. More than once since then I have deliberately tried to stand under that iron bridge while a train thundered overhead. Believe me, it takes a deal of nerve. On our charges the result was terrific. Two jumped forward and disappeared round the bend. The other five bounded back, with noses to the ground and tails in the air. Two of them barged through the hedge into a field of standing barley on the left. Another jumped a wooden gate on the right, while the remaining two scorched back for home as if seven devils were after them as well as in them.

To describe how we got our stampeded swine together again, and finally into Dingwall, only half an hour behind scheduled time, would be too painful even after the lapse of half a century. It must suffice to say that get them in we did, and that the two shillings reward did not seem so generous as when we so blithely took on the contract.

CHAPTER VI

AT thirteen I had already done two years in the ex-sixth standard. As a further year's attendance at school was still necessary, and as the family finances would not stand the strain of sending me to a Higher Grade school, it was decided that during the next year the old dominie would give me special tuition in subjects which, in consultation with my parents, he thought might lay a useful foundation in learning for one destined for the Church—which holy career they had decided I should follow. The choice of subjects showed worldly common sense: Greek, Latin, Agriculture, and Accountancy were the selection. A sixpenny text-book in each of these subjects was duly procured and I was to start in immediately after the annual School Inspection in March. But never a lesson out of these books did I ever learn. It would almost seem that a watchful Providence, concerned for the reputation of the Church, decided to intervene. Anyhow, what did happen was this.

The day of the Inspection came on wild and stormy. By night there was a gale blowing. During the day, my father, concerned for the newly thatched barn-roof, had laid a wooden slab horizontally on top of the thatch. To keep weight on the slab he set up a long ladder so as to lie on top of it, and to keep weight on the ladder he rested a heavy granite boulder a few rungs from the ground. He and I went to do "the eight o'clock" —*i.e.* supper the beasts and see them all right for the night. We had to carry *muileans* of straw from the barn to the byre. The lantern blew out in the gale. In the pitch-darkness I stumbled over the bottom of the ladder. My hands went to the ground; the big stone shook from its place and fell on my left hand. When we got back into the barn it was seen that half a forefinger was gone and its neighbour crushed to a pulp.

I never went back to school. By the time the damaged hand had recovered, my father was down with pneumonia and I, at the age of thirteen and a half, put down that year's turnip crop—dunging, drilling, sowing, and all— quite the proudest youth in Scotland.

What a joy to be free of school and those confounded lessons that didn't seem to lead anywhere! And, when you come to think of it, if pleasure and pride in personal achievement are eliminated it makes the world a dreary place for all but folks of the butterfly type, who are content if they contrive to get what they call "a good time" without doing anything to earn it. Fine I mind the thrill it gave me as I rested the horses for a breather and looked critically at the ploughed rig. There were the furrows—*sgrioban*, we called them—as like each other as the ribs in corduroy, straight and true and well packed, with not a blade of grass showing above. What a perfect bed for the seed that would be soon scattered on it.

And the sowing itself! Who that was ever a two-handed sower can forget yon lovely April morning when the seed-bags stood like sentinels along the ploughed field that was emerald-bordered by the new-coming grass? When the lea was in good fettle and the larks sang riotously overhead? And the seed-box was replenished by a bonnie lassie? And when he himself stepped out so grandly, with a swish and a swing of the arms, to arch the handful of grain like a rainbow so that it fell with a patter which to the attuned and practised ear gave the assurance of uniformity?—who, I say, that was ever a sower can ever forget that poem of a morning or his delight in his own achievement?

That mood lasted for three years. Then one morning, as I was spreading dung in the potato drills, all clarted up with mud and filth, didn't my cousin pass my way *en route* for the town office where he had found employment. Somehow I had never particularly noticed before, but that morning, as I looked at his beautifully creased trousers, polished shoes, dickey and tie AND kid gloves, a first glimpse of realities came to me. Good gosh! Here was I, mud to the knees of my moleskin trousers, spreading dung and planting potatoes, with not a glint of a hope of anything better in all my life.

After Jockie passed on I sat on the dyke for quite a while thinking out the whole position. That was a bitter morning. A lump as of lead seemed to press on my heart —and more or less remained there for three or four years. A dull aching pain, with a terrible longing for a way out; but never a ray of hope.

The chief solace in these awful years of bitter thoughts and frustration was reading. In the little hall we had built for our social evenings was a Library presented by Andrew Carnegie—the Dunfermline boy who had become America's Steel King. There was a good selection— Scott, Dickens, Thackeray, Burns, Biography, Travel— 600 volumes in all. What a revel! I read practically all of them, and many of them many times over. There were also some battered volumes of an early edition of the *Encyclopædia Britannica* (with the old "∫" for "s"), which proved a veritable mine of delight.

There was the further delight of debate during our winter sessions. Not infrequently, one of the next week's leaders in debate would come and ask me to give him a hand with his paper—for the affirmative side. Then the leader for the negative would come with a similar request.

With the greatest pleasure I undertook both commissions, and on the night of the debate would speak in support of what appeared to be the weaker side.

Another godsend was the "night class" started one winter by the new schoolmaster when I was about twenty. In two winters there I learned more than I had learned in my eight years at ordinary school.

Then there was another interesting development. In my capacity of secretary of our Literary Society, I one day received a letter from a man who signed himself "George G. Esslemont." The letter was headed : "Aberdeen and North of Scotland College of Agriculture." Mr Esslemont asked if he might have the use of our hall for a series of lectures on agriculture. The request seemed to me to be a queer one. What on earth could anyone lecture about on agriculture? Surely we knew all that was to be known about that! However, I politely replied that the committee would be delighted.

There was a good turn-out, mostly out of curiosity, but we all felt a little sorry for the man who was going to lecture to *us* on agriculture. And when he appeared—a smartly dressed *gentleman*—we were really embarrassed. The poor fellow! However, we were polite. The chairman said we were glad to see him, etc.

Mr Esslemont then got to his feet. He asked if there was any special *aspect* of agriculture on which we preferred he would speak. Aspect? We didn't know agriculture had aspects. You just ploughed and sowed and harvested and fed the beasts. Did the poor man think we didn't know about that?

When we could not suggest any special aspect and he suggested a talk on grass and clover seed mixtures we felt very very sorry. Grass and clover seed mixtures! Just perennial rye grass, Italian, Red, White, and Alsyke clover that we had sown from time immemorial and knew as we knew the back of our hand. But again we were polite.

And lo! Mr Esslemont opened a black tin box. From thence he produced neatly assorted specimens of some forty different grasses, each bearing on a tag its botanical name and the name it was commonly known by. We had never heard of more than four of them.

Then he proceeded to explain that it was the "natural habit" of certain grasses to be "shallow feeders" while others were medium and still others deep-rooted feeders, others again only survived for one or two years while some lived on indefinitely—so that, if you wanted a really good crop of hay and a superior sole of pasture you had better sow a well-selected mixture. It was the first time in my life that I felt an utter ignoramus. Many a time in after years when giving much the same lecture did I wonder if ever I made anyone in my audience feel such an awful ass as Mr Esslemont made me feel that night.

CHAPTER VII

THAT lecture on grass and clover seeds was followed by several others on various agricultural "aspects" (to the existence of which I was now thoroughly alive); relative values of different varieties of cereals, potatoes, turnips, and other crops; the scientific manuring of these in accordance with their varying chemical needs and the nature of the soil in which they grew; the "balancing" of rations to the different classes of stock so as to get maximum results with minimum waste—all such lectures were to me as a key which opened the door to a fascinating world of experiment and inquiry. The leaden heart became light and joyous. Ordinary humdrum jobs were humdrum no longer. Even a very elementary degree of understanding of the scientific facts and processes which underlay the most prosaic of field or midden operations invested them with an absorbing interest.

In the next half-dozen years I carried out for Mr Esslemont innumerable experiments for the purpose of demonstrating to myself and my neighbours how we might make better use of our time and land—and I am fairly certain that never were such experiments more meticulously carried out.

If only I could scrape together capital enough to take a small farm of my own! With this as an incentive I took on all sorts of piece-work or contract jobs, *e.g.*:

Felling Trees.—At five shillings per hundred, for larch-trees averaging fifteen inches diameter. This was the hardest and worst-paid job I ever tackled. We had to walk three miles to the wood each morning and three miles home at night. It was in the short days of winter. We did the walking both ways in the dark. Every minute of daylight—bar half an hour for the flask of tea and the "piece"—it was dobb, saw, crash! dobb, saw, crash! until we reached the daily quota of 120 trees—which gave us three shillings per man per day. Last year it took me over two hours to fell one such tree and I didn't get over the effort for a week!

Fencing.—For the erection of a wood-and-wire fence of six wires and posts seven feet apart our contract price was a penny-farthing per yard. Two of us could each earn four shillings per day when things went well.

Ploughing.—For horseless neighbours—at ten shillings per day for self and pair of horses. There would be a total of forty to fifty of such days each year.

Harvesting.—Rate ten shillings per acre for cutting, lifting, binding, and stooking. With the scythe I would have an acre cut in about eight hours. Meanwhile, my helpmate, Old Kate (and she was a top-notcher at the job), had followed up with the lifting and binding. Together, in the next two hours we would complete the binding and stooking of the acre. I, as "contractor," kept six shillings to myself. Kate got four shillings— big money in those days, but believe me, we worked for it. If you want to be quite sure—try it!

Thinning Turnips.—Sixteen shillings per acre. In dirty stiff land and wet weather this was heart-breaking work, and could easily take six days to complete. Under best conditions I could rattle off an acre in four days. But a "careless" hoe can ruin a crop, and a high-quality standard of work was a *sine qua non* of the contract.

Clipping Turnips.—Six shillings and sixpence per acre for yellows and eight shillings for swedes. I knew a crack hand who could turn off his acre per day of either. Personally, I never quite got up to that standard. As a back-breaker, clipping swedes must stand alone; and on a winter's morning when the frosted leaves crackled in your hand it was most exquisite torture—for the first few minutes; then your fingers burned as with fire.

Making Bridle-paths, Grouse Butts, and Hill Drains.—For such contracts I was indebted to my spendthrift friends the *sasunnach* shooting tenants. For several weeks in summer three or four of us would take to the hills, returning only at week-ends for "tommy" (food supplies). One summer four of us lived for six weeks in a sort of cave near a burn. That was a terribly hot summer. It was impossible to work in the heat of the day, so we breakfasted at four-thirty, worked from five till ten A.M., rested on our heather bed in the cave till four P.M. and then worked till nine. Between nine and midnight (midges permitting) we fished for trout in the burn and set snares for hares, to augment our provender. One evening, in three hours, four of us caught a total of 365 trout—mostly small, but all of eatable size. As it happened, too, they were all required, as you will see.

At this particular time we were billeted in a corrugated-iron shed, known as "The Stables," near the base of the last steep climb to Ben Wyvis and miles from the nearest human habitation. On the night of the big catch it came on thick mist just as we turned in at midnight. Four of us slept in the one bed, which was a sort of wooden platform six feet square. At one A.M. we were wakened by the deuce of a row outside. A party from Dingwall were on their annual pilgrimage to view the sunrise from the summit of the ben. They had got completely wandered in the mist and now came bang up against our iron-clad home, on which they rattled their sticks with momentarily terrifying effect. Soon, though, we discerned human voices and gathered who they were. It was evident, too, that they had not neglected the liquid refreshment side of the holiday. One of the revellers recognised the place as "The Stables." They decided to enter and light a fire. Not one of the party had the remotest idea that the place was occupied. Just as they were about to enter, our batman, "Jock," quick to offer hospitality, appeared in natal state at the door, holding a lighted candle above his head. That crowd got the fright of their life: with a yell of terror they took to their heels and vanished in the mist. It took much shouted explanation and assurance of our mortal state before they were induced to return. There were over twenty all told. The stove with its leaky lum was set agoing. Jock presided at the frying-pan. In an hour all the trout, our week's roll of bacon, a few dozen eggs, and a considerable quantity of "Dalmore" disappeared in a sort of Dagdal orgy amongst the pilgrims. A number of them rested in "The Stables" while the remainder, under our guidance, set off for the top. Above the Fuaran Mòr we walked out of the mist into a crystal-clear atmosphere vibrant with the dawn of day. We reached the summit just in time to see the white light in the north-east change in turn to pale green, violet, copper, crimson, and finally the sun, lighting up the summits of a hundred hills, appeared a ball of burnished gold. Even the revellers were hushed to silent adoration. No wonder our ancestors worshipped the sun.

We in this country are surely a prize pack of grousers in regard to the climatic conditions under which we live on the earth's surface. We are always complaining—of what? Of climatic variations that people in most parts of the world would give much to possess. For surely nowhere else in all the world is there greater variety and beauty in this respect than in this wonderful little country of ours, with its shades of summer green, with its lochs and hills and heather; with those glorious evening twilights and the rosy spreading dawns.   Ay, and there is a beauty, too, in the fertilising rains and in the frost and snow of winter, if we would but only see. . . .

CHAPTER VIII

A Domestic Bomb—Off on a New Tack—Reflections on the
Highland "Problem"

THIS chapter is going to have more of "I" in it even than
the others, but that can't be helped, as it is necessary to
tell how the Journey, at this stage, took a bend in a new
direction.

At the age of twenty-six I was what might fairly be
termed a practical crofter, skilled in a variety of country
crafts. My chief ambition in life was to save enough
money to enable me to secure the tenancy of a small farm.
Six months later I was a matriculated student of agriculture at Marischal College, Aberdeen, and destined for
a very different sort of career. This is how it happened.

One day in July, on returning home from some outside
job, I found Mr Esslemont waiting to see me. We walked
along the road together. He informed me that he had
been asked by the Governors of the Aberdeen and North
of Scotland College of Agriculture to look out for an
intelligent youth with a practical knowledge of crofting
and Gaelic who would take a course of training at Aberdeen with a view to appointment to the extension staff
of the College as Agricultural County Organiser in the
Hebrides. He had had his eye on me for some time and
was now asking if I could see my way clear to accept such
an offer. I would get financial assistance to the extent
of fifty pounds per annum while in training, and on taking
up the appointment would be put on a salary of eighty
pounds per annum with reasonable travelling expenses.

Only one with a previous experience similar to mine can
quite appreciate the stir which such a proposition caused
in my mind. A course at a College! A certain yearly

salary of eighty pounds! Travelling all over the Hebrides! The whole thing was fantastic. Go? There was no shadow of doubt that I would *like* to go; the sobering question was: *could* I go?

My father—who had never quite recovered his health and strength—had plenty to do in attending to the innumerable lighter jobs on the place. For years I had done all the heavy work, and had become an integral part of the domestic team which kept the home together. Mr Esslemont appreciated the difficulty. He did not press for an immediate decision: it would do if I let him know within a week or two. Meantime—not a word to my parents or anybody else!

There was no sleep that night. Till six in the morning I thought and planned, seeking for a way that would let me go, yet leave the home intact. A hired man, to do the ploughing and heavy work, must be found. After much cogitation I decided who the man should be—if he could be got to come. Let me say here, he did come, and proved so thoroughly unsatisfactory that he had to go within a month; and during the next four years some half a dozen men came and went in embarrassing succession. I suspect the meticulous standard of work demanded by my father—which he had got from me as a result of early training and unquestioned insistence— had a good deal to do with these frequent changes. Anyhow, luckily, I did not foresee them!

Finance had to be carefully worked out. The fifty pounds annual grant would do little more than pay for the ploughman. There was no family fund to draw on. That meant I would require to keep myself during the training period in Aberdeen. I had saved thirty pounds in cash and owned—as my own property, grazing on a neighbouring croft which I had rented—six stirks and twenty sheep. With luck these would realise some seventy pounds—giving a total of, say, a hundred pounds to cover living in a city for two years. In my ignorance of city life, and all that that almost inevitably involved in the way of spending, a hundred pounds seemed fairly ample. Here—to anticipate again—I was soon to realise my mistake, and some heroic wind-raising measures had to be resorted to before the two years were out.

But the biggest hurdle of all was that I would require to break the news to my father. For in those days, in our circles, despite extraordinarily strong (but inarticulate) ties of family affection there was a stern lack of chumminess between sons and fathers, which made the thought of having to tackle my male parent in the matter almost paralysing. I felt like one about to throw a bomb in the family kitchen!

But, anyhow, it had to be done; for my mind was made up, and that very day I placed the whole proposition before him. He listened without a word while I unfolded the story of the opportunity which had come my way and my plans thereanent. When I finished with:

"But, of course, if you think it can't be done—well, I'll just stay on," to my surprise and unspeakable joy he just said:

"Well, boy, I will not advise you in a matter of that kind: you must make your own decision. All I can say is that, if you see your way clear yourself, I will not stand in the way, and if you go I hope you will make a success of it—and we will manage at home *some* way." Somehow that made me feel that I had never quite understood my father before. I now felt such a surge of pride in him and such gratitude towards him that I fear I fell from the old tradition by indulging in a momentary mumbled confession of such emotions—which greatly embarrassed us both.

That was in July. By the end of September the crop

was all in and thatched; everything about the place in
apple-pie order; the new ploughman engaged; the
stirks and sheep converted into cash; my trunk packed
and everything ready for my journey to the opening of
the session at Marischal College, Aberdeen, on the 8th of
October.

Now, after over thirty years of the comparatively
sheltered, genteel, non-perspiring career, first of an
Agricultural Lecturer, and later of a Civil Servant, I
much doubt whether the change-over has been to my
advantage in the things that really matter in life; but
I am certain that no such argument would have weighed
with me when the opportunity for change came. Then
I just grasped it with both hands—and I have no regrets.
I would only add this reflection:

Every now and again a new champion enters the public
arena and demands the re-peopling of the Highland
straths and glens. The thesis that it is a good thing for
the country to have the biggest possible number of people
living contentedly in the Highlands needs no elaboration.
Unfortunately, its practical application is beset with
difficulties. For some men and women of philosophic
outlook life on the land—cultivating, seeding, tending
and harvesting of crops, the breeding and nurturing of
stock—even if unaccompanied by much in the way of
monetary profit, is of absorbing interest. They are
happy.

But such are in a minority. The majority of agri-
culturists, big and little, are ordinary, mercenary human
beings, maybe enjoying some of the æsthetic pleasures
of the life, but grimly materialistic in desiring monetary
reward; and when this does not come they are dissatisfied and, as opportunity offers, go elsewhere. This
has happened in the case of a great many crofters and
their families throughout the Highlands in the past half-

century: and were it not for that sense of filial duty which is so strong in crofting families the exodus would have been much greater. These are the simple facts—facts which "reformers" seem to be ignorant of, or forget. The truth is that those Utopian dreams of regenerating the Highlands are indulged in mainly by prosperous, elderly, estimable people who forsook the Highlands in their teens for "success" elsewhere and now cherish sentimental recollections of their early years. Life in a Highland glen seems to them a grand thing—in retrospect; and (now that they have grown older) maybe in prospect. But it didn't appeal to them when they were young any more than it appeals to young people of to-day.

It is unreasonable to expect educated young people to stay contented and happy in an unremunerative calling while bigger prizes are offered elsewhere; not even for their country's good or in order that a few reformers and politicians may reap public honour or continue to sit in the high places.

In this connection it is an interesting fact that, as a result of prolonged unemployment in industrial centres prior to the War, and now of the precarious thing which the War has proved life in a big city to be, a new light is coming to many: new standards of values are being set up. It is now a matter of general comment among young people in both town and country that a job in a city is a very uncertain thing. Conversely, many of them have come to appreciate the solid advantages that go with life on the land. To a young countryman a job at three or four pounds per week looked wealth. Now, in the city, he knows that even when such a wage is assured it has a habit of vanishing in umpteen ways of which a country-man wots not, and he realises he would be much better off in the country, earning a quarter of that amount in addition to the potatoes and milk and butter and cream and poultry and eggs and the dozen other substantial things which he could produce on his own holding. He also knows that in the city he is more or less of a serf, while on his holding he is a king in his castle.

By all sensible means let us seek to re-people the Highlands and so strengthen the strands of the fabric of nation; and if I were asked to state in two words the improvements which would do more than any other to make life on the land in the Highlands more attractive these words would be *roads* and *houses*. Not merely main roads, but roads —and good roads—to and through every glen and clachan and croft, and my houses would be of attractive design, with hot and cold water and electric light and power. Most of the many other necessary improvements would follow: but it is futile for those elderly sentimentalists or pushing politicians to imagine they can realise their dream by talking down to and advising the young folk to stay in, or return to, the Highlands. Young people nowadays resent being talked down to, and are perfectly capable of deciding a matter of this kind for themselves.

PART II

CHAPTER IX

The Novice at work—Contrary Winds—Keeping the Horns on!—
Elphin and Cnocan—Mistaken for a Tramp—Tinker Hospitality
—The Fight at the Inn—Conscientious Objectors

As a pioneer instructor in the science and art of agriculture
I had a wide territory, comprising as it did not only the
whole of the Outer Hebrides—"From Butt of Lewis to
Barra Head"—but also the western seaboard from
Durness to Glenelg. A faithful "Rudge" was my main
means of locomotion.   On it I did around four thousand
miles per annum. Soon its beautiful nickel-plate and
polished ebony succumbed to the island elements, to be
succeeded by a uniform rusty hue, to which one became
reconciled in the knowledge that it couldn't go worse and
conferred complete immunity in the matter of future
cleaning; but in the qualities that mattered that bicycle
was superb. With unfailing efficiency it carried my then
180-pound person (plus rucksack, spraying machine, and
other paraphernalia that sometimes weighed over half
a hundredweight) upwards of 20,000 miles of the worst
roads in Britain, often battered with rain, caked with mud
or soused in sea-water—and it was still going strong
twenty years after it had passed from my ownership.

For the first winter I (full of enthusiasm and in-
experience) prepared a neatly tabulated itinerary designed
to avoid loss of a single day or hour. Och, och!

On the Monday morning that was to be the first day of
a succession of visits and meetings during a week in South
Uist I was not a little annoyed to see rain falling somewhat

heavily. The night before had been fine and promising, so that this bolt from the blue was all the more so.

"It can only be a shower?" I surmised to the landlady, whose "Och, maybe, and maybe no," sounded rather ominous.

Reluctantly I postponed the start for an hour; but the "maybe no" was right. Before the end of the hour a gale (as I then deemed it) was driving a mixture of rain and hail and sleet and snow with remorseless fury across that rather unbieldy country. That continued all day, so I sent off half a dozen telegrams cancelling meetings and wrote a long letter to friends on the mainland telling of the terrible storm—two things which, in light of further experience, have often caused me to smile!

On Tuesday the storm was worse; on Wednesday it was still crescendo, and so it continued for the week. By this time it was being borne in on me that storm-severity conceptions are largely a matter of upbringing: that the people of the island were going about their ordinary avocations—with oilskins and sou'westers their only evidence of respect for the elements. So on the following Monday I pushed off on my Rudge, determined to have *some* entry for the official diary. There was still more than a capful of wind and occasional showers. That day, too, I observed for the first time a peculiar phenomenon in regard to the winds of the Hebrides: *no matter what direction you may be cycling in, the wind is always against you.* Meteorologists may dispute that statement, but I will never concede more than that it may be a slight exaggeration. This day the wind was dead against me to Dalibrough.

"I'll get a side-birl from there to Pollachar," thinks I. But from Dalibrough to Pollachar it was head-on again! At every little rise in the road I had to get off and push. On one such occasion I noticed a small tent by the roadside, heavily staked down with ropes, and with smoke fitfully issuing from its narrow doorway. Near the tent were a lot of Highland cows, and I noticed that one of these had a horseshoe dangling over her nose and suspended by a rope tied round the horns. Parking the bicycle in the roadside ditch I made for the tent, in hope of shelter from an oncoming shower. A voice in choicest brogue invited me "insoide," and in minutes I was enjoying the beautifullest "cup-o-tay" from the jovial Pat who, it transpired, was also new to this "counthrie." The horseshoe on the cow's nose had intrigued me, and before starting off again in a glint of watery sunshine I asked Pat if he had any idea of its purpose or meaning. Was it some local superstition, or what?

"Shure I didn't noatice it before at all at all!" said Pat. Then with a stab of Irish humour: "But, bejabbers, it'll be to kape the horns from blowing aff wid the wind, for the loikes of this counthrie for wind I nivir saw in me bliddy loife!"

As a matter of interest I may explain that later I saw many cows similarly adorned, and learned that the horseshoe is put there for the purpose of restraining a beast with a bad reputation for fighting and bullying others in the fold. The plan is said to be very effective too.

There was that other day of cycling—years later—with its one adventure after another.

If you look at a map of the Highlands you will see in the gusset of Sutherland that stabs into Ross-shire the names "Elphin" and "Cnocan." In the common phrase of the unthinking these Highland hamlets are "miles from anywhere"—implying a superior status for the "anywheres" and a corresponding insignificance for the places so far from them. In reality, of course, it is the other way about. For, in the things that really matter, it is the Elphins and the Cnocans of the world that are to be congratulated and envied, and the "anywheres" that are to be commiserated: the poor cities with their glare and their blare and their shams and their shames.

Anyhow, notwithstanding my views of such things, and my knowledge of the standard of social amenities and natural dignity that is so characteristic of quiet country places, Elphin and Cnocan came as a delightful surprise. In most places I had first visited in my official capacity, just what I was and represented seemed somewhat hazy in the local mind. Not so in Elphin: there they knew all about the Agricultural College and its activities. They knew of my appointment; they even wondered why I hadn't paid them a visit sooner! So I didn't have to explain myself. That *was* a new and pleasant experience.

At the meeting that night in the joint recreation hall and reading-room—well supplied, by the way, with daily and weekly newspapers and a selection of the best monthly magazines—there was not a vestige of the awkwardness which had been a characteristic of many of my first meetings. Without any palaver one man moved that Mr So-and-so take the chair. Mr So-and-so, in response to general acclamation, did so. He thanked them for the honour and made just the correct introductory remarks with the ease and practice of a Member of Parliament.

On inquiry later I was given to understand that the quite remarkable up-to-dateness of these townships originated years earlier with a schoolmaster of progressive views. In face of considerable old-world opposition he conducted *secular* as well as sacred singing classes, founded a literary and debating society, collected funds for the erection of a hall where the members could meet and read and debate in the long winter evenings—yes, and dance too!—thereby winning for himself the anathemas of the old and the enthusiastic regard of the young, and finally of the whole community—— But I started to tell of the adventure that befell on a day of cycling.

It was in Elphin one Friday afternoon that I got a telegram to say my brother had arrived home on holiday from South Africa. I had planned to cycle home on the Saturday in any case, and now decided to start off straight away. The distance was fifty-seven miles. It was now four o'clock. I should make it by ten or so.

Passing Ullapool I decided to carry on rather than waste time over a meal. Bitterly did I regret this an hour later when walking up the Coire Shalach brae. There hunger assailed me, and a cloud of weariness. In desperation I determined to call at a keeper's house for something to eat. My knock brought, not the keeper's wife, but a stranger, to the door. But "hunger's power is strong"; so I doffed the battered hat and made known my need. Very likely I did look the perfect tramp. Anyhow, the woman (wife of an English butler, I learned later) was taking no chances. She practically ordered me off the premises!

Indignation overcame hunger as I strode away; but that lasted only for a little while. Soon the awful urge to eat came on with renewed force. A mile past the keeper's I saw, some two hundred yards off the road, a tinker's encampment, with its three rugged horses, two dogs, a few hens, and a swarm of children all complete. There were still three miles to walk and then six to cycle before I could reach Altguish inn.

I went straight to the tinker's tent. The "Royal Family" had but newly arrived. A swarthy woman in the thirties was preparing a meal at the camp-fire.

"Good evening," I greeted her. "I have come a long way and there's still a long road in front. I'm very hungry. Could you give me a cup of tea or anything to eat?"

"Surely!" came the hearty response.

"I thought I might get something from the keeper's wife," I added, "but she is not staying in the house just now."

"Don't I know that! Didn't I call there an hour ago and found only yon blank, blank, blankety blank of a creature who said she would send for the police!" my new hostess indignantly informed me.

In minutes she had spread on the grass a white cloth, with bread and butter and honey and two boiled eggs; there was a large bowl of fragrant tea to wash it down. That meal still remains in my mind a rare and refreshing feast.

I was terribly grateful and said so, but a far-off hint of financial recompense was emphatically turned down.

"Not a penny," said she; "I never know when I may be needing a cup of tea myself."

In excellent trim, though now well behind scheduled time, I sped on my way. It was after ten o'clock when I approached the old inn at Altguish—still eighteen miles from home—but the night was fine, and it would never do to pass genial old Davie of the inn without a word in the by-going.

"It's the good Lord that sent you," said Davie in the Gaelic, "and you must stay the night."

But no: I must push on—just a shout on the way, etc.

"Oh! but you must stay," Davie insisted. "There are two scoundrels of tramps in the kitchen. They were drunk when they arrived at midday; they had a bottle with them. They are now very drunk, and threatening to burn the house down if they don't get more whisky."

Just then we heard loud voices in the kitchen.

"There they go again," said Davie (who was old and very lame). "For God's sake go and try to get them to go away."

I had a keek in at the kitchen door. The tramps were displaying the contents of a tin box—some bootlaces, a few collar-studs, a box of hairpins, and such like treasure —and offering the whole job lot for a half-mutchkin of whisky. The women looked scared but refused to trade. The tramps were very tight, but determined; they threatened unspeakable consequences if whisky wasn't immediately forthcoming.

One was a sturdily built man, wearing a short beard and a semi-nautical suit. The other was a weedy-looking specimen of pallid countenance. The inn was miles from the nearest house. They had never dreamed of anyone being about the place but the two old women and the lame Davie. It must have come as a shock to them, therefore, to hear a strange voice say: "Hello! Hello, gentlemen! And what is all the row about?"

Paleface simply wilted and sneaked outside. Not so the sailor.

"And what the h—— is that to you?" he demanded, coming towards me in anything but chummy mood.

But before he was prepared for it I got a good grip of his jersey high up at the back, rushed him along the lobby, out at the front door, and landed him in the side-drain across the road. Davie promptly locked the front door, while I bolted round the house and in at the back door, which we also locked. So there we were: all trouble over and a peaceful night ahead. We thought the night-cap well earned.

Soon we were disillusioned: the sailor came round to opposite our window and yelled his frank opinion of us. It was far from flattering. But it was only when he started again his threat of setting fire to the house that we took serious notice. I tried to reassure Davie, but he was highly nervous. When he heard the scratching of matches he got really scared.

"There's a cartload of bog-fir outside the back door," he remembered, "and it will burn like paraffin!"

Meantime the sailor, at the back door, was demanding admittance, and in spite of my remonstrance Davie went to open it.

"Wait," I insisted, "and I'll go out and speak to him, but he must not come in."

I opened the door just enough to allow me to slip out. There was the sailor, with an ugly-looking knobkerry of fir-root in his hand.

"If you don't let me in I'll bash your bloody brains out," said he, frothing mad. There was no doubt he meant it too. Now, I was never much "a man of my hands." Indeed, I have always preferred sweet reason-ableness to fisticuffs in an argument. But clearly the smooth answer would not serve here. So with my fist I hit him on the chin as hard as I could. It must have been pretty hard for, to my astonishment, he dropped like an old log. For a few moments I had a wild fear that I had killed him! But like a Jack-in-the-box he was up and kicked me one in the stomach, that partially winded me and nearly made me vomit. Then I went mad. There followed the wildest rough-and-tumble of my life. It was an all-out catch-as-catch-can and no-quarter affair. We rolled over and over, first one on top, then the other; crashed through the garden paling, flattened Davie's cabbages and brussels sprouts, and got badly lacerated amongst the gooseberry bushes. Davie was hopping about on his crutch hoping to get in a helpful blow with his heavy iron-clad stick.

"Will I hit him?" yelled Davie.

"Yes!" I bawled, not in the least concerned with the niceties; and Davie brought a terrific whack down *on my thigh*!

I howled—and cursed—and very nearly fainted with

the pain. Only dire necessity kept me conscious and enabled me to continue the fight.

I am morally certain that if that sailor hadn't been drinking all day he could—and would—have murdered me. He was as strong as a horse, and had some scientific holds that I knew nothing of. But his wind was going: he couldn't stand the pace. I managed to wriggle on top and all of a sudden the fight went out of him. Davie brought a plough-rein, with which we trussed him up good and tight. We left him thus, lying amongst the ruined vegetables, while we went to remove the blood and grime of battle and apply sticking-plaster to the bigger wounds. There was also a matter of refreshment attended to.

In half an hour the sailor was howling for mercy. The rein was cutting into his arms and legs.

"For God's sake cut this bloody rope!" he pleaded.

Perhaps I did a very foolish thing, but who could see and hear a man suffering like that? Anyhow, I undid the rope. The "word of honour" which I had extracted from him as a preliminary very nearly didn't stand the strain when he found himself freed again; but the sight of Davie's iron-clad stick—which I now controlled— saved it. He walked stiffly but in the right direction.

Next morning at six Davie came to my room in great agitation. Our two friends of the night before were sound asleep in the stable! When they wakened up the whole trouble would begin again! I would be gone and not a soul would come near the place till the mail coach came at noon!

It was arranged that the sleepers would be left undisturbed. In passing Garve I would call at the police station and ask the constable to start for Altguish immediately.

The constable was doing his morning ablutions in a tin

basin of cold water at the gable-end of his house when I arrived at eight o'clock. He was off on his bicycle within twenty minutes.

I got home in time for a late breakfast. In the afternoon I changed into another suit and started for Achterneed station to join the train for Dingwall. That day the train was unusually punctual. I nearly missed it. It was actually moving off when at the end of a two minutes' desperate sprint I just managed to tumble in. Panting, I sat down. Then I looked at the others in the compartment. Paleface and Sailor!—handcuffed together with the policeman in charge! I nearly jumped out again. But, taking my cue from the Arm-of-the-Law (who betrayed not a glint of recognition), I soon saw that neither prisoner was likely to link up this well-dressed young man with the ruffian of last night at Altguish; nor did they.

Next week the Chief Constable of Ross-shire thanked me for "aiding the police," and (unofficially) complimented me on the battered condition of the sailor's features.

And now for a confession—and a bone for the psychologists to chew on. That was my only fight as a grown-up man and I *enjoyed it*. In fact, it gave me the grandest thrill of my life. Which makes me to believe that:

(1) In primitive man there is a natural lust for blood and battle.

(2) All our "civilisation" hasn't succeeded in greatly altering man's primordial instincts.

(3) In certain circumstances the most conscientious of conscientious objectors would fight like a fiend— and enjoy it too.

CHAPTER X

WHEN I went first to the islands I was full of enthusiasm for my work, but ignorant of most of the agricultural customs and practices of the district. Many of the latter struck me as old-fashioned and in direct opposition to the accepted principles and practices of good husbandry in other. districts. A little reflection and observation, however, soon caused me to modify my view and to realise that there was some sound basis of common sense and experience for many of the accepted ways of doing things out there. Consequently, any visions I might have had of rapidly revolutionising the agriculture of the islands soon vanished.

"Go dead slow"; "Don't pose as a wise man from the East"; "Look for ways in which you *can* really suggest improvement" were some of the warnings I gave myself. And even then I would require to go very canny because, when a man is accustomed to do certain work in a certain way—and his father and grandfather did it that way too —he very naturally resents any tactless suggestions for "improvement" from an outsider—and a comparative youngster at that. It was with a full appreciation of these facts and with appropriate humility that I one day decided to approach Calum on the question of the best method of sowing corn.

Now the native method of sowing the corn had for some time been in my mind as a possible subject for demonstrating a more up-to-date method. It *had* struck me as rather contradictory that when sowing corn a man should step backwards instead of forward. Actually that

was what I found.   The sower started at the end of the
ploughed rig and, stepping *backwards*, scattered by one
hand the seed from a pail which he carried in the other.
The sowing was done by irregular, spasmodic jerks of the
hand and the sower stepped backwards to do a new area
when he had sown the part in front right up to his feet.
The general effect was that of a man shaking pepper over
a gigantic plate of soup.   The process was terribly slow;
it would take the best part of a day to sow a couple of
acres.   While the sower (usually the father) was busy in
the soup-peppering manner the son, with the horses
yoked in the harrows, rested till the rig was sown.   He
then got busy with the harrows while the sower rested
on the seed-bag and had a smoke.   By the time the sower
had had his rest and smoke the horses and their attendant
were ready to rest again till the next rig was sown—and
so on, turn about till the job was finished.   It was all very
interesting and picturesque but far from speedy—and
in that uncertain climate often resulted in protracted
sowing, with correspondingly late harvest.

Calum had just started sowing a three-acre field on
the morning that I decided to make my venture.   His son
and horses were there to harrow when they got the
opportunity and the work was proceeding in the good
old-fashioned way.   Calum and myself exchanged the
usual courtesies relating to weather prospects, family
welfare, etc.   We spoke in Gaelic and the whole of our
subsequent conversation was in that language, and this
tale loses a lot in the English telling.   I then remarked
that he was busy at the sowing.

"Very busy," said Calum.

"You will take a good while to sow the field," I
opinioned.

"Yes, indeed," agreed Calum.   "It will take me all of
to-day and maybe a bit of to-morrow too."

"You have never tried any other way of sowing?" ventured myself.

"Other way?" inquired Calum. "No. I never heard of any other way; and am I not busy enough?"

"Oh, yes indeed," I agreed, "you are busy enough, and making a very good job, too; but where I come from we sow in a different way. It will not be any better than your own way, but I do believe it might be quicker."

"Indeed?" said Calum, a little curious.

"Yes indeed, I think so," said I.

"Indeed," said Calum again; "and what way would you be sowing it?"

"Och!" I protested, "it will not be any better than your own way, but it will be quicker right enough"; and then I added: "If you do not mind I will sow a bit to let you see."

"Surely," invited Calum, "indeed I would like fine to see you doing it."

The pail was just an ordinary pail, but I had to make the best of it. I tied a piece of rope by the middle, close to where the handle joined the pail at the side furthest from my tummy; then passed the ends of the rope round my waist, tying them firmly at my back. This made a sort of improvised seed-container. I then suggested to Calum that his wife and daughter should come to the field with other pails to keep me supplied with seed; but as a pail of seed was sufficient to keep Calum sowing for quite a while he couldn't see any necessity for this; he himself would replenish my "box" when required. So my first pail was filled by Calum, and as I crossed over to my starting-place at the end of the rig Calum sat down on the seed-bag and proceeded to fill his pipe preparatory to watching the performance.

Here I may say without boasting that I was (and I am still) a really good two-handed sower. On this occasion

I stepped out at my very best, broadcasting the seed in those rhythmical rainbow sweeps that always give the sower a peculiar joy. After advancing thirty yards or so I stopped to get Calum's opinion of the job. Calum was astounded. He hadn't even completed the filling of the pipe. The sight of his seed being scattered in this quick and seeming reckless fashion was too much for him.

"What do you think of it?" I inquired.

"May the Lord look upon me!" replied Calum, "but I'm not sure. It looks a very careless way of throwing the seed about, anyway. But wait till I see."

He came over and carefully examined the bit I had sown, and to my relief pronounced: "It *looks* right enough, whatever."

On this I assured him I had sown fields and fields of corn in that way and that the crops had grown quite well. I offered to carry on and finish the field for him.

"Carry on," agreed Calum, "and I will get the wife and lassie out to keep you supplied with seed."

When the wife and daughter came out Calum's field became the scene of unwonted activity. For effect I deliberately sowed faster than ever I had done before. The two women had to run to keep me going. The horses were nearly running in the harrows but couldn't catch up.

I had taken the precaution of ascertaining from Calum the exact quantity of seed he customarily sowed in that field.   He told me in *pecks*, so that I had to do some mental gymnastics to translate pecks to bushels. I took good care to come out just right at the finish.   In less than an hour the job was completed, but by this time there was a gallery of a dozen neighbours who had walked over to ascertain the cause of all the commotion on Calum's field. They carefully examined the still unharrowed part and were frankly outspoken with their comments. In the interest of fair play one man was constrained to admit it "*looked* right enough anyway," but this qualified optimism was douched by another who dolefully remarked:

"Och, yes; it may *look* right enough; *but the man who lives longest will see what will come of work of this kind!*"

Calum himself was a complete convert. He said he was in his eighty-fourth year but, old as he was, he would like to have a try of the new way. (Actually he didn't, but I did have the satisfaction later of initiating his son to the sowing "step and cast," with sand from the shore as "seed" and in a "box" made by the local blacksmith.) Meantime Calum proceeded to remark on the extraordinary wonders a man might see in the course of a long life.

"Of course," he remarked, "I might hear of the like of this, but *seeing is believing*. Look you," he explained, "some of us have never been to the mainland of Scotland. For myself I have never been further than the Pier in my life, but we are not so simple as to believe everything we are told! And indeed some of the commercial travellers that come to the shop, though very nice men, are not above telling us some tall stories."

I agreed that some of the commercials' tales might require a pinch of salt.

"Indeed yes," concurred Calum. "There was one of them here a fortnight ago—a very nice man too—but och! the lies he tried to make me believe in half an hour!"

"Ay, ay," said I.

"Yes indeed," said Calum, shaking his white beard; "and do you know what he was trying to make me believe at last?"

"No," said I.

"Yes," said Calum, digging the joke into my ribs and chuckling at the recollection of this Ananias of the road, "*that they can hatch out the chickens nowadays without hens at all!*"

We all laughed heartily at the audacity of the man who could so presume on native credulity.

It is interesting to know that within a very short time there were several incubators in use in the islands and that Calum lived long enough to revise his opinion of the commercial's veracity, for when I visited the island ten years later this delightful old man had not yet passed on to The Land of the Ever Young.

ON the old croft we had a great big barn; at any rate,
being the biggest "room" I had seen bar the church and
the big classroom at the school, it seemed to me to be a
tremendous size. I could hardly believe myself recently
when, measuring out the barn from its old *larach* (site), I
was forced to the conclusion it couldn't have been so
terribly big after all.

Anyhow, anything is big or little only relatively, and I
prefer to think of the old barn as very big.

And what tales that old barn could have told had its
walls the power of speech! New Year dances, wedding
dances, political meetings, Land League meetings,
prayer-meetings, christenings—the old barn gave impartial
hospitality to all.

For a real big occasion like a wedding dance care was
taken to have the barn as clear of straw, etc., as possible.
What little straw or sheaves there were, were piled up
neatly at one end, and formed an excellent perch from
the top of which we youngsters could look with some
amazement at the unwonted riotous ongoings of our
elders.

Who, for instance, that had only seen *Donncha Beag*
plodding with heavy step in the wake of the harrows, or
solemnly wending his way to or from church, would
recognise in him yon sprightly lad who flung his feet so
high at the *righil a'phosaidh* (wedding dance) that he would
kick the candle off its stone wall-bracket six feet off the
floor, and who, at the change-over from the reel to the

reel o' Tulloch, would give a hooch that would all but lift
the thatch from the rafters! *M'eudal air!*

And again, under the same wall-bracket, I have seen
the same Little D.... of the dance sit at prayer-meeting
with devout and .... countenance drinking in the
terrors of hell and .... with never a doubt of their
reality!

One of the biggest wedding dances I can remember was
when an uncle of mine got married. For that night, at
any rate, the rather drab routine of the croft was forgotten
in dance and song and revelry.

One of the brightest and gayest of the guests was a deer-
stalker who had come for the occasion from his home in a
glen fully twenty miles away.

I can see him yet, with red whiskers and redder cheeks
and tall athletic figure, getting full value out of the general
merriment—and what a shock it was when news came to
the glen within a very short time that our robust, jovial
stalker friend was dead—treacherously killed by one of
his own stags!

The story, as I remember it, was that the stags were
being hand-fed during a heavy snowstorm. In such
circumstances, of course, stags become as tame as sheep.
One day this stalker had been at either church or a funeral
—I forget which—and on returning, without waiting to
change into his ordinary tweeds, he went out with a feed
of maize to the stags. A big stag—and known to be rather
cheeky—either mistook him for a stranger or objected to
the dark clothes and set on him furiously, with the tragic
result that so awed us.

That was the first time I realised that stags could on
occasion be very dangerous animals.

I had another sharp lesson in that direction many years
later. A friendly keeper and myself were having a day at
the hares in October. Late in the afternoon a wounded

hare crossed through the deer fence into the forest and dropped dead within view, but some two hundred yards in. Leaving my gun at the fence I went through to retrieve the hare. There was some very rough bouldery ground immediately beyond, but I never noticed any deer there, and even if I had would probably have thought nothing of it. I picked up the hare, and was more than half-way back to the fence when I heard a noise behind me. I turned round to look for the cause of it, and there was a big stag coming straight at me at full gallop! In a flash I realised that I was in a very perilous position and one that brooked of no delay. Believe me, there was none! At the time I didn't think, I ran! The other side of that fence was the most desired thing in my world! How I did it I can't yet understand, but I did manage like a rabbit to shoot through between two wires of the fence with about five feet to spare between my pants and the antlers of the infuriated beast. It didn't take me long, now on the safe side of the fence, to grasp my loaded gun. My recent pursuer, evidently appreciating the altered circumstances, had about-turned and fled, but I did have the satisfaction of getting a fairly effective "right and left" of No. 4's well planted round his apology for a tail!

It was a lucky escape, and my only regret was that there was no official timekeeper with a stop-watch, for I am morally certain that on that occasion I made a time for the hundred yards that would stagger Jesse Owens!

You may well think that that experience should have been sufficient to last me a lifetime and that in future, unless adequately armed, I would give stags in October the widest of wide berths.

Yet there is some contrary streak in most of us, and it wasn't so very many years afterwards that I let myself in for another real scare with a stag.

One day in late October I was plugging along on my Rudge on the road from Lochmaddy to Locheport. The road for most of its length of eight miles passes through open moorland. About half-way along I heard a stag roaring on my left. I came off the bicycle to look. He stood on the skyline some six hundred yards away and was facing at right angles to my line of vision. A right noble silhouette he made too, as he roared another challenge to any stag that cared to take it up.

Little dreaming of consequences so embarrassing, I thought I would like to try to see how near I could achieve to a realistic "roar" myself. With the notes of the stag's last bellow still fresh in my ears I let out the best imitation "roar" I could. It must have been a surprising success, for like shot that stag whipped round to face my direction.

"Gosh!" I thought, "that's interesting."

He gave another roar and tossed some heather with his horns. Elated with success I gave yet another "roar." I had no sooner done it than I began to realise what an idiot I was. As swift and smooth as a swallow that stag came galloping towards me! While he was still some four hundred yards away I jumped on the bicycle and was off as hard as I could pedal it. But a glance over my left shoulder showed me that my utmost speed was less than half that of the stag.

Scarcely realising what I was doing I came off the bicycle with some wild and futile idea of throwing it over his antlers when he actually attacked me. To my unspeakable relief, as soon as I got off the bicycle and stood still I saw that the stag stopped too.

He was now about a hundred and fifty yards away. He roared a roar that made the hills echo and re-echo for miles round and gave me the queerest of colly-wobbly feelings in the pit of my stomach. I did *not* answer that challenge! The stag stood staring with eyes which, even at that distance, I could see flashing. He roared and he roared again. I thought of all sorts of plans for escape, well knowing they were equally futile. Two or three times I tried to slide away on the bicycle, but every time I did that the brute raced towards me again till I stopped. Then he stopped and roared. How long this cat-and-mouse business went on I couldn't say, but to me it seemed hours of acutest funk, with that maddened beast now not fifty yards off, and not a house within two miles.

And just when I sort of made up my mind to face the inevitable as bravely as I could, if that stag didn't about-turn and flee as if the devil were biting at his heels! I nearly collapsed with relief and had to pull myself together.

It was with a mightily thankful heart I saw the last of the stag as he spanged over the skyline.

Then I cycled on towards the road end, leading to the gamekeeper's cottage. There I met the keeper, to whom I told my story. I was not a little hurt to notice he was inclined to be incredulous, but after a bit he had to believe me.

"What sort of a beast was it?" he asked.

"It was a fairly big stag, blackish at the neck and a nine-pointer," I replied, rather annoyed.

"Oh! I know that beast, and indeed I'm not saying but he could be nasty enough," admitted the keeper. "What did you do that set him off like yon?" he inquired.

"Nothing that I know of: he just went off all of a sudden."

"When did you light that cigarette?" he asked.

Truth to tell, till he asked, I hadn't noticed I was smoking a cigarette at all. It was now nearly finished.

"Really, I can't tell you," was my reply.

"Well," said he, "I can tell you. You lit that cigarette

at the moment the stag ran away—and it was the flash of the match which probably saved your life. It is not the first time I have seen a stag bolt at the flash of a light."

Well, well! That was a tip I'm not likely to forget—but indeed it isn't me that will invite trouble like yon again!

CHAPTER XII

In the Highlands the crow has ever been held in somewhat sinister repute. Always it has been credited with something more than mere bird-wisdom. Only a very reckless person would deliberately destroy a rookery, even if its proximity to the house made it an annual nuisance. There was no harm in shooting young crows at the rookery: that was an annual sport. But destroying the rookery itself was a very different matter—a very unlucky thing to do.

Who that was brought up in the country has not observed the cunning of the crow on potato-stealing bent? While the crows are intent on digging out the potatoes, one at least of their number mounts guard on a fence-post or tree near by, so that never a chance of a shot at the raiders can a man get.

Their sense of location of the potato in the earth, too, is rather uncanny. With seldom-erring accuracy the bill is bored into the side of the drill right to the tuber at its middle. Another well-directed stab and the potato is impaled by the bill. Off flies Mr Crow to some spot where he can guzzle in safety on his titbit—leaving a hitherto flourishing potato-plant to wilt and die and a farmer to grouse at yet another of his innumerable afflictions.

Often I have seen a kestrel—which had probably been showing too keen an interest in the crow's nursery—harried to distraction by a crowd of crows. Sometimes too I have seen the crows' attack strengthened by a few gulls, and even by some linnets, who joined forces to teach a lesson to the common enemy.

77

I did not know that crows ate mice until one day a good many years ago. It must have been about the month of June, for we were threshing the last stack in the yard. As is not uncommon in the case of last stacks, this one harboured swarms of mice. These we ruthlessly slew with the joint help of dogs, cats, and sticks.

Out of curiosity a few of us youngsters counted the dead mice and placed them in a *dalachan*—a sort of corn riddle, or container, made by stretching a calf-skin over an ordinary riddle-frame. There were over 300 mice, and the *dalachan* was placed on the top of a strainer post before we went in to dinner.

During the meal we heard an awful rumpus, and on looking out we saw a great number of crows struggling and fighting with each other to get at the mice. Off went every lucky crow with a mouse in his beak. In less than five minutes not a mouse was left in the *dalachan*!

Quite recently, in Thurso, the hotel in which I usually stay was packed to the door with summer visitors. I counted myself lucky in getting an attic room very high up. It was a delightful room though, and gave one a sort of thrill, as of sleeping near the top of a lighthouse.

Bright and early in the morning I was awake and enjoying the luxury of lying in a comfortable bed and looking out of the open window at the bonnie sky which you sometimes get in the far north. By shifting my head slightly I found my view somewhat obstructed by a chimney-stalk whose top was little more than level with my window. There were four cans on top of that chimney. From the volume of smoke which issued from one can it was obvious that down below preparations for feeding the multitude were already under way. The other three cans —probably bedroom vents—were "idle." The smoking can was second from the left and the smoke from it blew over the two cans on the right.

While I was speculating on the inequalities of this life's luck, which permitted of my lying snugly in bed the while a fellow-creature was already afoot and labouring for my further comfort in the shape of an appetising breakfast, what should hop on to the idle can on the extreme left but a crow. He wasn't more than twenty feet from my bed. He alighted on the side of the can furthest from the smoking can. Then he side-stepped round till he was on the side nearest the smoke. To my amusement he stretched his head over into the smoke, but withdrew it in a moment and vigorously shook it, as if the smoke were irritating his eyes. But again and again he did it, and then—after obviously and comically making up his mind to take the plunge—he hopped on to the far rim of the smoking can, spread first one wing and then another right into the thickest of the smoke, and stood there maybe a matter of five seconds, when he hopped back to the can in lee of the smoke, blinking his eyes and ruffling his feathers and obviously very proud of his bravery.

Soon he repeated the process.

The most comical part of the programme to me was the obvious screwing up of courage that was necessary each time before he took the plunge. Each time he got back out of the smoke I could almost hear him chokingly gasp to himself:

"That'll do now! This is pretty awful! You've had enough!"

But after getting his vision and breath again he seemed to be lured back for one more plunge.

For quite ten minutes he continued this off-and-on disinfecting process—for so I concluded it must be—taking about a dozen smoke-baths in all.

Finally he carefully preened every wing and tail feather in turn, before flying off with a triumphant "caw," presumably to look for a well-deserved breakfast.

But the most interesting experience I ever had with a crow was at Inverlael, by the side of Lochbroom—in 1912, as far as I can remember.

I had cycled from Strathpeffer that morning—nine miles to Garve, including the Tarvie Brae near the Falls of Rogie—and then off on the thirty-two miles to Ullapool.

It was a hot day. The long pedal up the *Direadh mòr* against what little breeze there was was pretty tiring. Then down from the top at Loch Droma—past the Coire Shalach with its well worth seeing falls, and along past Braemore and Inverbroom to Inverlael within a few miles of my destination.

At Inverlael there is another brae to negotiate. The sun was hot. I was tired and rather ahead of schedule. The lure of a grassy slope in the shade of some hazel bushes which grew between the road and the shore of the loch was too strong. Indeed that is the sort of resting-place that has a particular attraction for me. As you lie on your broad back on a warm day in a grassy glade mother earth seems to draw tiredness from your body as a blotter draws ink from paper. Half an hour of that and you are a new and invigorated man.

It was while lying there on my back and with my head in my hands that I saw the crow. I was first attracted by his peculiar form of flight. He was "towering" like a shot pheasant. Up and up and up he towered till maybe fifty yards off the ground. From there he let drop a cockle and swooped down after it. It fell on the sand and Mr Crow was at it in a second. But the cockle was still intact! That crow's face bore a most comical expression of perplexed disappointment. He cocked one eye at the mollusc, then the other, and you could practically hear him say, "Funny!"

But up he flew again with the cockle, circled round a bit and again dropped it. Down he swooped again, and again the same result. This time his expression said quite clearly, "Dashed funny!"

Up again, a wider circle, drop, swoop; nothing doing!

"Well, I'm . . . . . . !" said that crow.

But he was persistent. He picked up the cockle once again, circled wider than before, and again dropped it. Whether by chance I know not (and who dare say?), but this time the cockle fell on a patch of gravel, splitting its shell and exposing the succulent contents, which Mr Corbie soon transferred to another receptacle with gurgles of greedy delight.

If his luck was accidental he certainly had intelligence enough to profit by experience, for in the next ten minutes he picked up six more cockles and never dropped one on sand.

CHAPTER XIII

MORE than once, from certain vantage points in the Uists,
and with the right sort of visibility, I had discerned the
dim outlines of St Kilda, far away and lonely to the west:
a sort of *Tìr nan òg* with a magnetic pull on one's imagination. Now, while St Kilda had not been expressly
included in my sphere of official operations, neither had it
been expressly excluded. So there you were. *It might
be my duty to go there?* Anyhow, it wasn't long before I was
looking for an official excuse for a visit; nor did I have
long to wait.

One spring morning a crofter on one of the smaller
inhabited isles of the Uists, while bringing in seaweed,
noticed a buoy floating near the shore in shallow water.
Closer inspection showed it to be an inflated dog-skin to
which was attached a short piece of rope, which at its
other end had tied to it a small block of wood, some
twelve inches long and six inches square in its other
dimensions. On one side of this block, burnt in by a hot
poker, were the words: "FINDER PLEASE OPEN."

The interior of the block of wood had been scooped
out after the primitive boat-building plan. Several
letters addressed to various people in Glasgow had been
placed in the hollow. On top of these lay a note
addressed: "To the Finder."

A half-inch-thick piece of wood had then been closely
fitted on to form a watertight lid. This lid was with
some difficulty prised open to disclose the contents of the
unusual post-bag. The note to the finder was addressed

and dated from St Kilda about a fortnight previously. It asked him or her to be good enough to post the other letters at the nearest post office. It also stated that there was distress amongst the inhabitants of St Kilda on account of lack of the necessaries of life.

It was my good fortune to be on that small island that day and to meet the crofter on his way home with his interesting find. As I was crossing to the mainland of North Uist that same day he asked me if I would take the buoy, box, and letters to the post office. Of course, I did; and handed the lot over to the postmaster—who gave me the interesting information that by the rules of the post office the finder of such postal packet was entitled to a reward of a half-crown. In a couple of days the newspapers were ablaze with stories of famine in St Kilda.

Let me say here and now that the "famine" report was first cousin to the report of that historical death which was said to have been greatly exaggerated. It is true that stocks of conventional necessities like tea, tobacco, and other stimulants were running somewhat low, but the starvation story (with milk, potatoes, over fifty cattle and several hundred sheep on the island) was just an audacious and astute ramp which on more than one occasion in the history of St Kilda and other Hebridean islands has brought "succour" from a credulous, kindly British public to the "starving" natives.

In this connection there was exquisite humour in the reply I once got from a native of the Hebrides in relation to one of those "famine" scares. Some newspapers went the length of publishing maps of the island with darkly shaded parts showing the daily spread of the famine! When things had grown very black indeed I met my old friend the native, and with a solemn face asked him in the Gaelic if the famine had yet reached his particular township. Well did Norman know that I knew the truth, and nobly did he rise to the occasion. His eyes twinkled through the surrounding whiskers; then a flicker of a smile and said Norman:

"Well, indeed, I am never very sure myself till I read the newspaper!" ("*Gu dearbh, cha 'n eil mi fhein robh chinnteach gus an leugh mi am paipear naigheachd.*") But this is by the way.

The day after the publication of the St Kilda famine story I wrote H.Q. suggesting that perhaps an official visit should be paid to the island. My Chief played up splendidly: it was urgent that I should go to St Kilda first opportunity. First opportunity came the following week, when the S.S. *Hebrides* called in at the pier *en route* for St Kilda on her first official call at that island since the previous September. By the way, she brought with her a Christmas mail, and I'm not yet sure whether it was meant for the previous Christmas or the next.

There were some threescore *sasunnach* holiday-makers on board. At our pier four others joined: the local excise officer, the district nurse, a native home on holiday from Canada, and myself. There was also on board MacLeod of MacLeod's factor from Dunvegan, the late Mr John MacKenzie, who was paying his annual visit to St Kilda for the purpose of collecting rents. He was a veritable mine of information regarding the island, its people and customs, and we were tremendously interested in his talk. Incidentally, he explained that rent "collecting" was somewhat of an Irishism. Actually, it was an annual settling of accounts between proprietor and tenants. The latter produced to the factor their year's harvest of oil and feathers got from some of the millions of sea-birds which frequent and nest on the island's precipitous cliffs. Each family was credited with the value of its collection of these commodities. Sometimes the value of stirks and sheep and wool was also brought in on the credit side. From the usually quite substantial total was deducted the rent—mostly under two pounds per croft —and the factor handed over the balance in cash.

We were given to understand that the independent character of the St Kildeans had of late years been sadly sapped by "tipping" and largess introduced by tourists. Formerly, young men took pride in giving gratis exhibitions of cliff-climbing. Now their amazing expertness in that direction was strictly commercialised. There was nothing much to complain of in that, but apparently the natives had become cute to the extortionate stage in the art of "milking" the *sasunnach*; and we were warned to be on guard.

The voyage out was in perfect weather. Going through the Sound of Harris—which can be navigated only in daylight because of numerous submerged rocks—was a thrilling experience. The ship was steered on lines of "landmarks" and when a new set of these came in line she would be swung hard round in less than her own length.

It was bright and sunny when we anchored in St Kilda's horseshoe bay. Out came several boats loaded with people and a great assortment of knitted garments and webs of handmade tweeds, blankets, rugs, etc. It was just like what you see at Madeira; and, believe me, the St Kildeans were no less expert traders. In the first half-hour £300 must have been transferred from the *sasunnachs'* pockets to theirs.

When it came to going ashore the Gaelic-speaking quartette got into a small boat in charge of a white-whiskered native and a youth—both wearing cheese-cutter caps. Now there was nothing in our external appearance to suggest to the boatmen that we were anything but just four of the *sasunnach* "towrists" and we never said a revealing word. The nurse had a grand sense of humour and was idolised by her patients, but it must be admitted that whatever Fate it is which confers beauty on mankind at birth must have been on vacation on her natal day. Not the most biased of fond parents could call her facially well-favoured: far, far from it! But no one knew that better than herself and little did it bother her! As we were being rowed ashore the youth sized us up with a stealthy glance and then, gazing at the sky as if discussing the weather, said to the old man:

"*Ciod e chuiridh sinn orra, saoil* **sibh?**"   ("What will we charge them, do you think?")

The ancient then had a look at the sky and said hopefully: "*Fiachaidh sinn da thasdan*" ("We'll try two shillings")—and promptly placed his inverted cheese-cutter in front of the nurse with the announcement: "Two shillings, mem."

"Two shillings!" exclaimed the nurse in horror, and her best English accent. "What for?"

"Take you there, take you pack agaane," explained the ancient. "Chape chape too," he added.

There followed heated protests on both sides, but the nurse was adamant: she would give a shilling and not a penny more! At last the mariner gave up the unfair contest (he was at a heavy disadvantage with the language) and, speaking in his native tongue, gave vent to the cryptic soliloquy:

"*A Dhia! nach e an te ghrannd tha cruaidh!*" ("God! isn't it the ugly one that is hard!")

Retorted the ugly one: "*Ma tha mi grannd* **a** *dhuine, tha mi onarach.*"   ("If I'm ugly, man, I'm honest.")

Never have I seen an island gentleman so distressed and embarrassed—and we got off for the shilling.

CHAPTER XIV

Delicate Doings—Advisory Committee—Island Wooing

IN the few years preceding the date of our visit the population of St Kilda had slumped heavily. By then it was down to 79—which, by the way, was also the age in years of the oldest inhabitant—a woman. By 1930 only 39 people were left on the island, and these, at their own urgent request, were evacuated by the Government to the mainland of Scotland.

I am not, here, to go into a detailed description of our interesting six hours on the island of St Kilda, but there was a sequel so unique in my experience that it is well worth the telling.

Just before we left to rejoin the ship the then minister-cum-teacher-cum-doctor on the island (whom I had previously met in the Uists) took me aside and entrusted me with the following intriguing information. A native of the island (it will serve if I call him "Erchie"—which was not his name) was going with us on the *Hebrides* to the *Tìr Mòr* (Big Land). His mission was one of peculiar delicacy. His wife had died a few years before, leaving him with a family of very young children. After allowing him a decent interval for mourning, the old men of the island—a sort of self-elected Witenagemot, known as the "Mod," who advised on and decided all vital matters affecting the interest of the islanders—pressed strongly on Erchie the advisability of "getting someone to look after himself and the family." Erchie protested that, however desirable that might be in theory, there was the practical difficulty that every woman on the island, who might be otherwise eligible, was too closely related to himself. The Mod had been compelled to admit the validity of

Erchie's protest, but for a year now had urged the bolder
step of going further afield to look for a wife.   And that
was what Erchie was going to do in the *Tìr Mòr*—and,
wife or no wife, he must return by the *Dunara Castle*,
which left him ten days for his quest.   The minister, etc.,
suggested I might be able to help, but pleaded that I
would not let the story go round amongst the *Sasunnaich*
on the ship, as Erchie was anxious to avoid publicity in
the matter.   I promised to do my best.

Shortly after we up-anchored and left the bay I went
alongside the terribly lost-looking Erchie, who brightened
up visibly on being spoken to in his own tongue.   First,
I asked him about St Kilda.   Then, I got on to the
subject of his journey.

Of course, he had been to the *Tìr Mòr* before?

No, no—he had never been out of St Kilda in his life.

Oh! He would be going to the markets?   Maybe to
buy a cow?—or sell?

Well, well, he might be going to the markets—he
wasn't very sure.   Oh, yes, he might buy a cow too.

Then I tried him on domestic affairs.   Of course, he
would be a married man?

Och! well—yes: he *was* and he was *not*!

Och! Indeed, indeed! That was very sad. Was
there a family in it?

Yes, indeed.   There was; four of them—all young.

Och! Och! And who was looking after them?

Och! Indeed! Nobody but himself.

Och! Och! That was bad, bad! It was not *right*.
It was not fair to the family. *He should try to get a sensible
woman to look after them.*

At this stage Erchie caught me by the arm, looked
round apprehensively and "*Tuiginn a so*" ("Come here"),
said he, leading me away to a quiet spot near the bows.
Then in a dramatic whisper: "*Eadar sinn fhein, sin mo*

ghnothach air an turus so" ("Between ourselves, that is my errand on this journey").

I heartily approved the plan, and suggested that the other Gaelic speakers aboard—who knew everyone in the *Tìr Mòr*—should be let into the secret; they would certainly be helpful. At first Erchie protested against letting the cat out of the bag even to that limited extent, but ultimately he agreed.

We collected in a quiet corner of the saloon, and in our capacity of advisory committee solemnly discussed the business in hand. The Canadian—who had a strong belief in the efficacy of a dram in all critical situations in life—suggested a drop of whisky. But no! Erchie had promised the minister that he would not drink a drop of whisky while away. So we had the dram ourselves, and Erchie had a glass of "lemonade"—of peculiar sparkle. Things brightened up a bit after that. By the time we reached our port the exciseman—who naturally, with his very intimate local knowledge, became chief adviser— had prepared a list of seventeen "possibles." He wrote down not only their legal names (which wouldn't convey much to anybody) but also the names they were known by, and placed them in "order of call" as one proceeded clockwise round the island. Erchie couldn't read a word, but I have never met an apter pupil. In half an hour he had mastered the name and address of all seventeen; and that very afternoon the wooer started off on his quest. By the way, his entire "luggage" consisted of a walking-stick.

For a week there was only one topic in our island. We at H.Q. were in a fever of excitement. Every morning the postmen coming from the provinces brought in news. One day it would be "nothing doing." Next it would be two—or maybe three—wives for Erchie; but on the third day it would be back to zero again. On the seventh day

Erchie himself returned, weary and dispirited. He had called on the whole seventeen—and on a good many more —but no success! He could have a harem if he stayed on in the *Tìr Mòr* but not one would marry him and go to St Kilda; and as Erchie himself put it: "*Ciod e 's fhiach sin dhomhsa ?* " ("What is the good of that to me?")

It was clearly a case for further "lemonade"—which we duly attended to. But we all felt terribly dejected, till the exciseman had a brain-wave. Why not cross by that afternoon's boat to a neighbouring island? The *Dunara Castle* called there on its way to St Kilda three days hence —and Erchie could have a three-days' hunt on fresh ground before it came. True, we didn't know so many of the "possibles" there, so the list was a short one, but you never know your luck! Inside half an hour, with hope restored, Erchie was packed off on the *Lapwing*.

It would be after six o'clock that evening by the time he could get ashore. We had made him promise to wire success or failure—indeed had provided him with the message appropriate to either eventuality—but did not expect any news till the last minutes of the last day. But after office hours that same evening down to the hotel came the Postmaster himself, with a telegram handed in less than an hour after Erchie's arrival. It read:

"Excise Officer (*Tìr Mòr*). Successful. ERCHIE."

In this tale of truth it must be recorded that we had something approaching a little spree that night.

.   .   .   .

My colleague Archie Campbell loved the story of the St Kilda wooer, and would have it again and again. He was quite frank about the matter: he *knew* it wasn't true, but it was a good story!

Many years later *chaidh mi cheilidh air* (I went for a sociable evening) at his house in Aberdeen. When I arrived, there was a middle-aged, pleasant-looking lady sitting yarning with his wife. Mrs Archie proceeded to introduce me to the stranger. The latter smiled; there was no need for such formality: we were friends of long ago. For the life of me I couldn't place her—time and frocks fairly beat me in that way—but I did my best to hide the fact. Cautiously I went probing for firm ground:

"It's a good while since we last met," I chanced.

"It is that," agreed the lady; "it's getting on for twenty years."

"Do you know," I admitted, "I can't for the life of me remember just where it was."

"And I won't soon forget," said she. "It was yon day at *Tìr Mòr* pier when the man from St Kilda joined the boat to go to —— to look for a wife."

"*Archie !* " said I.

"Well well," admitted Archie. "'*S gu so fhein bha mi deimhinn gur e bhreug bhriagha bh'ann!* " ("And till this minute I was sure it was just a bonnie lie!")

CHAPTER XV

THE MacBraynes steamer service to the West Coast and Islands has been so frequently the subject of popular scorn and public reproach that a defence of it requires no small degree of courage. But it is always so easy to criticise and condemn: mankind in the mass seems to have a sadistic streak which finds pleasure in that sort of talk. Yet as one with over thirty years' experience of that service, in fair weather and foul—more foul than fair —I do feel constrained to put in a warm word of respect and approbation. It is all so very easy to quote "extortionate" freights and "scandalous" conditions; but when such accusations are submitted to dispassionate investigation and analysis by any unbiased person I make bold to say that factual support for sweeping condemnation is hard to find.

Even before the day of the present fleet of miniature luxury liners—in the days (and nights) when the old *Plover* and *Lapwing*, and *Lochiel* and *Shiela*; the tiny *Cygnet* and the tubby *Handa*, and other boats of that generation, were the shuttles that ploughed their way from port to port carrying merchandise, mails, and passengers — the service was never so bad as it was painted. True, the saloon might be small, and there was no guarantee that you wouldn't find yourself rolling on its floor amongst the debris from the dinner-table which, as the result of an extra "big one," had been debunked of its broth or finnan haddies and general crockery. But MacBraynes didn't make the Minch; nor do they control the strong tides or raging gales that so frequently rouse it to furious wrath.

And the boats, if somewhat cramped, were sturdy craft of a marvellous pertinacity.

As for the men-in-charge, from captain to cabin-boy, they were a courteous, courageous breed. None so fully as they knew the thin line which so often marked the difference between "making it" and disaster; but their seamanship was superb and their courage great. May I say in passing that their successors of to-day are well maintaining the old traditions; and so far as I am concerned the only point on which I should like to be assured is that so hardy and hard-worked a class of men are adequately remunerated, and that they can look forward to a pensioned retirement from which they may in comfort look back with reminiscent pleasure on their stirring days of sailing.

One winter night many years ago I was to join the *Plover* at Lochmaddy for Lochboisdale. She was due to leave at nine P.M. and to arrive at twelve midnight. A fresh easterly breeze had blown all day. By seven o'clock it had risen sharply. By nine it looked like blowing up for a real nasty night. It was not till ten that the *Plover* berthed at Lochmaddy. When I went to go aboard Captain Black—a great little sailor—shook his head doubtfully.

"It's bad outside the loch: I was glad to get in. If it doesn't slacken soon we will have to lie here all night," was the verdict.

I confess the decision was to my liking, for the wind was playing terrifying tunes with the masts and rigging. But with an early-morning start in view it would be as well to go on board for the night. So I did.

Instead of abating, by eleven o'clock the gale had developed into a hurricane. We were storm-stayed for the night and old "Angus the Pier," after consulting with the Captain, went off to his bed.

But within an hour the unbelievable happened: with amazing suddenness the wind died down. By eleven-forty-five it was dead calm. A few stars appeared.

"Most extraordinary!" was the Captain's comment. "But if this lasts for a little we'll go yet."

By contrast the calm seemed eerie; but it continued. At the Captain's request I helped to cast off the shore ropes, and off we slid out the loch.

Just as we passed the Big Maddy rock, and rounded the bend to set a course down off the east coast of the islands, the stars disappeared. From the east an ink-black canopy came climbing up the sky. In a quarter of an hour we were blotted out from everything as completely as if covered by a gigantic shroud and we moved on through a Stygian night.

I was up on the bridge having a yarn with the Captain and just thinking of turning in. Suddenly the ship seemed to rise on top of a big wave that might be a legacy of the gale that had so recently and so eerily died down. But then she heeled over to starboard to such an alarming degree that we wondered if she was going clean over. It was when she was on the back roll from that that the monstrous sea struck her. Later the Captain told me it was the worst wave that had struck her in his experience. The towering fluid monster swept across her deck as if bent on her instant destruction.

Poor little *Plover* shivered, as a bantam boxer might well quake on finding that he has to fight for his life against a Dempsey. But surely a stouter-hearted bantam never donned gloves, for, while she was as yet recovering from the initial blow, she was struck by a sudden wind that was as the very breath of the Furies.

Never could I get the happenings of the next eight hours into reasonable sequence: but if the order of events gets all mixed up in my mind the recollection of that terrible night as a whole is vivid. The ship rolled and reared and pitched and tossed continuously; but it was when the bows got buried and the stern rose till the propeller raced in air, and all but stopped when it suddenly got a grip of the water again, or when the bow from the crest of a high wave shot upwards and then came slap down on the water, so that the ship, like a sentient suffering creature, shuddered from stem to stern, that one felt awed by the devastating powers of nature. It is doubtful if anyone on board really believed that the *Plover* could survive that terrible storm.

As the gale was from the east, the Captain's greatest concern was to steer well clear of the rocky coast to the west. So he set a course calculated to keep her well out in the Minch. Setting a course was one thing, but the extent to which the helm in that terrifying turmoil of waters could effectively impel the ship in the desired direction was a very different matter; for in addition to the disturbing strength of the water there was the problem of the immeasurable drift-effect of the wind. If only we could get one blink of the Usinish Light! But though we looked for it till our eyes ached—and we looked the whole night through—never a beam from that good light managed to pierce the awful darkness.

Not until about eight in the morning did the outline of South Uist show ever so faintly to the west; and although the sea was still running hills-high the relief which came with the certain knowledge of where we were is indescribable. For nearly eight hours now the gallant *Plover* had taken such a hammering that somehow one wanted to embrace her! Now in the light we felt cheered and confident and safe.

Meantime, in Lochmaddy, at six A.M. the Piermaster looked out of his window to confirm if the storm was as wild as it sounded. Looking in the direction of the pier he wondered why he didn't see the headlight of the *Plover*. It was pitch-dark, but the pier was only a hundred yards away. If the light was there he was bound to see it! Hurriedly Angus got into his clothes, lit his storm-lantern, and made for the pier. No *Plover*! He fought his way to the house of his nearest neighbour. The neighbour was nearly sure he had seen the *Plover*'s lights going out the loch about midnight—the wind had gone down by then. By seven Angus roused the Postmaster. The mails had been put on board last night at ten-thirty but the Postmaster understood the boat wouldn't start till morning.

Then came a telegram from Lochboisdale: Was the *Plover* still at Lochmaddy? This looked bad! The indications were that the *Plover* had left Lochmaddy at midnight; to Lochboisdale was only a three hours' run. Even making more than usual allowance for stress of weather she looked long overdue. More telegrams flew up and down the islands. The men at the lighthouse hadn't seen a sign of her! And that awful night!

Within half an hour the alarm spread. Alarm soon changed to conviction. The *Plover* was lost with all on board! Well, well! She had been a grand boat. Many's the hammering she got in her day but the Minch had beaten her at last!

But the Minch hadn't. At half-past nine, to the surprise and joy of the crowd on the pier, the *Plover* turned in to the shelter of Lochboisdale and was soon lying snug in her berth.

"A wild passage, Captain," said the hotelkeeper.

"Och, indeed! not too good," said the Captain.

CHAPTER XVI

Bride's Dilemma—Long Telegram—Happy Sequel

In the darkening of a winter's day I pedalled along the roughish road that encircled the island. Wind as usual dead ahead, at every turn I had to stand on the crank to keep the wheels moving. Walking would have been quicker, but youthful vigour disdained that indignity. So, with ten miles to go, and a hunger that would not shrink at fried frogs, I stubbornly shoved along at something like three miles an hour.

Soon I would be passing the schoolhouse, where the restful arm-chair by the big peat fire harmonised so perfectly with the refreshing cup and cordial welcome which were the portion of all callers at that oasis. But I was in a hurry to reach journey's end and had already dealt with this temptation of the schoolhouse; firmly had I set Satan astern and was even now taking to myself full consolatory credit for that manly resolution.

Just then, all of a sudden, didn't that schoolhouse door open wide, to throw a magnetic path of light from it to my front wheel! Alas for good resolution, and *Ochanee* for human frailty! Without conscious guiding on my part if that wheel didn't turn straight for the schoolhouse door! Any chance there might have been of recovering self-respect was completely shattered by the lady teacher who now materialised in the doorway: a bonnie lassie, whose hospitality was only equalled by that of her aunt, the much-loved District Nurse, who lived with her.

But there was unwonted tension in the atmosphere of that fireside that evening. One sensed it immediately. Clearly the teacher had something on her mind; nor had the Nurse offered us one of her fund of original jokes.

"What on earth is it that's stringing you up?" I asked.

"This," said the Nurse, pointing to a huge parcel which I had already noticed.

"And what's that?" I asked, wondering.

"It's her wedding frock," said the Nurse, indicating her niece. "She is getting married in Glasgow on Wednesday of next week. The frock was made by a Glasgow firm and it arrived here by post only half an hour ago."

Of course every soul on the island knew the *Banamhaighstir sgoile* was getting married, but we were hazy about the date.

"Hooray!" says I. "Good luck! And I hope the frock is a good fit."

"That's what's bothering us," said Nurse. "From the glance we've had of it it looks on the big side—and of course we can't try it on!"

"Just that," I agreed, well knowing how unlucky a try-on of a wedding frock might be. "But surely we can have a good look at it any way."

"Certainly," agreed Teacher, loosening the strings and removing the tissue.

With trembling hands she held up the frock for our inspection. The done thing on such occasions is to exclaim "Beautiful! Exquisite!" But there was a something about that frock, evident even to a masculine eye, that forbade commendation.

"Gosh!" I gasped, "it looks bonnie enough, but it certainly does look on the big side."

"Oh! I'm sure it's far too big for me," moaned the bride, who was rather petite in her proportions. "It looks to me to be big enough for Aunty!"—with which conviction I agreed; and Aunty was *not* petite!

"Look here!" I protested. "You can't risk appearing

in that at your wedding. Circumstances are desperate, you know; you must have a try-on."

"But even if we know it's a misfit there's no time to have it put right now," she cried, loth to risk her luck.

"You would look just fine in your Harris tweed," I suggested.

But that was too much for those ceremonial days.

"Anyhow," helped Aunty, "you must try it on till we see, and we'll just chance the luck."

"Off you go, the two of you!" I urged; and the two women disappeared with the precious parcel.

In a couple of minutes or so there came from the bedroom shrieks of hysterical laughter that might easily change to weeping. Then the bride sailed in in her wedding frock. Literally, it took my breath away. It wasn't merely a misfit: it was a monstrosity. It was big enough to overlap even Aunty's ample form! A few minutes were devoted to saying things of the Glasgow firm and their precious traveller that should burn up all their ears.

The traveller, by the way, had called at the schoolhouse that same afternoon to give the soothing assurance that the frock would be by that evening's post. If only he had waited to see this awful thing! But no. He had pushed on to be in time to get across the ford. He was now on the other side and a good dozen miles away

There are rare times when it is given to ordinary mortals to rise and shine: to overcome the impossible. "I'll have a shot at it any way," I promised; "and even if I fail you will be no worse off than you are now."

From a work-basket an inch-tape was produced. Within five minutes the Nurse and myself, working co-operatively, had taken and noted all measurements that mattered (we hoped!). In a jiffy I disposed of a substantial meal. The old Rudge was brought forth and off

I set towards the ford. There, of course, what had been dry sand two hours before was now deep in the tide. But the old postman had a boat, and knew every turn and sandbank of that treacherous ferry. The urgency of the case was explained to him—and he was game. For hours, it seemed, he piloted that boat with the sureness of a seal, finally landing me in the dark on the rocky shore on the other side. There was a mile from that rock to the beginning of the road and then five miles to the hotel where I hoped to catch up with my traveller man. Peat-bogs and ditches made heavy going as I humped the old Rudge from the rock to the road, but that night I felt like a knight of old inspired by a great resolve.

In pleasant contemplation of rest well won the traveller was ensconced in the hotel's deepest arm-chair, with a spot of comfort in a glass on a near-by table. Did he have a rude awakening! . . .

To him it was clear that a bloomer had been made in the dispatch department: the wrong frock had been sent!

Within half an hour a five-and-ninepenny telegram giving correct measurements and demanding the production without fail of a brand-new frock for the wedding morning was on its way to Glasgow. Nor—as I learned later—did the Glasgow firm let us down.

That happened a long, long time ago. Shortly after the event I met the young couple. We never happened to meet again.

But last autumn, in a Highland glen I learned that a new teacher had recently come to the school; a young lady not long qualified.

"What's the name of your new teacher?" I asked one of the youngsters. The reply threw my mind in a flash back over the years. "Can it be?" I wondered.

I would call. I did. At the schoolhouse there was an

elderly little lady with wavy white hair. "But I thought the teacher was a *young* lady!" I stammered.

"And so she is," smiled the little lady; "she is my daughter."

"Gosh! and I would know *your* voice anywhere!" said I.

"And I know yours," said she. . . .

Then her husband came in about, and for quite a while we spoke of the little school at Cladach on the island—and of an outsize in wedding frocks—and of a long telegram and its happy sequel.

CHAPTER XVII

WHAT between the Land League activities of the eighties
and nineties, the never-ending demands for roads and
paths and piers and postal facilities, and the land-raiding
which followed the last war, the Highlands and Islands of
Scotland must have given more headaches to politicians
and governments during the past half-century or so than
all other parts of the realm put together. It is simply
amazing how the comparative handful of electors in these
fastnesses of professed liberalism and practised con-
servatism manage to make each successive government
sit up and take notice. No doubt this mainly accounts
for the fact that practically every Secretary for Scotland
(or Secretary of State for Scotland, as the title now goes)
has, at some stage of his tenure of that uneasy office, paid
a personal visit to—as the newspapers with unfailing
humourless loyalty always announced—"inquire at first-
hand into the various problems affecting the Highlands
and Islands." As these investigational visits usually
take the form of an autumn holiday on board one of the
Fishery Cruisers—a most delightful experience, as I know
—it is permissible to smile at the idea of the annoyance of
some future holder of that high office were he to learn
that, as a result of his predecessors' efficiency, all such
problems had been solved! But I hasten to assure
aspirants to the office that it is a little doubtful if that joke
will ever materialise.

Anyhow, it was often part of my duty—and usually
pleasure—to prepare the necessary itinerary and pilot
the great man safely round with a wary eye on treacherous

fords and dangerous political swamps. At that time of year weather conditions were nearly always favourable. Being but human, there were times during these trips when I would have welcomed weather which would have given the visitors a conception more approximating the average of the year. Only once were my silent prayers thereanent adequately answered.

My Departmental Chief had come out to the islands to attend a series of agricultural shows. It was his first visit. He crossed a Minch like a mill-pond. He found the islands bathed in sunshine. In from the Atlantic came that warm gentle breath which shimmers in visible waves over the machairs, and sends the larks skywards in scores to pour on pedestrians their torrent of joyous song like a choral benediction from heaven.

The Chief was enchanted. What a country to live in! What a paradise! My feeble attempts at painting another side of the picture he ruthlessly brushed aside. In his view a week of that was well worth a winter of wind and rain!

Day after day, across the fords from island to island, and for nearly a week it was the same story: the same glory.

But for me it was somewhat annoying. If only he could get one real sample of the islands' weather-wickedness! But no! We crossed over to Dunvegan in an evening of unspeakable charm.

Next morning, looking out from my bedroom window I was cheered to see a mist curling down from the top of MacLeod's Tables. There was also hope in the general cheerlessness of that morning's atmosphere. Ah ha! Might I not soon have reason to chide myself for recent lack of faith in the efficacy of silent prayer?

At the door I met the Chief. He had noted the change but was not perturbed.

"There might be a few showers to-day," he informed me.

"I think there will be just one," I ventured; "but it might last all day," I added, not without a touch of genial venom. He pooh-poohed this, and reiterated that there would probably be a few showers in the forenoon but the sun should come out by midday.

We were bound that day for Kyleakin by car, and thence Kyle by ferry-boat. He took the seat of honour next Rory the driver. There he sat, a slim figure in light brown overcoat, stand-up collar and red tie, and a jaunty brown-felt hat.

I deemed it wise to don oilskin and sou'wester (which experience had advised as a routine part of the travelling outfit) and I sat in the back—and hoped and hoped.

As we started from the hotel the first big drops began to fall. At Fairy Bridge the rain no longer appeared as individual drops but as rods of water, which stotted up from the road—and from my Chief's head—with a grand ferocity. By Sligichan there was no change—unless perhaps an intensification of the downpour and of my unholy joy.

Half-way up the famous hill at Druim nan Cleochd it was still going strong. From the Chief's whiskers rivulets of water poured into his lap and were finding their way slowly but surely to the most intimate parts of his person. The road was a running burn and deeply tracked. The going was delightfully slow. As we were just about to top the summit there was a grand bang from the near rear tyre. The car stopped. Rory's announcement was brief but comprehensive:

"Butched!" said Rory.

And in very truth "butched" it was; for in those days, in the matter of providing against the possibility of *en route* repairs, Skye motor-drivers attained to the acme of optimism. A spare tyre was looked on as the last word in pessimism. The most that passengers could hope for was two or three ravaged repair outfits which between them might provide the wherewithal to patch a puncture in the inner tube. Rory ran true to type. His outfits— and an empty oil-can and some rusty levers with which he hoped in the next hour to wrench the tyre from the rusty rim—were deposited in a cavity underneath the Chief's seat. The Chief had to come to earth to let Rory get to his Pandora's box.

Oh, that lovely lingering mending! The first patch blew off as we were squeezing the cover over the rim. So we had to start all over again, including (in the absence of sandpaper) the "cleaning" of the patch-area with a mixture of spit and lucifer match. It took over an hour to complete the job, and all the time the rain continued to fall in torrents.

At Kyleakin there was a smart wind blowing and "white horses" out on the ferry. The ferryman was reluctant, but ultimately agreed to row us across. About half-way it was really rough.

Maybe the ferryman looked at me; maybe I looked at him. Maybe there was a word in the Gaelic. I can't right mind. Anyhow, the ferryman was a highly intelligent man, with skill in his job. But somehow, yon big wave took him unawares; and so it took my Chief unawares—a good half-ton of it right on his crown. And while he was still gasping for breath there came another one. The ferryman was profuse with his apologies.

I still see that drookit creature shivering on the shore at Kyle. Hat, coat, boots, and whiskers were one soaked whole. There was a gruesomely suggestive blood-red ring round his throat—but that was only the dye in the tie that had run.

CHAPTER XVIII

Moloch of Speed—Moorland Mixture—An Ardent Angler—
Troubles of a Stalker's Wife

THIS worship of efficiency and speed to which we are now so prone has no place for praise of the more haphazard and leisurely transport systems of not so many years ago. Then, a stationmaster was master in his station; a guard could, for a sensible friendly purpose, stop a train off the official schedule; even a porter could be a man, and the driver of a mail-coach wielded the power of a commander-in-chief.

But indeed this modern craze for efficiency and speed is only symptomatic of our attitude towards life generally. From the cradle to the grave life is becoming a senseless sort of sprint that is just idiotic. Mark our parental pride and approbation when wee Johnnie cuts his first tooth a month ahead of our neighbour's bairn!—or if he is first to pass the "Ta-ta" or "Daddy" tape! Later, his speed at "learning" in school is equally acclaimed. In adolescent days, by common consent, his "success" is measured by the speed with which he accumulates wealth or rank or power. Yet when we come to shake round the advantages to the average person of this high speed and efficiency business we are left with mighty little in the sieve; we may well wonder why all the hurry or where does the real advantage come in? This speeding merely intensifies the process of accumulating hustle; and the necessity for hustle is one of the great delusions of the age. Hustling! Hustling for what? "Saving time" seems such a comical idea—as if time were in limited supply!

Yet we are all apt to be caught in the whirl. I know a white-haired commercial gentleman who used to enjoy a sixty-mile journey in the old mail-coach that was supposed to do the run in eight hours (but never did), or who chugged along at ten miles an hour from pier to pier (D.V. and W.P.). He now flashes from place to place in an aeroplane at 150 miles an hour and grumbles if the thing is a few minutes behind schedule. In the old days he took a friendly human interest in every house and person by the way. Even with the cats and dogs and cows he was on friendly terms. Now he has "no time"; he rushes past the interesting, friendly things in life. Soon, as a result of the ever-increasing speed of the means of locomotion, our capacity for abstracting pleasure from the contemplation of the homely things by the wayside will be lost. . . .

When resident in the far north it was sometimes necessary—or so youthful enthusiasm decided—that, in order to catch a passenger train starting at five A.M. from a station further down the line I must leave from the terminus by an overnight goods train. For the right to travel in luxury in the guard's van you had to pay first-class fare, and sign a declaration that in the event of being killed in transit you wouldn't make a compensation claim against the company. One winter's night on such a journey I was flat out and sound asleep on the hard seat at the rear of the van. A sudden stop pitched me off the seat and sent me rolling along the corrugated floor.

"What's up?" I asked the guard.

"She's stuck in the snow," he explained. "You better get up and give a hand."

We were at one of the bleakest parts of the moor: not a house within miles. Against such emergencies several shovels were carried in the van. All the available strength—driver, fireman, guard, and self—set to work on a drift quite ten feet deep. Fortunately it wasn't very long. In an hour, by the light of the moon, we made substantial inroads on the block, the engine was backed for a charge, and pouff! we were through.

Half an hour later we were jangling along about the middle of the moor. I was just dozing off again when, for no reason that I could think of—we were miles from a station—the train gradually slowed down and finally stopped. Then, of all unexpected things, the high note of a pipe-chanter with a background of dance music from a melodeon! Just at first I thought I was "hearing things," but soon there was no doubt: the music was real enough.

"What on earth is it?" I inquired of the guard, who was looking out at the van door.

"Och! just a little splore," he explained. "We are at the surfaceman's house at ——. His daughter got married yesterday and there is a bit of a dance at the house to-night. We canna pass without wishing them luck." And off out he went; and so did the driver and fireman and myself, and in we went to the cottage, that you could see only as a snow-covered mound with fiery window eyes and an open door. We got a tremendous welcome. Inside there were over a score of friends doing justice to the occasion in song and dance and feasting. Nothing would do but each of us in turn must have a dance with the bride. Fortified by generous drops of the *creutair* we had a strenuous half-hour of revelry before puffing off on the train again, and were just in time to catch up with the "passenger" at five A.M.

A favourite guard was Jimmie. He was gifted with a magnificent thirst and thrice blessed with a marvellous instinct for spotting opportunities for quenching it. The day there was nothing in your flask he just walked along the corridor giving you a cheery wave in the passing. He came in to speak to you only when there was "something doing." Just how he divined was a mystery, but he was seldom wrong, and it was seldom in the length of the train that he drew a complete blank. One such depressing day, at a remote station the train was held up for longer than usual. Passengers looked out at windows to ascertain the cause. They saw a group of railway officials, including Jimmie, gathered near the van. One had a hammer with which he solemnly tapped an axle. The driver held an "ile poorie" in his hand.

"A heated axle, but she'll be right in ten minutes," explained Jimmie to the nearest passengers. The news was passed up from coach to coach and passengers sat back resigned. I happened to be sitting opposite the gate at the side entrance to the station. Through this gate sauntered the young red-headed porter. But when he got the station between him and the train he sprinted like a hare for the hotel—some two hundred yards to the rear. In a couple of minutes he sprinted back again, came slowly through the gate and sauntered towards the group at the heated axle. They all disappeared into the van. Very soon they were out again. The driver and fireman hurried forward to the engine.

"All right now!" bawled Jimmie, for general information, and waving the green flag.

A little later he was passing up the corridor much more cheerful as to countenance.

"It's a good job you noticed it at the station," said I.

"Wasn't it?" he grinned.

As might be expected of one of Jimmie's particular gift he was an ardent angler and missed no opportunity of plying the gentle art. Against possible chances he always had with him in the van a smart little trouting rod.

The first time I saw him in action was at a certain station where a nice stream runs below the railway bridge just about where the van is when the train stops. It was a north-going train and considerably behind scheduled time. This meant that we would have to give way to the south-coming train—not due for nearly half an hour. Some travellers went the length of saying that Jimmie manœuvred matters so that such delays must happen. Indeed I wouldn't put it past him! Anyhow, this day he was not long in getting to work with his rod and within twenty minutes I saw him put five nice trout in the basket.

.   .   .   .

Then there was yon day the mail-coach driver stopped to collect a letter from the stalker's wife. We found the lady in an embarrassing dilemma. That morning her man and his fellows, with a number of terriers, had gone miles away to a *saobhaidh* (foxes' den) to try to exterminate Reynard and all his pernicious brood. The men might not be back till to-morrow night. At home there was a fretting infant who could not be left alone. There wasn't a neighbour within miles. And if that brute Molly (a rakish red cow), with the perverseness characteristic of her sex, hadn't chosen that very morning to display unmistakable and determined manifestations of an urgent desire for an amorous liaison! The nearest entire male of her species was stanced at a farm nearly four miles down the glen. To a stalker a calf is a calf, especially a spring calf, and for that it was already late enough in the season. Clearly, measures had to be taken.

Molly was separated from her sympathetic but futile companions. A rope was tied round her horns. I sat at the back of the coach grasping the other end of the rope. The driver gathered the reins. The stalker's wife with a supple hazel switch helped to give us a trotting start—and off we were.

Of course we couldn't go too fast, but after a while it seemed the purport of the unusual form of convoy must have dawned on Molly's intelligence, and for the last mile she put her best foot foremost with a will.

Less than a year later the driver told me he had the satisfaction of carrying, shrouded in a sugar-bag, the outcome of Molly's liaison, and that it had been sold at Dingwall for three pounds ten.

CHAPTER XIX

Reformers' Troubles—The Cult of the Pig (ancient and modern)

IT was with no little self-complacency I read over one of my early annual reports before dispatching it to headquarters. The section dealing with

SUGGESTIONS FOR SCHEMES OF WORK

AND

FUTURE DEVELOPMENTS

was particularly satisfactory. It had afforded full scope for my genius in that direction. A less biased reader might have detected in it signs of that smug arrogance which emboldens some people to make rude intrusion into the affairs of others by advocating fundamental changes in their customs, habits, and beliefs; that arrogance, for instance, which pious elderly ladies and others display in rendering financial aid to those proselytising activities which for the most part result in the questionable "conversion" of Jews or in transforming happy Hottentots into perplexed and doubtful Christians.

But such sobering reflections were to come only later. In the meantime, there was my report with its masterly survey of "defects" and of the required "remedial measures"—*Eg*.

I. In the Hebrides there was a large area of sandy loam soil, an abundance of seaweed, and a mild climate. The combination made circumstances ideal for the growing of early potatoes and other vegetables. Yet few other vegetables were grown, and not one early potato. *Ergo*, "Go to it," as the phrase now runs.

II. *Poultry.*—But for (*a*) the accident of weddings—which might involve her in a violent death and accord her an honoured place on the Hymeneal board, and (*b*) occasional disease-epidemics—which rendered her liable to a lingering death and subsequent indecent exposure and putrefaction—the Hebridean hen might hold her place on the home midden for years without number; indeed the older she grew the more firmly did she become established in the affections of her mistress. Clearly a reforming bomb must be dropped on this department.

III. *Pigs.*—Except for a pig or two at the hotels, not a pig in the place! And an abundance of potatoes and house and dairy swill going to waste!

I determined to make pigs my first concern. I recommended that three breeding sows should be placed with selected "custodians" at convenient centres. In course, piglets would be made available on such attractive terms that every crofter in the neighbourhood would be in the new industry. From small beginnings a big industry would develop. Even the necessity for a bacon-curing factory was visualised.

Unaccustomed as I then was to the strain which so revolutionary a proposal would place on the Departmental digestive system, I was much hurt when at the end of a fortnight no official approval of my pig scheme came through; indeed it didn't even receive any official acknowledgment. In a month I was enthusiastic about something else. In three months pigs had faded from my immediate outlook. Then one morning I received a telegram:

"Three farrowing sows left Oban by *Lochiel* to-day arrange with custodians."

By the way, the S.S. *Lochiel* was due to arrive at midnight, but oftener than not she would sail in around three

A.M. One of the custodians I had had in mind lived six miles from the pier, another eight, and the third a good ten miles away. Weeks ago they had given up any idea that the pigs I had spoken of would ever come. Besides, they were far from enthusiastic in the matter at any time, and sensitive as to what their neighbours would say about them. From forenoon till after dark I cycled feverishly from place to place arguing and cajoling crofters—the wives had to be won over too—to agree to take a sow and —when a grudging assent was finally extracted—helping to build suitable accommodation in the steading for the unwelcome addition to the live stock.

As per usual in such matters, news of the coming of the pigs went round the island like a broadcast. There was a record gathering that night to meet the *Lochiel*. Thank heaven, my three "custodians" had come with their carts, but they were anything but happy in their rôle of pig-pioneers and I was mortally afraid the chaffing of their neighbours would send them off home before the boat arrived. From midnight to three A.M. that night was for them and for me a nightmare of discomfort and apprehension. It required considerable liquid bribery ("closed" hours were then and there happily unknown) to keep my men till three-thirty, when Captain Mac-Dougall, after one of his worst crossings of the Minch, at long last berthed up at the pier.

The Captain met me at the top of the gangway.

"The sows . . . " I began.

"Blast the sows!" said he, with a horrible heartiness. "Squealing stubborn brutes; and one of them can go back home: her six young ones were born in the middle of the Minch. They were all dead and were thrown overboard."

"Say not a word about that on the pier," I warned him sternly. "There is plenty trouble without that!"

To the accompaniment of blood-curdling porcine protests, the terror of the horses (which had to be held by half a dozen men apiece), and the humorous comments of the crowd on the pier, each pig was put into her cart. It was ten o'clock next morning when I got back from seeing each sow established in her new home.

The fortnight that followed is one which I would fain forget. From the custodians came daily complaints. The sows' appetite was far in excess of anything they had anticipated. Then one day a telegram from No. 1 custodian demanding my immediate presence at the croft. There I was met by a distracted couple. Their sow had given birth to seven young ones but not a drop of milk had she for them! In major grunts and minor squeals old and young bewailed their lot. Neither the crofter nor his wife would keep the brutes another hour. I must take them away that very day!

Just then along came the wife of custodian No. 2. A wrathful woman! Her sow had eaten them out of house and home and still showed no signs of having any young ones. This—God forgive me!—caused me to express surprise. While I was frantically trying to extemporise a solution for this peck of troubles along came a boy on a bicycle with a message from custodian No. 3. *His* sow had given birth to nine. She had made a breakfast of five, smothered the remaining four, and was now troubled with an unwanted flow of milk!

Grateful for small mercies I collected the seven starving piglets in a box and had them straightway transferred to the now desolate and penitent cannibal, in whose milk I soused them so that the fostering was soon successfully completed. That fortuitous combination was the only bright patch in my precious plan for establishing pigs in the Hebrides. But even for the survivors there were no bidders on the island. Within a year the pigless

Hebrides were pursuing their wonted blissful way.   That year, too, I came across a book written just a hundred years before my advent in the Hebrides.   There had been an "improver" there then too; and he too recommended the keeping of pigs.   And just as I write this— thirty years after my own disillusionment—I have officially submitted to me "for observations" a report from the present-day Agricultural Organiser in the Hebrides—and *he* sees a great future for pigs there! Good luck to him!

CHAPTER XX

Harvest on the *Machair* —Milkmaids at the *Buaile* — Standard of the *Sugan*

As a good character and repute are as desirable in a crofter as in a king, the selecting of a tenant for one of our holdings always caused me much concern. It was while questing for confidential and reliable information regarding an applicant for a holding that I received from an old native the mystifying reply:

"*Och! Faodaidh e bhi mar sud no mar so, ach gu dearbh cha chuala mise riamh gu do chaill aon de'n t-seorsa sguab as an t-sugain*" ("Och! he may have his good points and his bad; but indeed I never heard that one of his kind ever lost a sheaf from the *sugan*").

Here, clearly, was the retort parabolic, but it was a new one on me; so I asked for light.

"Och," said he, "it is just a way we have here of speaking well or not so well, but at least truthfully, of a man according to the reputation of his forebears."

"But what is the whole story?" I asked, keen for light on darkness. So we sat for an hour on the *garadh-fail* (feal dyke) while the old man expounded the intricacies of a highly developed communal system that is as interesting as it is instructive. The system was still in full operation in his township and in some of the others, but it worked so smoothly that an outsider might live on the island for a lifetime and never know anything about it. Here is my attempt at the picture.

On most estates in the Hebrides the subdivision is mainly of the "township" nature. A township comprises an irregular number of crofts whose tenants in addition to having individual lands have common use of certain areas. In the township which the old man described to me the croft was made up of a share in three different areas of land, in addition to the land held in individual occupation. The three shared lands were:

Machair (sandy land near the sea);

Geàrraidh (superior pasture-land for milch cows);

Monadh (hill pasture for sheep).

The individually occupied *Dubhthalamh* (black or loamy land) was where his house and steading were built, and came in between the *Machair* and the *Geàrraidh*.

The *Machair* is the flat sandy land (though sometimes broken with bent-covered sand-dunes) which lies between the seashore inwards to where the *Dubhthalamh* begins. A dyke or fence roughly parallel with the shore separates *Machair* from *Dubhthalamh*. The *Machair* (which may extend to several hundreds of acres) is subdivided into large fields. A field is known as a *sgat*. On each *sgat* there are as many rigs as there are crofts in the township. Always, two or three or more *sgats* are in cultivation. After bearing crops for two or three years in succession the *sgat* is allowed to rest for some years. It is not sown out to grass but left to natural regenerative processes. By the end of a year or two it will be well covered with a variety of more or less useful pasture plants.

It follows that each year a *sgat* will fall due to be left out of cultivation and that another which has been long rested must be brought into cropping. At the beginning of winter the township "Constable" calls a meeting of all the tenants to decide which *sgat* should be thus brought in. The Constable, by the way, is one of the crofters who has been appointed by the *Bàilidh* (Factor) as his local agent. After the *sgat* for cultivation has been decided on there is a meeting on the ground to allocate to each man his rig. This is done by a form of double ballot. The rigs are numbered. For the first draw the Constable puts papers in his hat numbered up to the number of tenants. The men approach the hat for the first draw not in any regular order. But that draw is only to decide the order in which each man will approach the hat for his second draw. It is the number on his second paper that determines the number of his rig.

This rig is his until that *sgat* is left to rest again two or three years hence; and from the moment that his lot is known his main concern in life seems to be the manuring of that rig. Throughout the winter and spring, in fair weather and foul, he is cutting and collecting and carting incredible quantities of seaweed on to it. There is sharp, all-round rivalry as to who will get the best crop out of his rig. The effect, in early autumn, when two or three *sgats* of maybe thirty acres each are bearing beautiful crops of barley, potatoes, *coirce-beag*, or rye, is very impressive indeed; and the stately herds of Highland cattle as they move with majestic leisure, grazing over the pastures of the *Machair*, complete a remarkable scene of rural beauty and peace.

Lying inland from the *Dubhthalamh* is the *Geàrraidh*, with its rich pasture, where the milk cows are summered. From the day they are put out to the *Geàrraidh* till the approach of winter they never enter a byre. Each evening, after milking, they are driven into the *buaile* (a spacious stone-built enclosure or fold) by the *buachaille* (herd), who lets them out again for milking in the morning.

Buachailleachd is often an hereditary job. As part of his remuneration he occupies, rent-free, a small house and croft within the township. During the summer and autumn when all the cows are out at pasture—and there may be well over a hundred of them to look after—the *buachaille* is provided with a daily assistant. This assistant —often a lad or an old man or woman—must be supplied

from each house in the township in turn. On Monday
the assistant will come from No. 1 house; on Tuesday
from No. 2, and so on, right round and round every croft
till the end of the season. The croft from which the
assistant comes has also on that day to give the *buachaille*
his dinner. As may be surmised, than the *buachaille* there
is no sounder judge of the standard of culinary skill
amongst the housewives of the township!

One of the sights of the islands is the morning and
evening trek to the milking. In the morning each family
group of cows, recently released from the *buaile*, hangs
around looking with expectant eyes for the coming of the
mistress, who sometimes brings the gift of a specially
succulent titbit, in return for which—and bewitched by
a Gaelic song—"*Ciabhag*" cheerfully acquiesces in the
theft of her progeny's birthright. After milking, each
cow strolls off to begin that almost never-ending foraging
that will ensure filled pails again in the evening.

The number of cattle a crofter may keep is regulated
by his "souming"—usually expressed in cows, or *cailep*,
which is the eighth part of a cow. Thus if the "souming"
for a croft is 8 cows, that equals 64 *cailep*. A three-year-
old beast equals 6 *cailep*; a two-year-old 4, and a one-
year-old (or stirk) 2 (calves are "off the coupon");
and so long as he does not exceed his total souming a man
may make up his stock in any way that suits him best.
For instance, on such a place he would probably have:

$$
\begin{array}{llll}
5 \text{ cows} \times 8 & = 40 \ \textit{cailep} \\
1 \text{ three-year-old} \times 6 = & 6 & ,, \\
2 \text{ two-year-olds} \times 4 = & 8 & ,, \\
5 \text{ stirks} \times 2 & = 10 & ,,
\end{array}
$$

Total   64 *cailep*

Bulls were supplied from the big-farm folds, of which

in those days there were some very good ones. No money passed. The farmer loaned the bull to the township in return for a specified number of days' work to be provided by the crofters at harvest, peat-cutting, sheep-smearing, etc.

The wintering of the bull was also an obligation on the township. At the end of harvest a meeting was held to decide whether the crop that year was a big one, a poor one, or a middling one. On that decision depended the daily ration of the bull throughout the winter: he was fed in accordance with the bountifulness (or otherwise) of Providence.

The exact measure of the bull's big, little, or medium ration was governed by the *sugan*. The *sugan* was a short rope made of pleated bent-grass. It had a loop at one end. Towards the other end there were three knots, each about six inches from the other. The obligation to provide the day's ration for the bull fell on each crofter in the township in turn. Each evening, to-day's supplier would pass on the township *sugan* to to-morrow's supplier. The ration was in the form of sheaves of *coirce-beag*. The *sugan* was stretched on the ground. Sheaves were laid on it to the number which would allow of the burden being tightened by the *sugan* to the appropriate knot for that year. But, as everyone knows who has tied a burden in that fashion, the degree of security of the load will depend on the degree of tightness of the rope. Therefore, when loop and knot met, if the burden was still loose— in other words, if you hadn't put enough sheaves in (or more plainly still, *if you were trying to cheat the bull*)—the chances were that some of the sheaves would fall out before you reached the bull-house with your burden. What clearer evidence of mean dishonesty and disgrace: *you had lost sheaves from the sugan*. And so to this day in the island a man is well spoken of (or not so well) according as his forebears were honest (or not so honest) with the feeding of the bull.

"Now," concluded the old man, "you will understand my answer to your question about Norman: 'Och! he may have his good points and his bad; but indeed I never heard that one of his kind ever lost a sheaf from the *sugan.*'"

CHAPTER XXI

The Magic-lantern—High Jeenks—A Sheep and a Lamb—
Controlling the Shebeen

LITTLE did I dream, as I waited for the mail gig in the dark and wet and wind of that March morning, of the stirring time which was waiting for me round the corner. "Round the corner" is really a figure of speech, though; for there were seventeen miles to travel to the ferry in yon hideously plain and battered dog-cart that on alternate days carried His Majesty's mail to the outposts; and then a two hours' row in a boat before I would reach my destination—and, as it happened, the locus of an unexpected experience.

Meantime (six A.M.) at the town post office the angular "shalt" that supplied the motive power for the dog-cart champed his bit and did some semi-prancing that might have encouraged a stranger to think he would make short work of the miles once he got a-going. I was saved that pitfall, for well I knew how soon the initial burst of speed would slacken to a sober trot that would so readily come to a dead stop on the slightest prospect of a wayside gossip. Most of the way it was that jog-jog, jog-jog, jog-jog which only the combination of a slow-trotting horse and an ill-balanced dog-cart can produce. By the end of the second hour you felt that the eternal nid-nid-nodding of your head was seriously threatening your mental equilibrium and your one comforting reflection was the knowledge of the rousing effect on your liver. With the exception of restful minutes at road-ends, where there were exchanges of courtesies and news, and the driver was entrusted with a variety of commissions, this physical-jerks process continued during the four hours which the old horse took to do the seventeen miles to the ferry. To add to the charms of the drive, business-like showers of sleet came pelting along every half-hour or so. It takes a very special arrangement of rugs and oilskins to success-fully resist such sleety onslaughts, and I know of no more dismaying moment than that in a dog-cart when you suddenly realise that all your careful sartorial dispositions for securing immunity for your person have failed: that even now your posterior is in direct and chilling contact with a pool of ice-cold water!—and that there are still many miles to go!

When we emerged refreshed from the ferry-house we were gladdened by a decided improvement in the day. It looked as if a whimsical Weather Clerk, regretting his earlier scurvy treatment of us, was trying to make amends. He succeeded too; and the row down the loch in the shelter of a friendly island was in genial sunshine.

At the landing-jetty a small crowd of young men were waiting. Even before we landed they shouted to ask if I had brought my magic-lantern with me. This lantern, by the way, had proved an excellent "draw" at lectures; but as it happened I hadn't brought it on this journey. It was only when the situation was fully explained that I understood the keen disappointment which this omission caused amongst the lads on the jetty. Here was their story.

Two months previously the younger spirits in the township had decided that, as one item in a general effort to raise funds for a cattle-show, a concert should be held. But never in history had a concert of any kind desecrated that stronghold of Calvinism. The daring promoters got their first rebuff when the local school-management committee, headed by the minister, refused them the use of the school. Also there had been some pointed pulpit references to the "freevolities of the rising generation."

Somewhat daunted, but wholly determined, the lads applied to the School Board, who, greatly daring, granted them the use of the school in face of the local ban. But this had caused delay. The concert, which had been fixed for a date early in February, had to be postponed. It was now timed to take place on the very evening of the day of my arrival. But alas! feared by the frown of the Church, most of those who had been depended on to contribute songs and music had asked to be excused. Defeat was staring the committee in the face. Then came a hope when they heard that "*Fear an ìm*" ("The butter man"—I used to lecture on butter-making) was coming and that he might be bringing his magic-lantern— now of considerable local renown. They had telegraphed the previous evening asking me to be sure to bring it— but now realised that the telegram could not possibly be delivered before I left that morning. The position was desperate. Would I send a telegram at once to instruct that the magic-lantern be sent to the ferry by special hire that day? They would themselves boat it in good time from the ferry.

There was only one thing to do; and it was done. Moreover, unlike some island last-minute efforts of that nature, there was no disappointment: the magic-lantern did arrive in good time to take an honourable place at a memorable concert.

Meantime, local excitement was running high, the pro- and anti-concert elements doing their respective bests. For better or worse I, of course, was in the camp of the former.

"What sort of a programme are you hoping to get together?" I inquired (an hour before the concert was billed to commence) of the Secretary, a genial giant with a noble contempt for ministerial inhibitions.

"There's no programme at all yet; but och! we'll

soon make a programme when we see who turns up," said this optimist.

At eight P.M. the Chairman, Secretary, members of Committee, and myself, accompanied by a band of enthusiastic supporters, set out to walk the two miles to the school—this with a charming indifference to the announcement in the handbills: "Doors open at 7 P.M. Concert begins at 7.30."

We arrived at eight-forty-five to find the school in total darkness. The schoolmaster was in the opposition camp, so merely left the school door unlocked. We lit the solitary hanging lamp. Not a sign as yet of an audience, but that caused no concern to the officials.

"They'll turn up all right before ten o'clock, you'll see," declared the secretary.

He was right: at about nine-thirty voices and footsteps were heard approaching. Within ten minutes a very large crowd had gathered at the door. Meantime, dispositions had been made for dealing with the two essentials—taking the money and preparing a programme. I was entrusted with the former duty and collected the shillings as fast as I could allow the people to pour in. It was a simple cash-down business. I just threw the money into an enamel milk-basin set on a near-by table.

The Chairman and Secretary (with the unsolicited assistance of ardent but not always unanimous advisers) prepared the programme. Their *modus operandi* was delightfully simple. The Secretary, with a double foolscap sheet of paper and pencil in hand, stood inside the door. The Chairman stood beside him acting as chief spotter. Every time he saw a likely artiste passing in he whispered to the Secretary to add that name to the rapidly increasing list of victims, who were as yet in complete and blissful ignorance of the honour conferred upon them.

By ten o'clock the big classroom was filled from its

back wall to within a desk-breadth of its inner side. In triumph the Secretary produced to the Chairman and myself his programme. The list of names extended over nearly two pages of foolscap: over seventy names in all. I ventured the opinion that that was on the big side: that indeed half that number would be more than enough.

"Och! we'll soon sort that, then," said the indomitable Secretary; and straightway, with a blue pencil, he proceeded ruthlessly to obliterate more than half of the names whose owners had so nearly but unwittingly attained to local fame. The names so summarily blotted out were of those judged to be less efficient performers, but the final list was not adjusted without some considerable differences of opinion amongst the small coterie of self-appointed advisers—who succeeded in getting one or two "reprieves." But in regard to a certain Donald MacLeod whose name had suffered blue-pencil extinction, when one admirer protested that the name should be left in because he (the admirer) had recently heard the same Donald sing beautifully at a certain wedding, the evidence was summarily rejected.

"Just that," agreed the Secretary: "very likely he would do well enough at a wedding but he's much too sober for to-night."

At ten-thirty everything was in readiness for a beginning with the concert. It was now the Chairman's turn to shine; and he did, spiritually and physically. He was a delightful old man with the heart of a lad of twenty. With singular independence he had scorned the carping criticisms of his coevals and given wholehearted support to the concert. There he stood now, rather tightly encased in his wedding suit of many many years ago. The coat had yon elusive pocket secreted in its tail. He had much difficulty in extracting from this hidey-hole a large-sized handkerchief needed frequently and urgently for wiping his profusely perspiring brow. His whitening beard still showed streaks of its pristine red. Normally his cheeks were of fresh and youthful colour: to-night, partly as a result of unwonted excitement—and partly no doubt as a result of frequent visits to the little class-room where a supply of liquid refreshment for the Committee and a few other privileged people had been cached —they shone like American apples, and his whole countenance radiated geniality all round.

Prompt at ten-thirty he got up to make his opening remarks. There was a gloriously defiant challenge in his voice and eye:

"Ladies and Gentlemen. Here we are at last, all ready to begin the first concert in the history of this parish. I am very pleased to see such a grand turn-out and I'm not going to say a word about those who ought to know better than to be in opposition to this concert. But I am glad to see that so many have more sense than those who are supposed to be their betters.

"And now the first item on the programme is a tune on the bagpipes by Johnnie Murray."

"No! No!" interposed the Secretary. "Johnnie was to come to the first concert but he was afraid to turn up to-night."

"What!" exclaimed the inspired Chairman. "I am not going to say a word about those who ought to know better than to be in opposition to the concert, but I cannot let the concert start without a piper."

"But there is no piper here, man! Just make a start with a Gaelic song and it will do fine," urged the Secretary.

"Never!" retorted the implacable Chairman. "I am not going to say a word about those (etc. etc.) . . . but if we start without a piper they will think we were afraid."

There was some desperate talk of sending some of the lads down to the Lodge (over two miles away) to see if the gamekeeper could be induced to come with his pipes; but it transpired that the keeper was from home.

The impasse was complete, so I whispered to the Chairman that if only we could get a set of pipes I would try to give them a tune myself and let him get on with the concert.

"What!" ejaculated the astonished autocrat. "Can you play the pipes?"

"Only a little and not very well," I protested, "but it would let you get on."

He was on his feet in a jiffy: "Ladies and Gentlemen. I am not going to say a word about those who should know better than to be in opposition to this concert, but we must begin the concert in proper style with the bagpipes. I am sorry to say our own piper has not turned up to-night, but we are very fortunate in having with us our good friend Mr MacDonald who is an old hand at the pipes, and he will give us an opening tune. The pipes are down at the keeper's. Three or four of you boys· there run down, like good lads, and get them here as quick as your legs will carry you. The men can light their pipes and have a smoke or make love to the lassies till the boys come back."

On the instant (eleven P.M.) half a dozen youths ran off over the moor in the direction of the keeper's house—where, it was surmised, the wife would still be afoot.

The principal "officials," including the prospective piper, repaired to the little classroom. Perhaps it was an illusion associated with this visit to the classroom, but anyway it did seem to me the boys hadn't been more than ten minutes gone when they were back with the pipes. A preliminary trial assured me that the pipes, though lacking tartan bag-cover and drone ribbons, were all right in the essentials. Again, the little classroom may have had something to do with this, but I do really believe that at that midnight hour, to open the concert I played as I never played before—nor since. Of one thing I have no doubt at all: never did I receive such an ovation.

The Chairman was riotously triumphant. He was not going to say a word, etc. . . ., "but that was a grand opening to the concert. The next item on the programme is a Gaelic song from——"

He peered through his spectacles but failed to decipher the name. Then, for the first time, everybody noticed that the single paraffin lamp was smoking so badly that the globe was black with soot. It was also discovered that the globe was cracked, so that cleaning without breaking it was out of the question. There was only one thing that could be done: the wick was screwed down, and we were left in all but complete darkness. But the Chairman, whose rosy countenance now reflected what little light there was, brushed the lamp incident aside as too trifling a matter to dim the happiness of great minds. By the light of a match he and the Secretary scrutinised the programme and agreed that the first item was due by Miss Mary MacLeod. But the point wasn't so easily settled as that: there happened to be several ladies of that name present and each one of them was now being urged by her immediate neighbours to step forth and sing. All of them refused the honour in quite emphatic terms. The ambiguity was removed only by the Chairman's explanation that the lady whose name was on the programme was Mary, the daughter of Donald, the son of Angus, the son of Big Malcolm. On that the persuasive efforts of the whole audience were concentrated in the direction of this highly honoured but embarrassed young lady. Her protests were of no avail. Out she had to go, propelled towards the floor by many muscular arms. But sing she did, naturally, easily, sweetly, one of those haunting Gaelic songs that go so near to making a bairn of a grown man. She was encored twice—and so, for that matter, was every one of the other singers; who, by the way, were announced in similar fashion and made similar initial protests against the unexpected honour. But the concert was now in full swing and going merrily.

By four A.M. we were well down towards the finish of the first half of the programme; but we were destined never to hear the rest of it, for just then the Chairman had an inspiration which would make a mere concert pale into insignificance as a red rag to those who ought to know better . . .

"Ladies and Gentlemen," he announced, "I am not going to say a word about those who ought to know better than to be in opposition to this concert, but I am sure that you will agree with me that we have had a most enjoyable evening so far [*loud cheers*] and now, as it is as well to be hanged for a sheep as for a lamb, I propose that we have a DANCE."

This startling announcement was greeted with frenzied cheering. In five minutes the seats were piled up at one end of the room. In less than another minute the floor was crowded with couples all set for a reel, with the Chairman and his lady at the top end. The piper was perched on top of the teacher's high desk and—*Hooooch!* they were off.

The dancing was the heartiest and most strenuous I had ever seen; and through it all that prince of diplomatists, that most dauntless of leaders, the Chairman, was a sight for the gods of Mirth as he stepped and stamped and swirled, hooched and mopped up the perspiration with the large handkerchief—which now for convenience was partly jammed inside the waistband of his tight wedding trousers and partly floated like a victory banner when he did an extra quick whirl.

This was no paltry dance-and-rest affair. Every couple

danced to the point of physical exhaustion, and when they
sat down to recover, others, fiercely fresh, joined in.
There was no respite for the piper, who played for a solid
hour and a half. Fortunately, at nearing six A.M., he
was relieved by a fiddler, who by the spiritual intoxication
of the dance was emboldened to play.

With a throat like a smiddy file I headed for the wee
classroom—only to learn that the supply had gone done
half an hour ago. It was a bitter blow! But the
Secretary suggested that if I went outside and saw the
policeman he might be able to save my life. I soon
found the guardian of the law and hinted to him that
piping was hard on the throat. He led the way to yon
usually unused little building that stood in a corner of
the country school playground. He squeezed his ample
form in past the door. I followed. With a match the
policeman lit a stump of candle fixed in a bottle set on an
up-ended beer-box. There was plenty plenty more too.
Just for company the policeman bar-tender had one or so
with me. Then I heard him murmur something about
"two shillings" but didn't just catch the drift.

"That will be two shillings," he said now quite pointedly.
He then explained that the Committee's supply was free
but that on this side-line they were trying to make a little
for the concert funds—so the control had been placed
in the safe hands of himself!

"Of course, of course; just that," I agreed, as I handed
the cash to the constituted authority, and returned to the
revels in the school.

The morning lights were high in the east when tired
but triumphant we skailed our ways homeward.

PART III

CHAPTER XXII

The Lure of Lewis

THE island of Lewis seems to possess an irresistible attraction for "improvers." Again and again in the course of its history it has been bought or invaded by people who seem to have discerned in its somewhat sterile exterior possibilities of profitable development or exploitation. In the seventeenth century a syndicate of Fifers—who came to be known as "The Fife Adventurers"—made ambitious plans for the exploitation of Lewis, but soon found themselves in such a hot water of native opposition that ultimately—and not without considerable bloodshed—they were compelled to abandon their project and quit the island.

At a later period Sir James Matheson, a wealthy Eastern merchant, bought Lewis. Sir James made earnest and costly endeavours to improve social conditions by reclaiming land, establishing industries, developing the fisheries, etc., but with such meagre success and at such heavy cost that in the long run he had no alternative to throwing in the towel—having all but bankrupted himself in a most gallant fight.

The latest victim of the Lewis allurement was Mr T. B. MacAulay, a wealthy Canadian with genealogical roots in "Eilean an Fhraoich" ("Isle of Heather"). Inspired by a mixture of loyalty and sentiment Mr MacAulay some years ago fostered and financed a sustained effort to demonstrate the practicability of scientifically reclaiming the peat-land of which Lewis has so large an area, so that it might grow profitable crops instead of only rather inferior pasture. How far this effort has succeeded I am not to say. Certainly, surprisingly good crops have been made to grow on the MacAulay peat farm, but at what cost seems somewhat obscure. Beyond doubt the cost was big; the "reclamation" is doubtfully permanent. Incidentally, it may be explained that most of the arable land in Lewis had already over the centuries been reclaimed from peat by the slow but simple process of removing for fuel all but a little of the peat, which was then mixed with the underlying clay to form a not-too-bad crop-growing medium. This laborious but interesting process of "skinning" the land of peat and then preparing it for crops is still to be seen in operation: it is fairly common to see the year's requirement of peat drying on the "bank" of the hag while a crop of potatoes or oats is growing alongside in the bottom of the hag from which last year's peat was taken. Reclamation by this process is certainly slow but it has the merit that it doesn't cost cash; "elbow grease" and time are the two essentials— and in normal years there is a good deal of both available in Lewis.

But the most spectacular of all the Lewis "improvers" was the late Lord Leverhulme. The great industrial magnate had again and again proved his remarkable genius for successful business enterprise. Towards the end of the 1914–18 War I suspect he found himself in the same dolorous plight as the great Alexander with no more worlds to conquer. Inactivity to a man of Lord Leverhulme's dynamic personality was intolerable. Then, by some chance, Lewis began to attract him—as it had so many others. The more he studied the fishing industry out there the more he was intrigued by its tremendous scope for organisation and expansion; so he bought the island.

Now Lewis, as usual in time of war, had contributed an astonishing number of men to the fighting forces. Those —or what were left of them, for the toll was cruel—were being demobilised at the time their island passed into the new ownership. The first reaction of the natives to the news was one of hopeful anticipation. What could not a wealthy proprietor do to help settle them in crofts on their beloved island?

To a materialistic outsider seeing a typical Lewis croft for the first time this agricultural unit might well appear but a miserable affair. But how far, far wrong he would be in that estimation! To a Lewisman that croft is the most precious spot on earth: to it he is bound by a thousand ties of memory, sentiment, and HOME. For, wherever he may go in pursuit of wealth or fame, or even for a mere livelihood—and they are world-wide travellers —in his heart of hearts there is only one HOME: that little house with its few acres of land in Eilean Leodhais.

This intense love of the Lewisman for his island home is told in that inexpressibly beautiful Gaelic song *Mo Dhachaidh* ("My Home")—a verse or two of which are rendered somewhat freely on the following page.

Imagine therefore the consternation of the returning warriors when the rumour went round that the new proprietor was set dead against making any additional crofts on the score or so of still remaining large farms. Their first hopeful anticipation gave place to strong and angry resentment. Meetings were held in every principal township on the island, from which emphatic resolutions were forwarded to the Government demanding the break-up of the farms into crofts; and threats were not lacking that, failing legal sanction, forcible possession would be resorted to.

The reason for the new proprietor's refusal to countenance the formation of additional crofts lay in his honest

Doh is E♭

{ :s .f | m :- .d :d | d :- .m :s | d' :t :l | s :— }
  My | heart it is buoy-ant, my | steps gay and free,

{ :f | m :- .d :d | d :r :m | f :m :f | r :— }
  At | close of the day, as I | steer straight for thee,

{ :f .f | m :- .d :d | d :- .m :s | d' :t :l | s :— }
  Where the | love of my life and my | bairnies a - glee,

{ :f | m :d :m | r :t, :r | d :— :— | d :— }
  Are | waiting to welcome me | home—   HOME.

{ :d .d | d :- .r :m | m :- .m :m | s :- .m :m | m :— }
  What are | tur - ret - ed cas - tles and | dwellings so grand,

{ :m | f :- .m :f | r :- .m :f | s :m :d | d :— }
  To | one who was reared in yon | cot by the strand?

{ :s | l :- .f :f | d' :t :l | s :f :m | d' :— }
  Yon | snug but and ben with its | wee plot of land,

{ :f .f | m :d :m | r :t, :r | d :— :— | d :— }
  Is my | palace, my lode - star, my | heart - - home.

My heart it is buoyant, my step gay and free,
At close of the day, as I steer straight for thee,
Where the love of my life, and my bairnies aglee,
Are waiting to welcome me home—HOME!

*   *   *   *

Away the false pleasures of wine cup and gold!
So transient, so sordid, so shallow, so cold,
Compared with the uplift, the rapture untold,
That streams in the beam from thy window.

*   *   *   *

My heart, etc.

conviction that crofts were "uneconomic." In face of threatened land-raiding he was assiduous in efforts to explain this to the people, in the hope of getting them to agree with his view that under an industrial régime they would be much better off. At the Castle he gave a series of dinners and entertainments to which he invited in relays most of the influential people of the island. But, whatever degree of success attended this stratagem, the demand of the returned soldiers and sailors was overwhelming and insistent. Raiding broke out in several centres; soon the island was in a ferment.

One day in the north, when I read in the *Scotsman* of the trouble in Lewis, with a shrewd instinct for self-preservation I tried to get officially "lost" in the wilds of Sutherlandshire. But a rascal of a telegraph messenger—a really bright lad—proved too efficient. With untiring tenacity he tracked me to my hidey-hole to deliver the inevitable yellow envelope which contained the curt instruction to proceed to Lewis immediately!

There was the usual crowd on Stornoway pier next night, awaiting the arrival of the *Shiela* (now mouldering in the bed of the Minch whose wild waters for so many years she so gallantly rode). Many of those on the pier were old friends and soon I was generally spotted as "the man from the Board." Questioners in Gaelic and English demanded to know what the Board were going to do. I evaded the point as best I could; I could not say anything until I got my instructions.

Next morning I called at the post office for instructions, but found none!—and let me say now that during the whole of that six-weeks' stay the divil a guiding instruction did I get! No doubt there were good reasons for this policy of silence but it was mightily embarrassing for the official on the spot, and made him feel an awful ass.

Would the Board back Lord Leverhulme in his industrial schemes—which ruled out the prospect of any additional crofts—or would they use the power they had to provide crofts for the returned soldiers and sailors? It was an answer to that question which was demanded of me by emissaries of both sides who came in force to see me during the next week.   Easier asked than answered!

As I write this, at a time when the mightiest armed conflict in the history of the world is raging round diametrically opposed human ideals, the trouble caused to a landlord and to the British Government of twenty years ago by the natives of an island in the Hebrides in demanding the right to live "freely" on the land in preference to a life of "servitude," which industrialism threatened to impose upon them, may seem a trivial matter.   Yet I believe there is a direct relationship; that the urge for "freedom" (and what life is so free as that on the land?) which actuated Lewismen then is of the very essence of the great urge which now animates the opposition to Hitlerism; and that even in that little struggle in Lewis there lies a lesson for our statesmen of the future.

CHAPTER XXIII

Meeting with Raiders—Greek meets Greek—The Philosopher—
Bodach an t-siapuinn—The Optimist

THE atmosphere into which I stepped off the *Shiela* that
night at Stornoway was highly charged. From the Army,
the Navy, and the Mercantile Marine hundreds of men
had already returned to the islands, hundreds more would
be demobilised soon (hundreds, alas! would return only
with MacCrimmon). The lads had been led to believe
that crofts would be ready for them. Not only were
there no crofts ready, but with a hostile proprietor, and
a hesitant Government, their prospects of being settled
on the land were anything but bright. Disappointment,
succeeded by intense anger, surged through the island.
Just before my arrival mere threats of raiding had
developed into reality. Land-raiding became general.
In one case there were three raids in two days on the one
farm. The new factor (from England) was thoroughly
scared. Lord Leverhulme appealed to the Government
for the protection of the law. The returned soldiers
appealed to the Government to have the farms broken
up immediately. The Press revelled in the situation,
and the whole atmosphere became electrical and highly
embarrassing to the Government and the Scottish Office.
It was at this juncture that I received instructions by wire
to proceed to Stornoway immediately.

It is not to be inferred that here was a case of the silent
strong man being called upon to extricate the Government from its difficulties. The simple fact is that a
representative had to be on the spot, and I was selected
merely because I was the one of the staff who happened
to know Lewis best, and its language; and I went in

anything but heroic spirit. Yet I am grateful for being privileged to have taken an intimate (if somewhat futile) part in the Lewis Drama of that time, because of the intensely interesting insight it afforded of the views and motives which actuated the protagonists. For it was intensely interesting; and if I succeed in passing on to others even a little of that interest and pleasure I shall be very glad.

It was indeed no easy matter for the Government to decide on any active course. If they decided to break up the farms Lord Leverhulme would abandon all those schemes which, if brought to fruition, might bring hitherto undreamed prosperity to Lewis. On the other hand, if they decided to support Lord Leverhulme by refusing to break up the farms they were up against the fact that the returned soldiers were in illegal possession and that nothing short of armed force would compel them to quit. It was in very truth a dilemma. But this is digression, and I am mainly concerned to tell the story of the meeting between Lord Leverhulme and the raiders.

Lord Leverhulme called to see me one morning. He was my first millionaire and Industrial Magnate and I shall not soon forget the occasion. At very first glance one would put him down as a rather insignificant little fellow. That impression lasted for a shorter time than it takes to write it. Charm, tact, decision, power radiated from the man's every word, look, and gesture. I had never met a man who was so obviously a megalomaniac and accustomed to having his own way. He had the sort of personality which immediately afflicts ordinary people with a pronounced inferiority complex. In these circumstances I realised that I must adopt one of two courses straight away: either accept the position and become submissive to the strong will; or make instant and silent appeal to the shades of my forebears to grant me strength to still retain at least a little of my own individuality—indicating a sort of resentment! I adopted the latter alternative and am consoled to think my appeal was not quite unheard.

After just the right amount of greeting and tactful flattery Lord Leverhulme informed me that he had arranged an open-air meeting with the raiders at eleven o'clock to-morrow and would like me to go along with him to the farm. I had no wish to go to the meeting and said so plainly. But he pressed that I should go. I would not go.

"Pity," said he, making for the door, "but I hope you will change your mind. Good-bye." Within three hours I received a telegram from H.Q. instructing me to attend the meeting. Almost immediately afterwards Lord Leverhulme reappeared.

"Well," said he, "have you changed your mind?"

"I have," said I.

"Good," he grinned, "I thought you would. I'll call for you in my car at ten-thirty to-morrow morning."

"Thanks," I grinned back, "but you needn't trouble. I'll have that much of my own way, and I'll go in one of Kenny Henderson's cars."

"All right: that must do. Good-bye," and off he went.

To-morrow at the farm steading we found over a thousand people gathered for the meeting; mostly men, but there was a fair smattering of women. It was a sullen crowd, resentful of the situation which had developed. One wrong note might have precipitated serious trouble. But no wrong note was struck; and if Lord Leverhulme sensed any danger he certainly showed no sign. He walked right into the middle of the crowd, made a little "ring" for himself and his interpreter, mounted an upturned tub (in which the farmer was wont to brew a real knock-me-down brand of beer), raised high his hat, smiled genially all round and said:

"Good morning, everybody! Have you noticed that the sun is shining this morning?—and that this is the first time it has shone in Lewis for ten days?" (This was a fact!)

"I regard that as a good omen. This is going to be a great meeting. This is going to be a friendly meeting. This meeting will mark the beginning of a new era in the history of this loyal island of Lewis that you love above all places on earth, and that I too have learned to love. So great is my regard for Lewis and its people that I am prepared to adventure a big sum of money for the development of the resources of the island and of the fisheries. Do you realise that Stornoway is right in the centre of the richest fishing grounds in the whole world? The fishing which has hitherto been carried on in an old-fashioned, happy-go-lucky way is now to be prosecuted on scientific lines. Recently at Stornoway I saw half of the fishing boats return to port without a single herring and the remainder with only a score of crans between them. That is a poor return for men who spend their time and risk their lives in a precarious calling [*ejaculations of assent*]. I have a plan for putting an end to that sort of thing [*the crowd is eagerly interested*].

"The fact is, your fishing as presently carried on is a hit or a miss. I want you to make it a hit every time. How can I do that? Well, every time you now put out to sea you blindly hope to strike a shoal of herrings. Sometimes you do. Oftener you do not. But the shoals are there if you only knew the spot—and *that* is where I can help you.

"I am prepared to supply a fleet of airplanes and trained observers who will daily scan the sea in circles round the island. An observer from one of these planes cannot fail to notice any shoal of herrings over which he passes

Immediately he does so he sends a wireless message to the Harbour Master at Stornoway. Every time a message of that kind comes in there is a 'loud-speaker' announcement by the Harbour Master so that all the skippers at the pier get the exact location of the shoal. The boats are headed for that spot—and next morning they steam back to port loaded with herrings to the gunwales. Hitherto, more often than not, the return to port has been with light boats and heavy hearts. In future it will be with light hearts and heavy boats! [*Loud cheers.*]

"I have already thought out plans which will involve me in an expenditure of five million pounds! But there has been some discord between us; we have not seen eye to eye. When two sensible people have a difference of opinion they do not quarrel: they meet and discuss their differences reasonably and calmly. This is what we have met for here to-day—and the sun is shining! But what do I propose to do with this five million pounds? Let me tell you." . . .

And then there appeared in the next few minutes the most graphic word-picture it is possible to imagine—a great fleet of fishing boats—another great fleet of cargo boats—a large fish-canning factory (already started)—railways—an electric-power station; then one could see the garden city grow—steady work, steady pay, beautiful houses for all—every modern convenience and comfort. The insecurity of their present income was referred to; the squalor of their present houses deftly compared with the conditions in the new earthly paradise. Altogether it was a masterpiece; and it produced its effect; little cheers came involuntarily from a few here and there—more cheers!—general cheers!! . . .

And just then, while the artist was still adding skilful detail, there was a dramatic interruption.

One of the ringleaders managed to rouse himself from the spell, and in an impassioned voice addressed the crowd in Gaelic, and this is what he said:

"*So so, fhiribh! Cha dean so gnothach! Bheireadh am bodach mil-bheulach sin chreidsinn oirnn gu'm bheil dubh geal's geal dubh! Ciod e dhuinn na bruadairean briagha aige, a thig no nach tig? 'Se am fearann tha sinn ag iarraidh. Agus 'se tha mise a faighneachd* [turning to face Lord Leverhulme and pointing dramatically towards him]: *an toir thu dhuinn am fearann?*" The effect was electrical. The crowd roared their approbation.

Lord Leverhulme looked bewildered at this, to him, torrent of unintelligible sounds, but when the frenzied cheering with which it was greeted died down he spoke.

"I am sorry! It is my great misfortune that I do not understand the Gaelic language. But perhaps my interpreter will translate for me what has been said?"

Said the interpreter: "I am afraid, Lord Leverhulme, that it will be impossible for me to convey to you in English what has been so forcefully said in the older tongue; but I will do my best"—and his best was a masterpiece, not only in words but in tone and gesture and general effect:

"Come, come, men! This will not do! This honey-mouthed man would have us believe that black is white and white is black. *We* are not concerned with his fancy dreams that may or may not come true! What we want is the *land*—and the question I put to him now is: *will you give us the land?*"

The translation evoked a further round of cheering. A voice was heard to say:

"Not so bad for a poor language like the English!"

Lord Leverhulme's picture, so skilfully painted, was spattered in the artist's hand!

But was it? When the cheering died down the brave

little artist looked round the crowd with eyes that seemed to pierce every separate individual. Finally he fixed a cold-steel look on the interrupter and in a clean-cut staccato accent said:

"You have asked a straight question. I like a straight question; and I like a straight answer. And my answer to your question is 'NO.' I am *not* prepared to give you the land" (here a compelling hand-wave that instantly silenced some protests), "not because I am vindictively opposed to your views and aspirations, but because I conscientiously believe that if my views are listened to— if my schemes are given a chance—the result will be enhanced prosperity and greater happiness for Lewis and its people. Listen." . . . And the indomitable little artist took up his work again in such skilful fashion that in a matter of seconds he had the ear and the eye of the crowd again—and in five minutes they were cheering him again. . . . Theatre! Play!

But the play was not yet over. A clean-shaven æsthete —a crofter-fisherman—cut in politely at a momentary pause in the artist's work. He spoke slowly, in English, with a strong Lewis accent; each word set square like a stone block in a building, and he made a great speech.

"Lord Leverhulme," said he, "will you allow me to intervene in this debate for a few moments?" (Assent signified.) "Thank you. Well, I will begin by saying that we give credit to your lordship for good *intentions* in this matter. We believe you *think* you are *right*, but we *know* that you are *wrong*. The fact is, there is an element of sentiment in the situation which it is impossible for your lordship to understand. But for that we do not blame you; it is not your *fault* but your *misfortune* that your upbringing, your experience, and your outlook are such that a proper understanding of the position and of our point of view is quite outwith your comprehension.

You have spoken of steady work and steady pay in tones of veneration—and I have no doubt that in your view, and in the view of those unfortunate people who are compelled to live their lives in smoky towns, steady work and steady pay are very desirable things. But in Lewis we have never been accustomed to either—and, strange though it must seem to your lordship, *we do not greatly desire them.* We attend to our crofts in seed-time and harvest, and we follow the fishing in its season—and when neither requires our attention we are free to *rest and contemplate.* You have referred to our houses as hovels—but they are our *homes*, and I will venture to say, my lord, that, poor though these homes may be, you will find more *real human happiness* in them than you will find in your *castles* throughout the land. I would impress on you that we are not in opposition to your schemes of work; we only oppose you when you say you *cannot give us the land*, and on that point we will oppose you with all our strength. It may be that some of the younger and less thoughtful men will side with you, but believe me, the great majority of us are against you.

"Lord Leverhulme! You have bought this island. But you have not bought *us*, and we refuse to be the bond-slaves of any man. We want to live our own lives in our own way, poor in material things it may be, but at least it will be clear of the fear of the factory bell; it will be *free and independent*!"

After a short silence of astonishment there came the loudest and longest cheers of that day. "That's the way to talk, lad!" "That's yourself, boy," and such like encomiums were shouted from all quarters. One voice demanded to know what "Bodach an t-siapuinn" [1] could say to that? Nobody thought he could say anything to that: the enemy was annihilated!

[1] The wee soap-mannie.

But we had yet to grasp the full fighting qualities of this wonderful little man, and we were soon to see him in action, at his very best. With a sort of magical combination of hand and eye he again commanded a perfect silence; he then spoke in modulated, cajoling tones that showed the superb actor.

Said he: "Will you allow me to congratulate you?—to thank you for putting the views of my opponents so clearly before me? I did know that sentiment lay at the back of the opposition to my schemes, but I confess I had not adequately estimated the strength of that element till now. My friends! sentiment is the finest thing in this hard world. It is the golden band of brotherhood. It is the beautiful mystic thing that makes life worth living . . . and would you accuse me of deliberately planning to injure that beautiful thing? No! No! A thousand times No! Then is there, after all, so very much between your point of view and mine? Are we not striving after the same thing?—by different roads it may be, but still, for the same goal? We are both out for the greatest good of the greatest number of people on this island. You have admitted, that the *young men* may believe in my schemes. May I again congratulate you? The young people will—and do—believe in my schemes. I have in my pocket now (fetching out a handful of letters) quite a number of letters from young men in different parts of the island, and I have received a great many more of the same kind—all asking the same questions— 'When can you give me a job in Stornoway?' 'When can I get one of your new houses?' These young men and their wives and sweethearts want to give up the croft life; they want a brighter, happier life. . . . My friends! the young people of to-day will be *the* people of to-morrow. Are the older ones who have had their day going to stand in the way of the young folk? Are we older fellows going to be dogs-in-mangers? No! The people of this island are much too intelligent to take up so un-Christian an attitude. Give me a chance—give my schemes a chance —give the young folks and give Lewis a chance! Give me a period of ten years to develop my schemes and I venture to prophesy that long before then—in fact in the near future—so many people, young and old, will believe in them, that crofts will be going a-begging—and then if there are still some who prefer life on the land they can have two, three, four crofts apiece!"

And the crowd cheered again: they simply could not resist it, and they cheered loud and long.

The artist knew when to stop. As the cheers died he raised his hat and said: "Ladies and Gentlemen— *Friends*—I knew the sun did not shine for nothing! This has been a great meeting. This will be a memorable day in the history of Lewis. You are giving me a chance. I will not fail you. I thank you. Good day." And off he walked to another round of cheering.

I tried to walk off too—unsuccessfully. An eager crowd surged round "the man from the Board": "When will the Board be dividing off the land?"

"You do not want the land now," said I, well knowing they did, notwithstanding the cheers.

"Want the land! Of course we want the land, and we want it at once."

"But you gave Lord Leverhulme the impression that you agreed with him," said I, affecting astonishment.

"Not at all," was the reply, "and if he is under that impression you may tell him from us that he is greatly mistaken."

"But why did you cheer him?" I inquired.

"Och! well: he made a very good speech and he is a very clever man, and we wanted to show our appreciation

—but the land is another matter"—and that, I knew, was the real position.

When I joined Lord Leverhulme later in a near-by shooting lodge he was in great form, and it was with keen regret that I began the task of disillusioning him. At first he was incredulous. He could not understand what he called such "double dealing." I tried to explain and let both sides down gently. When he realised the truth he became very downcast. But after a few minutes he brightened up and said: "Anyhow, that was a great meeting! They are an intelligent people, and I never give up hope so long as I have an intelligent opposition to deal with. Besides, there is not the same enjoyment in things that are easily won. I am enjoying this fight and I shall win them over yet!"

"I am very sorry," said I, "to have to resort again to the cold-water jug, but if you could see the position as I see it you would be less optimistic—unless you are prepared to compromise on the question of the land, which I venture to think you could do without material hurt to your schemes."

"I shall *not* compromise," he retorted with emphasis, "and as for optimism, I have always been an optimist. I am like the Irishman who fell from the roof of a New York skyscraper. His friend working at a window lower down yelled as Pat shot past: 'Hello, Pat! Are yez all roight?' 'Yes, bejabbers,' shouted Pat, 'so far!'"

CHAPTER XXIV

Dinner at the Castle

SOON after arriving in Lewis—to play so inglorious a part in the Leverhulme v. Natives clash—I called to see my friend the late Duncan MacKenzie of the Royal Hotel. It was always good policy to "get the breath" of that remarkable man on any question affecting the island. In half an hour I was well posted in the present state of the campaign, coloured with piquant side-lights on the disposition of the fighting forces of the two sides.

Dinners and dances at the Castle were in the forefront of Lord Leverhulme's strategy. There were several such per week, and nearly every person of influence sooner or later found himself—and his wife or daughter—at one of these delightful banquets.

"You'll be at a dinner at the Castle within the week," was Duncan's jocular prophecy.

He was right; and when the invitation came I could not suppress a smile. It was after the meeting at the farm described in the last chapter.

After the joke about the optimistic Irishman, Lord Leverhulme left the subject of the land and switched on to another.

"By the way," he inquired, "have you got any special engagement for this evening?"

It was then I smiled at the recollection of Duncan MacKenzie's prophecy; and before I could reply he added:

"I'll tell you why I ask. I am having a few friends to dinner at the Castle to-night and would be delighted if you could come."

"Thanks very much," I said, "but no! no! I'm not in the habit of dining with lords in castles!"

"You mean clothes?" said he. "Never mind about clothes! Come just as you like—so long as you don't come in pyjamas!"

"Right then!" I decided. "I'll be there."

"Good! My car will call for you at seven-thirty."

There was a big dinner-party and Lord Leverhulme was the ideal host who manages to give each guest the impression that he or she is someone just a little special. His "management" of the mixed elements in the party was a masterpiece. He seemed to exercise a sort of mesmeric power over his guests, that bent them readily but unconsciously to his will. Soon I felt I would have no will of my own at all, so potent was this influence. I was seated next but one to him. In a crude effort to retain a remnant of my individuality I challenged facetiously:

"Are you aware, Lord Leverhulme, that you are committing a breach of Highland etiquette?"

"Really?" he inquired. "And what is my crime?"

"I have been waiting for a lead from you with the bottle," I explained.

"I *am* so sorry," he jokingly apologised; and then, in the oracular manner which he readily affected, he proceeded: "Whisky is uncertain in its effects. It affects different people differently. Some of my friends who are ordinarily rather dull fellows become quite inspired by a glass or two of Scotch. They become eloquent, witty; they seem to think more clearly and quickly. Now if I were to take even the tiniest drop of whisky it would have the opposite effect. It would make me witless; my thinking would be confused. I cannot afford to let my thoughts get confused; so I do not take any whisky. But, please . . . please . . . !"

"Thank you," I said; "and I hope I may rank with some of your friends!"

How skilfully and unobtrusively that Bodachan dominated the situation from his chair at the top of the table; and later with equal skill and urbanity directed the social activities of the evening! There was music, dancing, and some very good singing—in English and Gaelic—and much merriment. At one stage a few of the young girls called for a song from Lord Leverhulme.

"Ladies! Ladies!" he protested. "You *know* I cannot sing. I just croak!"

But the lassies jingo-ringed him, chanting:

> "Lord Leverhulme for the Bathing song,
> Lord Leverhulme for the Bathing song!"

He pretended to be shocked: "That dreadful song!" But the insistent chant continued. Then with dramatic suddenness he agreed.

"Very well! If you insist I shall sing a song—and I shall sing the Bathing song."

It was quite true: he couldn't sing: he could only croak; and that versatile little man croaked heartily through a song which would make an Irish navvy blush. As encore, in the Lancashire dialect, he gave an excellent recitation displaying real humour and histrionic ability of a high order.

Soon after the recitation, when everything was going noisily and merrily, I felt a firm grip on my bicep and a quiet voice said in my ear:

"Let us go over to a quiet place behind the pillars. I want to have a word with you."

My hour had come!

We seated ourselves in a quiet corner. Not a trace of gaiety now on that alert countenance. His eyes fixed me with a "now-to-business" sort of look which must have stood him in good stead in many a tussle. His speech was as direct as his look. Perforce I adopted a similar manner and this is a fairly accurate record of our conversation:

L.L. "I should like to know exactly how I stand with you. Are you with me or against me?"

ME. "You mean: 'Do I think the Board will be with or against your schemes?'"

L.L. "Put it that way if you like, but please, *please* do not be evasive. You know, and you know that I know, that the Board will be largely guided by you in this matter. Are—you—with—me—or—against—me?"

ME. "I do not yet know. I have not made up my mind. I see both sides. You see only one. Tell me this. You said to-day at the meeting that you had arranged to spend five million pounds on your development schemes here. I cannot quite grasp what even one million means, but at least I have an idea that five million pounds is a lot of money. Do you expect to get a return from that expenditure?—and how?"

L.L. (*registering horror*). "I am not a philanthropist in this matter! I would not put a penny into this venture if I did not see that it would be a commercial success. Never have I seen the successful end of a venture so clearly as I do now. Not that I require—or desire—to make more money for myself. I am never sure on a given day just what I am worth in money, but last time my accountant reported to me it was in the neighbourhood of eighteen million pounds. In any case I have more money than I can possibly require. But I derive my greatest pleasure in life from business ventures which call for thought and vision. That is a great game: the creation of wealth— and thereby providing steady work and good wages for thousands of people."

ME. "I can understand that; but what on earth is

there in this rather barren island that offers economic scope for so huge a capital expenditure?"

L.L. "You appear to be intelligent. You probably are. But *vision* is also required here. You know this island. Did you know that, if you take a map, fix one leg of a pair of compasses in the town of Stornoway and describe a circle of a hundred miles radius, within that circle *you have the richest fishing grounds in the whole world* ?"

ME. "No. I did not."

L.L. "Quite. Well, you have. That is a very important fact. Fish is a valuable human food. That is also important. How can I link up these terminal facts? I shall create the necessary connecting links so that I shall have a chain leading from the bed of the Minch to the breakfast-tables of the world. First I must catch my fish. I shall soon have the best and the best-equipped fishing fleet the world has ever seen.

"My fish must be conveyed quickly to the railheads. I shall have a fleet of fast carrier-boats for that.

"I am in process of acquiring so substantial a block of railway company shares that there will be no fear of my fish rotting at the sidings!

"I am getting on! But am I going to incur all this expense and risk, and then allow another fellow to reap the reward? No! I have already purchased most of the biggest retail fish-shops in the big consuming centres. My fish will be sold in *my* shops.

"But I shall catch more fish than I can sell *fresh*. Well, I shall can the surplus. I have built what I believe to be the most up-to-date fish-canning factory in existence. I know little of the process of canning but I pay an expert from Norway two thousand pounds a year to advise me.

"I shall make my own cans—and I shall make my own labels. Labels are very important. I have recently had submitted to me various label designs. Some are from men who put R.A. or A.R.A. after their names. I have made my selection. It has red lettering on a white ground. The letters spell

LEWIS CANNED FISH

This is printed in slanting fashion three times in the full round of the can.

"I have placed a can with that label inside a window of the Castle. I have looked at it from every angle and from just outside the window and from twenty yards away. It strikes me in the eye from every angle and from every distance. I cannot escape it!

"Canned fish is like whisky: the longer you keep it (up to a point) the better it gets. When my first 'cure' is properly matured I send a consignment to my principal corner shops with instructions to make a good window display on the Saturday.

"John Smith has been busy in the office all the week (or so he tells the wife) and late home every night. On Saturday he goes home to lunch. Conscience-stricken he tries to make amends.

"'Mary, my dear,' says he, 'you've had a dreary week of it. What about a show to-night?'

"Poor Mary is overjoyed. What a considerate man is her John! On the way to the theatre they are held up at the corner for a car—the corner where my shop is. The light from the window shows up LEWIS CANNED FISH most attractively. It catches Mary's eye.

"'I say, John, what a lovely label! Lewis Canned Fish. I like the look of it. . . . Just a minute. . . .'

"'What is this Lewis Canned Fish?' she asks.

"'Madam,' says my salesman. 'It *is* Lewis Canned Fish and very delightful too.'

"'Can you recommend it?'

"'Thoroughly, madam.   I believe it is the best canned fish in the world.'

"'Thank you.   Will you please send along a tin?'

"Back from the show Mary is peckish.   That can just asks to be opened.   They have Lewis Canned Fish for supper.   They have never tasted anything so good.   *They lick their fingers.*   Nyum nyum!

"Monday morning Mrs Smith is in the back green hanging up the washing.   Mrs Brown is over the wall on the right.

"'Mrs Brown!   Do you know!   I made the most *wonderful* discovery on Saturday!'—and she lets Mrs Brown into the secret.   She also tells Mrs Jones on the left.   Each buys a can. . . .

"And so the great news spreads and spreads.   Within a year—certainly within two years—there is *only one canned fish that counts in the world,* and that is LEWIS CANNED FISH."

It is impossible to convey in mere writing the force, the eloquence, the abounding self-assurance that radiated from this visionary as he expounded his plans.   He was as an evangelist preaching a gospel.   He all but mesmerised me.   It needed a real effort to hang on to the one thing I knew to be true—namely, that nothing at that time could effectively stand between the returned Lewis soldiers and sailors and their land.

"Almost thou persuadest me," I quoted, "and I thank you for paying me the compliment of giving me a glimpse of your business methods.   Now I understand how your various ventures have been so successful.

"But, Lord Leverhulme, however much you may convince me that you would be equally successful in Lewis it would but mislead you if I said I thought you could convince Lewis men of that.   Certainly nothing you can promise them will induce them to drop their demand for crofts. But surely there is a middle way. The retention of the large farms is not essential to the success of your schemes."

"I need them for the production of milk for supplying the greatly increased population which will be one of the direct results of my schemes," he rapped at me.

"You can import milk from the mainland," I countered. "That is being done now—and better and cheaper milk than you can produce in Lewis."

"My agricultural expert advises me I must have the farms. In this matter I must be guided by him."

"I do not question the ability of your agricultural expert to advise you—in England. But—with respect—Lewis is not England."

"But I *must* have control of my factory hands! How can I have that in the case of men who are in the independent position of crofters? "

"That is just the point," I urged. "That is what was made so clear at the meeting to-day. These men will not tolerate being subject to your whim or charity. But if you initiate friendly relationships by giving them crofts you will have no lack of men willing to work in your factories. By opposing their desire you will but stimulate their opposition and in the end they will beat you. In one word my advice is—*compromise*."

"I will *not* compromise. I *must* control," he reiterated again and again.

"Then I am afraid you are only at the beginning of your troubles," I sighed; "but at least I sincerely wish you good luck—and no one will be more pleased than I if I should prove a poor prophet."

After events in Lewis proved Lord Leverhulme's optimism to have been no better founded than Pat's. His failure to understand and meet the views of the people led to the failure of all his projects. A little mutual compromise would have enabled both sides to attain, substantially, their particular ambitions.   But Lord Leverhulme refused to compromise until towards the very end—and then it was too late.   Farm after farm had to be broken up until at last he abandoned the whole venture and left the island—never to return.

Is that a matter for regret?   Or is it not?   I cannot say.   I have merely tried to tell the story of the most interesting incident in my official experience.

JOURNEY ENDING

The Journey is nearing its end.   This book gives but a sketchy glimpse of a few of its incidents.   How, as a whole, has it gone?   Listen—

Lerwick of the Silver Horde, North Isles, Muckle Flugga, Fitful Head—

Pomona, Stones of Stennes, Old Man of Hoy, Ola of the dreaded Firth—

Stacks of Duncansby, Dunnet Head, Deil's Brig and fearful Clett—

Ben Hope and Loyal, Cape Wrath of the angry waters, Canisp, Suilven—

Summer Isles, Lochmaree, Slioch, Ben Wyvis (*mo ghaol!*)—

Dunvegan, Duntulm, Fairy Bridge—and the snowclad peaks of Cuchuilein cutting the crimson of a winter's sunrise—

Loch Duich and the Sisters of Kintail—

Lochaber of the wild men and strong, Glen Finnan, Sands of Morar—

Glen of Weeping, Buachaille Etive, Ben Dòrain of the song—

Mull of the mountains, Coll and Tiree of rich pastures—

And then? And then! Behold the Hebrides! Enchanted Islands of the West! Sanctuary of soul-rest and heart-healing where time is properly regarded as the infinite thing it is; whose spell, once cast, is ever potent. Islands of bent-grass and seaweed, of salmon and sea-trout, of wild wheeling greylag, of curlew and teal; of song and of story, of Gaelic and homespun, of peat-fires so radiant, of hearts warm and leal :

> Muran 's Feamainn,
> Cladach 's Tràigh,
> Machair 's Mointeach,
> Céilidh 's Ceòl;
>
> Giomach 's Gealag,
> Liathag 's Leòbag,
> Glas-gheadh cho fiadhaich,
> Muinntir cho còir!

Truly, the Journey has been along a delightful road.